I0824905

BLOOM ACROSS CANADA

50 Inspiring Conversations

FOREWORD BY
LYDIA OKELLO

BEKA SHANE DENTER

BLOOM ACROSS CANADA

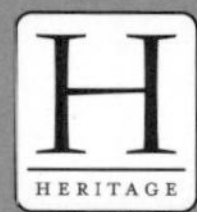

Heritage House Publishing Company Ltd.
heritagehouse.ca

Cataloguing information available from Library and Archives Canada
978-1-77203-500-1 (hardcover)
978-1-77203-501-8 (e-book)

Edited by Christine Jean-Baptiste
Proofread by Elysse Bell
Cover and interior book design by Setareh Ashrafologhalai
Full image credits on page 209

The interior of this book was produced on FSC®-certified, acid-free paper, processed chlorine free, and printed with vegetable-based inks.

Heritage House gratefully acknowledges that the land on which we live and work is within the traditional territories of the Lkwungen (Esquimalt and Songhees), Malahat, Pacheedaht, Scia'new, T'Sou-ke, and W̱SÁNEĆ (Pauquachin, Tsartlip, Tsawout, Tseycum) Peoples.

We acknowledge the financial support of the Government of Canada through the Canada Book Fund (CBF) and the Canada Council for the Arts, and the Province of British Columbia through the British Columbia Arts Council and the Book Publishing Tax Credit.

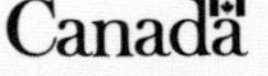

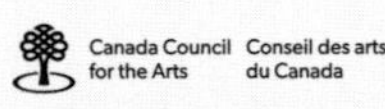

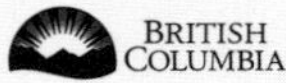

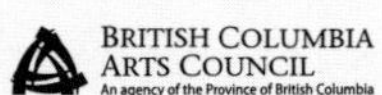

28 27 26 25 24 1 2 3 4 5

Printed in China

Cover images

(*clockwise from top left*):
Breagh Isabel (photography by Mo Phùng)
Jag Nagra (photography by Agata Matyszczuk)
Avis O'Brien (Nalaga) (photography by Nycky-Jay Vanjecek, Bluetree Photography)
Andrea Gzowski (self portrait)
Dawn Pemberton (photography by Wendy D Photography)
Becky Feasby (photography by Nikki Collette Photography)
Anna Williams (self portrait)
Thanushi Eagalle (photography by True Rosie Brix, Truzys Photos)
Mara Mennicken (photography by Jurga Prakapaite)
Carla Tak (self portrait)
Truc Nguyen (photography by Jenna Marie Wakani)
Jane Brokenshire (photography by Ryan L. Mackay)
Lindsay Kelloway (photography by Megan Bodker Photography)
Jill Pangman (photography by Cathie Archbould)
Sylvia Tennant (photography by Kristine Cofsky)
Andréanne Mulaire Dandeneau (photography by Danny Shumov)

For Cali & Elle—my two inspirations.

For Christian—my rock.

And for everyone who finds inspiration in these pages—this book is for you.

Contents

SASKATCHEWAN

ALBERTA

BRITISH COLUMBIA

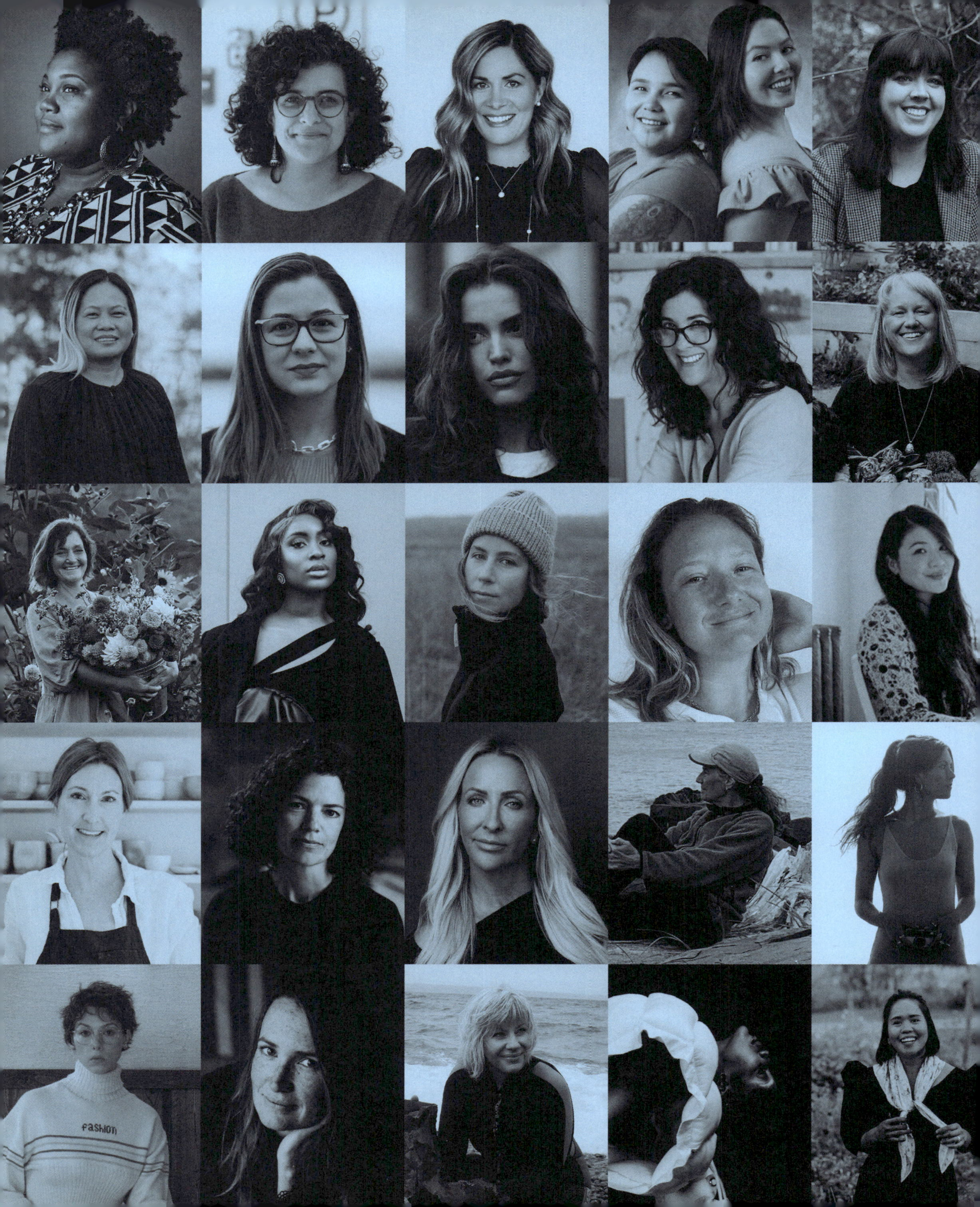
fashion

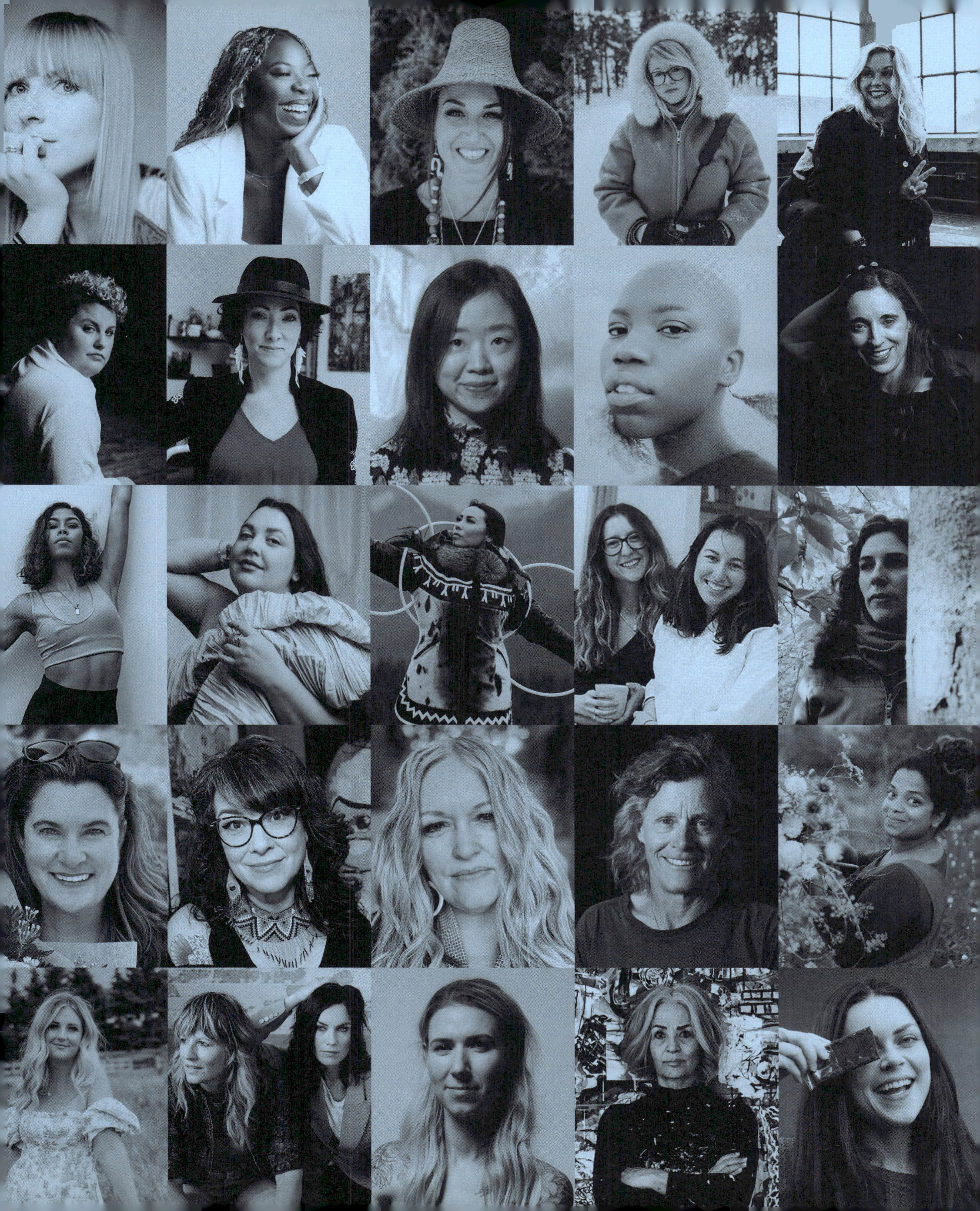

Watch out world, because we all have something so very special to contribute.

Foreword

THAT INEFFABLE DRIVE to express something within you—it's not an idea, but a calling. Many of us who have a creative practice, pursuit, or need to make or create know this feeling well. You can run and hide from it, but it's truly inescapable. It brews in us, planted from some unknown, and manifests where we are. In reading the first *Bloom*, there are many contrasts and many throughlines. An incredible attribute that many of the interviewees have in common is that their current life stage may seem, from the outside, to be in sharp contrast with their beginnings or past lives. But for each incredible subject, the past and present coalesce to create something that can uniquely be attributed to them and them alone.

Knowing how to start, whether it's baking chocolate chip cookies, starting a business, or training for a triathlon, can be daunting. Depending on the tools you've been given in life, you might know exactly where to look—or you might be the only one looking for *the thing*. When you are the first or the only one, forging a path and teaching yourself is a necessity, even if it's a messy one. I'm a recovering perfectionist. I've realized that *so* much of life is about preparing the best you can with the knowledge you have and surrendering to the fact that there will be a lot you would have done differently in hindsight. And that's the beauty of living; we get one go at something that argues could be improved upon with a couple of tries.

And so, we forge on. Sometimes with grace, other times fumbling in the dark towards something we can't quite make out the shape of. There are extended periods of treading water. Different phases of life are brimming with new experiences, growth, and wonder. Others are still challenging, seemingly attempting to break us, to put us under the weight of something that feels just a little too heavy to carry. It's all of it—the mess, the beautiful, finished project, the dinner that came together just so, the breakfast that burnt but the loaf of bread that could be salvaged. The everyday stuff of life grants us the fuel to make, to create, to spin something new seemingly out of thin air, to reimagine that which came before us for those who we'll leave here.

I have realized, both in conversation and reading her work, that something I have in common with Beka is a love of the written word and an early connection to magazines. I remember visiting my school library for *Chirp* and *National Geographic* and then realizing my public library had all these cool, sophisticated magazines like *Seventeen, Teen People* and *YM*. Growing up in the suburbs of Vancouver, I was so curious about the big world. What did cool people read? How could I be cool? Would I ever be cool?

It feels like some of us were born to be *inside kids*. I was one of those children who learned to read quite early and devoured the written word. I'd beg for library visits—making a pile of new discoveries in what felt like an endless trove. I was lucky to have a parent who was a voracious reader like me (thanks for the genetic inheritance, Dad) and would cater to this side of me. That said, I would often spend summer afternoons taking the bus to the library! AC and somewhat infinite reading materials? That sounded much more appealing than any walk down to the local gas station for slushies.

We were one of the few Black families in our communities—and I think that my magazine obsession was a double-edged sword. On one hand, it was exciting to immerse myself in a world outside the limiting and specific confines of suburbia. But I do think my obsessive pawing of these print magazines was a detriment to my self-worth. I chased after prescribed ideals—forgetting the very things that made me uniquely me and the things that would be beneficial to share with folks who felt a similar sense of being an outsider.

I moved a ton as a kid, and although I always found making friends easy, it instilled a restless nature in me. These days, I've stayed in the same city for thirteen years—but the wanderer in me reaches for new experiences, places, and people. This book feels in line with that spirit. No two interviewees have the same life experience, nor do they approach their practice or expression in the exact same way. It's exciting to live in a time when that is something to be celebrated. To live in a time where homogenous culture isn't the default—where the outliers and rebels can congregate and feel special, celebrated, and cared for. As much as we may have to fight to make that space, the call for it is undeniable. And that call keeps returning, making for art and books like the one in your hands now.

Beka began the first *Bloom* with, "My hope for this book is that it will inspire." I'm hard-pressed to believe that it wouldn't. I'd go so far as to say, "I dare you not to leave this book feeling renewed and brimming with inspiration." Regardless of your life phase, background, or current pursuits, these are stories of incredible folks and, yes, everyday folks like you.

LYDIA OKELLO

Introduction

WHEN WE FIND OUR THING, the thing we're good at, it's like a life raft in the stormy sea of life. Writing is where I go when nothing makes sense or when I feel lost. It's where I find my footing and feel my most authentic self. It's also where I feel inspired and how I make connections. A fascination with words started in early childhood. In December 2017, while cleaning out my mom's home after her passing, I came across a series of stapled pages. It was a magazine of sorts I had put together, filled with stick figures, hand-drawn ads for travel to exotic places and fashionable, affordable jewellery items, and a Q&A questionnaire. The *magazine* was to accompany my mom as a form of entertainment on a business trip. My one request was that she fill out the Q&A, which I would then edit upon her return. At the bottom right corner of the last page, I signed *Beka, age 8*.

My love for words expanded as I entered my teen years to include a passion for print, as magazines and song lyrics were found on the sleeves of the many albums in our home. Travel, music, and fashion magazines were at the top of the list; however, it was the infamous Proust Questionnaire section in *Vanity Fair* with which I became very familiar. As an only child, perhaps reading about other people gave me a sense of expanding the very small world that was my mom and I. Summer visits stateside to see my dad and his family in rural Pennsylvania were wonderful because I had four older cousins who would take turns entertaining and playing with the *Canadian cousin*, as I became referred to. Those summers were pure magic—always somewhere and someone to be with. And yet, I still found time to read the copies of *Architectural Digest* my grandparents had scattered around their house. My dad had stacks of *National Geographic*, which inspired my desire to travel and explore new countries and cultures. Back in Ottawa, my mom's selection would often include a variety of lifestyle and wellness magazine titles such as *Chatelaine* and *Yoga Journal*. It's no wonder that eventually, after several attempted career starts and stops, I returned to my first love and began writing.

Being raised by a single mother in a culture, a community, and a country that encouraged me to embrace and be accepting of all people fostered in me a deep desire to share the stories of the experience of doing and being. Everyone, I realize, has a story and a journey that is unique to them, be it the journey of a creative, an entrepreneur, or an individual in some stage of seeking. I wholeheartedly believe that the themes of our lives guide us to pursue a path that will hopefully be an authentic reflection of who we are and where we want to be, personally and professionally. The two are often connected for me in my work as a writer. As I learned in doing hundreds of interviews for the *Bloom* books, it appears to be a similar sentiment for many people.

Two beautiful quotes appeared on my Instagram feed the week I began work on this introduction. "The world shifts when the people who created you pass." Taquana Sears's words were a response to Paul Rudd's take on loss, shared in an interview on the *Today Show*: "When you lose a parent, the world is off its axis, and it never rights itself . . . you adapt or perish." Both heartfelt sentiments aptly convey the depth of sadness and the definitive change losing a parent can have on us. My professional and personal paths blurred together in the most meaningful way after my mom died.

The way forward through my grief after the loss of my mom, in 2017, was to embrace the tangle of what appeared at the time to be my life and the work of unknotting it. The world kept spinning, yet I remained still, stuck in a place that asked me to take stock. At first, this involved a three-month break from writing. I was in the *adapt* stage and realized that if I did not soon return to writing, I may actually *perish* or disappear into the gulf of grief that had gripped me in the months following my mom's passing.

The *shift*, as Taquana describes it, happens on so many levels. Professionally, there was an intentional shift in the type of writing that would better reflect this version of me. Where did I want to focus my time and energy? What and who filled my cup? The answer was easy: people and their stories, their journeys and what inspires them to pursue their passions is what made me smile. As I began to publish profiles on various platforms, the feedback from readers was a resounding *yes*. Profiles have remained where I feel most genuine as a writer. They allow me to shine a light on others, which brings me so much joy.

When the pandemic hit us hard in 2020, I, like so many others the world over, had to find a new way to move forward without losing sight of my purpose and what fuelled me. Still, moving through the grief overwhelmed me in unexpected ways; the pandemic simultaneously put a pause on my healing journey and gifted me the opportunity to heal by expanding my work into that of an author. Initially, I started to write short profiles about women specifically and how they were moving through the pandemic, both professionally and personally. In August 2020, the idea of compiling these stories came to me as I drove cross-country with my family from Ontario to British Columbia. Over the next three years, the *Bloom* books offered me, as an author, a space to be my true self, form connections, and find inspiration through the stories of others. Every person I interviewed for both *Bloom* books gave me a reason to move forward, keep writing, and keep believing in the uniqueness and creative power of others.

Grief continues to teach me how essential it is to be in the moment, to do what feels difficult, and to walk through this world with an open heart and mind. That has been my intention from the beginning with the *Bloom* books—to share the stories of others who give and gift their passion and creativity to others—be it in the form of a performance, a product, a flower farm, a book, a piece of clothing, a photograph. All the individuals featured on these pages generously offer an honest, insightful, and heartfelt recollection of what motivates them to keep doing and contributing in a positive way. Everyone here shares that it's all about celebrating being in the process—in whichever form it may take, because the outcome is not entirely known or guaranteed, and is often ever-changing.

The first *Bloom* book was in the early edit stages when I began working on this second edition. I felt that my work was not yet done. There was a strong sense of momentum happening not only in my life, but also in that of many entrepreneurs and creatives post-pandemic. I felt a strong responsibility to continue sharing the stories of a never-ending pool of talent. People are simply fascinating, and because of this, my work as a profile writer will never be done.

Although personal essays came easily, it was the interview format that intrigued me because this is how I discovered and learned about the people and places where I live. With many moves around the world, it's important for me to gain a sense of my surroundings. To better understand the place in which I find myself—be it Tokyo, Boston, the Philippines, or Canada—getting to know the makers and doers is what I've found to be the most rewarding way to discover the hidden gems and learn about the cultures in these places.

A few months before the manuscript deadline of this book, my family and I learned that we would soon be embarking on another new adventure. In July 2023, I moved to Denmark with my husband, Christian and two daughters, Cali, then 12, and Elle, then 10. A four-year posting in Copenhagen will most definitely again shift what I write about and shape how I approach my craft. I can't speak too much about this next chapter as by the time this book goes to print, I will only be one year into this new life. What I do know is that writing this book, in which we converse with a range of individuals doing meaningful work, has given me the strong desire to curate a mindful and inspiring collection of stories about the makers and doers in my home country.

Speaking with individuals across Canada has been a true gift, something above and beyond anything I thought possible just a few short years ago. From Newfoundland to Nunavut, with the wonders of technology, I can research, be moved by, and have conversations with the incredible individuals featured on these pages.

Many of the people featured in both *Bloom* books were and continue to be experiencing various life layers. These layers are not viewed as an obstacle or limitation, but as motivation to keep pursuing their path and passion. Oftentimes, there is an incredible story of struggle, survival, and strength. I think of the powerful and beautiful words of the great Maya Angelou: "Every storm runs out of rain." And when it does, watch out world, because we all have something so very special to contribute.

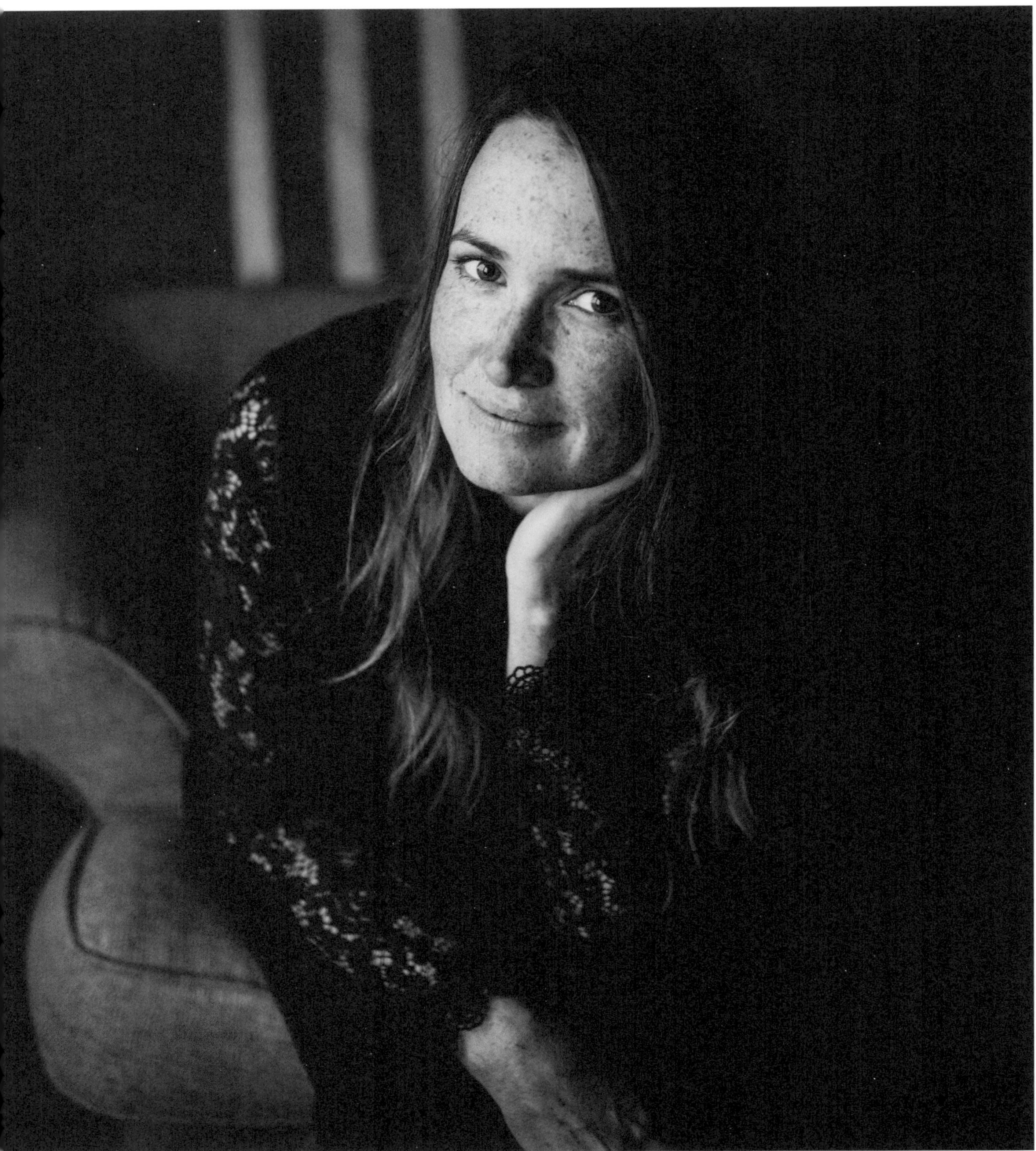

Jane Brokenshire

Lifestyle, Portrait, and Design Photographer

"Life can be busy, messy, and complicated. The way I take photos is how I cope with it all, by creating something that offers a sense of stillness."

What is your first memory of a photo that moved you?

It was an image taken by my dad back in the 70s. My mom grew up in a small community called Long Harbour in Placentia Bay. Depending on where you are on the Avalon Peninsula, the sun either sets or rises in your community. Long Harbour is on the sunset side. It was a magnificent image of so many deep oranges and pinks and shadows, and it hung in our house. For some reason, that is the one image that really made me first take notice of the feeling that photography can give you.

There's also another image worth mentioning. My grandmother had an image of her and my uncle sitting on a hockey bench. He was maybe eleven. It was a close-up shot of her coaching my uncle; he had his helmet on, and in big black letters across his helmet on masking tape, said the name *Brokenshire*. You could almost hear what she was saying, the passion, the absolute in her being. The image tells the viewer exactly who she was. That inspired me.

You were born and raised in St. John's. Then, you moved west to the ski town of Fernie. What inspired this move?

The move was inspired on a lunch break over a game of pool at The Breezeway at the Thomson Student Centre at MUN. One of my good friends said she was going to take a semester off and move to BC to snowboard in Fernie. I thought it was a great idea and jumped on board.

Growing up in Newfoundland, leaving was a kind of rite of passage, something that every young person either did or thought about doing.

My time in BC shaped me in a way that I don't think I ever would've experienced had I stayed in St. John's. The lifestyle in the mountains is completly different. It's driven by a love for adventure, not a career. People live there because they want something different. It's not easy living because you need to be creative in how you support yourself.

As a family, you decided to return to Newfoundland in 2014. What made you want to move back?

I couldn't quite settle out west. I had to know what it would've been like to go back home. I feel this is something that a lot of Newfoundlanders struggle with—the push to leave is as strong as the pull to return. There's also something so freeing about being home. I didn't realize it until we moved here. There's an ease about this place and underlying humour in every conversation or interaction. We laugh often.

Your previous work experiences out west were very different, with a focus on trades in male-dominated spaces.

The trades paid well and offered great job security, but once I had my children, I wanted to preserve as much time as I could for them. I bridged over to my work at Island Lake because it was an easy transition for me to make. I shifted my focus once I moved back to Newfoundland because photography was something I knew I wanted to do.

Within a year of returning to Newfoundland, you began taking photographs. What did this look like in the beginning?

In the beginning, I was on a mission to make it happen. The studying picked up where I had left off, and I spent a lot of time practicing, driving my family and friends crazy, and documenting everything. I don't enjoy being the centre of attention, so I quickly noticed that my photographs were better when I sat back and observed.

What have been some challenges and benefits of being a self-taught photographer?

I don't get bogged down by the way things should be done and I'm able to forge my own path based on the experiences I deem valuable. For me, simplicity and truth are how I see my work; accuracy is important, showing my projects as they are.

But the business side of things is challenging when doing it on your own. Finding the right people to support your business is key to keeping things moving forward.

We talked about developing a strong sense of self-assuredness as creatives. How do we change our inner dialogue with ourselves as we pursue our passions?

In an ideal world, a positive inner dialogue would come from the messages we receive from our parents and society. Kids today are fortunate because they seem to have a higher emotional intelligence, which will hopefully help with more positive self-talk.

The best way to support a positive inner dialogue while pursuing our passions is to continue to educate ourselves in our respective fields.

Who, what, and where inspires you and your work as a photographer?

My clients. I don't think there is ever a shoot where I don't feel totally inspired. I get to see the incredible work people are doing when doing commercial photography, from furniture makers, cabinet makers, and luthiers to curators, art galleries, incredible musicians, interior designers, architects, entrepreneurs, jewellery makers, toy makers, 3D medical supply printers, brew masters, and Indigenous drummers.

When doing portraits, I get a glimpse into people's lives. I've noticed that people have two sides: the one they portray to the public and strangers, and then the side of them that comes out during their time off. I enjoy breaking through that barrier in a very short period of time by asking questions, being vulnerable myself, and genuinely listening to their stories. These conversations are where inspiration happens for me.

> Being a highly sensitive person is a great gift to have as a photographer. When one can anticipate emotion and fire a shot at the right moment, we capture the parts of life where true joy, space, calm, or contemplation are experienced—the parts of life people want to remember.

How would you describe your work?

My approach to photography is to take images that are uncomplicated, to strip away the unnecessary. I like images to have space and room to breathe. Life can be busy, messy, and complicated. The way I take photos is how I cope with it all, by creating something that offers a sense of stillness.

Being a highly sensitive person is a great gift to have as a photographer. When you can anticipate emotion and fire a shot at the right moment, you capture the parts of life where true joy, space, calm, or contemplation are experienced—the parts of life people want to remember.

You have two children and shared that you're also passionate about teaching people how to grow their own food. What inspired this?

As a mom, I was inspired to provide the best possible food for my children. When we moved back to Newfoundland, I noticed that it was the opposite end of the spectrum from life in BC in regard to food growing. At the time, there was not much going on. Luckily, the principal at my children's school was also interested in growing food and enthusiastically got a school garden going.

We started with four vegetable boxes, eight the next year, and then received a grant for an 8 × 16 greenhouse. In 2021, we had forty pounds of tomatoes. It's been a seven-year process, and we've had a few different principals come and go, but every one of them has been extremely supportive. Our community has stepped up, and we have volunteers taking care of the garden in the summer. It's been a beautiful thing to see the passion the kids have developed over the years since we introduced gardening to them.

Dream place, space, or subject to shoot?

Fallingwater House designed by Frank Lloyd Wright, which symbolizes the harmony between nature and people. It's the epitome of *organic architecture*.

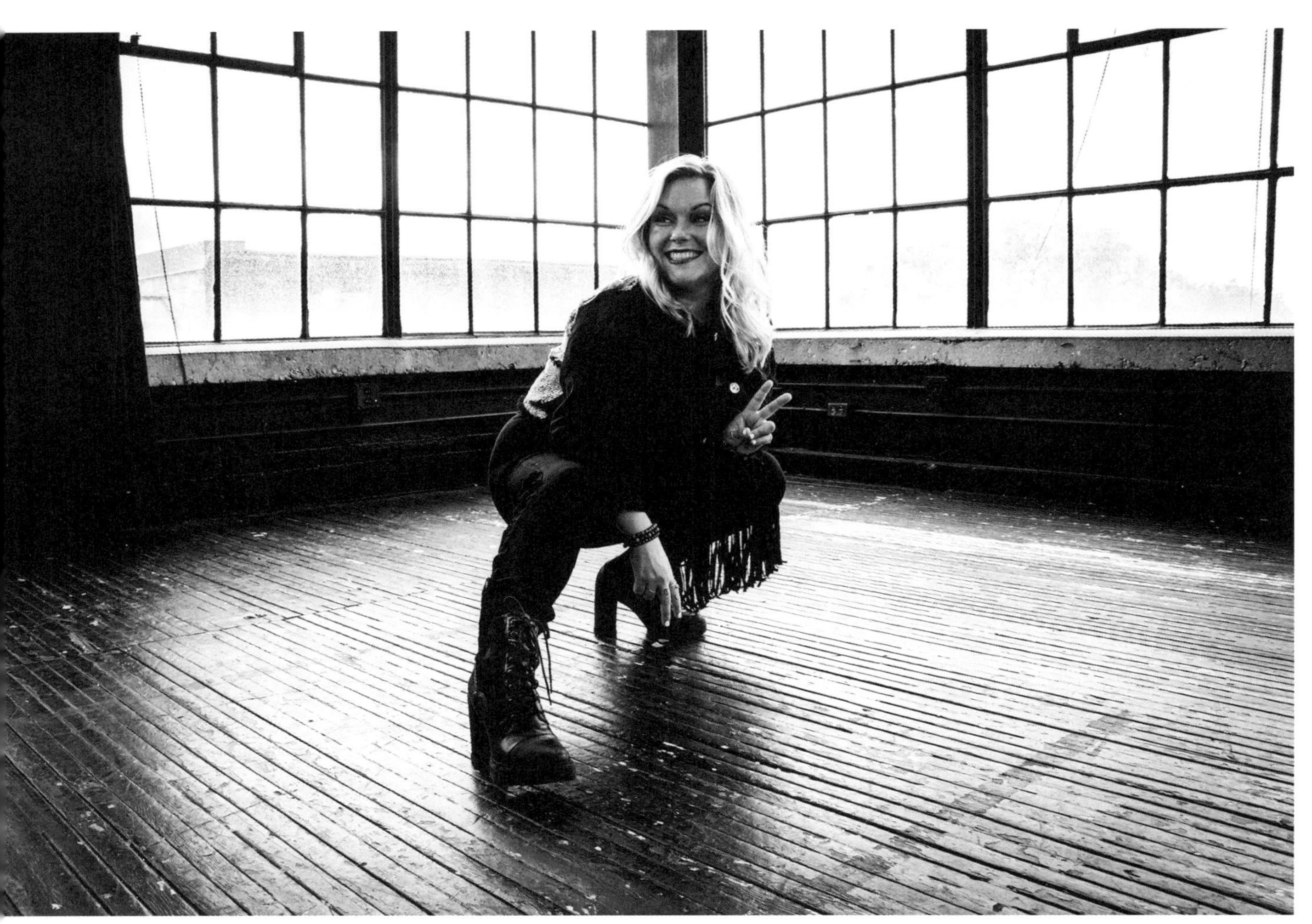

Sandra-Lee Layden

Music and Lifestyle Photographer

"I've found the benefit exists not in my gender but in my ability to create a connection with the artists. Being personable and friendly has gotten me further than being a female in the industry."

What is your first memory of a photo that moved you?

It was the photos from the CD inserts in the Woodstock 1994 compilation album. I remember listening to the album on repeat and burying myself in the photos of everyone in the mud—they were so raw and real—a sea of humans, soaking wet, dirty, naked, and rocking the hell out to music they loved.

Other photos would be those from Woodstock 1969 or Jimi Hendrix lighting his guitar on fire at the Monterey Pop Festival in 1967. Both represented freedom and a different side of photography that I hadn't explored as a small-town kid in rural Newfoundland.

You started shooting musicians and concerts as a teenager.

I started photographing small local bands from my area when I was around sixteen. I'd be front row at the rec centres or clubs with a cheap digital camera, probably a Kodak EasyShare, shooting my heart out.

I was twenty when I photographed my first real gig—for the *Newfoundland Herald*, and it was Blue Rodeo at the Mile One Centre, or maybe Backstreet Boys at the same venue. I remember how nervous I was going into it, not feeling completely confident in my abilities as I had only recently gotten the job and started photography school.

At what point in your life did you realize that you wanted to pursue music photography?

I was a late bloomer in deciding on what I wanted my career to be. After high school, I took a gap year and thought I wanted to be a chef. I lasted less than a week in that program, realizing that I love cooking for people I love, not for people to critique. I was twenty before I enrolled in college and realized I could potentially make a career out of this. The progression to a professional music photographer was natural. I was always front row at concerts and local gigs and would have my camera on me. Capturing bands how I saw them, as a fan, was something that brought me joy. I felt like so many music photographers were looking for *the* shot instead of trying to capture how the artists made you feel.

Music has always been one of the most important aspects of my life. The emotions and memories that music evoke remind me of the same feelings that a good photo brings out.

Music has always been one of the most important aspects of my life. The emotions and memories that music evoke remind me of the same feelings that a good photo brings out.

You've shared that you went to school for photography but felt that you learned so much more from being in the field.

I took a degree program at a local community college, where we learned on film cameras. However, the courses severely lacked. We were being taught how to be a Sears portrait photographer, not taught to explore our creativity and our own eye. You can learn everything on paper, but once you are in the field, it changes. Fifteen years later, I learn something new every time I pick up my camera. It's a constant state of improvement and bettering yourself.

Once I started working, I learned that to be truly successful, you have to differentiate yourself from the crowd instead of being a sheep.

You were born and raised in Newfoundland and continue to call it home. You also spend a lot of time in Toronto. How has each place shaped you?

Growing up in a small town in Newfoundland, I always felt a little like an outsider. I was born in Toronto to Newfoundlander parents, and we returned to the island when I was five. Moving to Newfoundland provided me with more safety and physical freedom as a child, but it was definitely a little more close-minded when it came to the exploration of the arts outside of the standards.

Newfoundland did provide me with rare access to influential bands, whereas music photographers were a dime a dozen in Toronto. I had a home advantage when bands came to town and forged some great friendships that way. In Toronto, I was a small fish in a big pond, but thankfully I had friends that supported me and helped me forge a great career in the city. It's a nonstop rotation of every band you could ever dream of working with, incredible local musicians, and a stunning arts scene.

Over the past few years, you've shifted the focus of your work to 75 percent music photography and 25 percent lifestyle. What motivated this shift?

I reached a point in my life where I wanted to find joy in my work. In 2017, one of my close friends lost his battle with mental illness, and it was a slap in the face that life is too short to be unhappy. I spent a decade photographing twenty-five to forty weddings a year and hundreds of family photo sessions, which is mentally and physically exhausting. Working in the music industry can also be both of those things, but the shows and shoots bring me so much happiness. I've never walked into a wedding and had the weight lift off my shoulders, but that happens every time the lights go down in a club or arena.

How would you describe your style as a photographer?

Authentic. What you see is what you get. I don't spend hours to get one photo. I capture the moment as it happens—creating a memory of that moment in history.

I like to shoot people in an environment that brings out their personalities and makes them comfortable. The more comfortable someone is when you're capturing them, the more they're going to trust you behind the camera.

Who inspires you?

My grandmother Annie Brennan inspires me to be a better person, to chase my dreams, and live life to the fullest.

What do you hope people take away when looking at your photos?

I hope people look at them and feel like they were right there next to me capturing the photo. I hope they walk away with a feeling of authenticity and having seen a different perspective than the usual.

I imagine being a female photographer in a predominantly male industry comes with its share of challenges but also benefits. Why is it important to pave the path of this profession for future female creatives?

Starting out, there weren't a ton of female photographers in the industry; we were few and far between. I was usually the only woman in the pit at big festivals, like the Much Music Video Awards and JUNO Awards, for years. I feel like I've worked twice as hard as my male counterparts, and it's taken me twice as long to achieve the accolades and recognition.

Unfortunately, some female music photographers may experience harassment, discrimination, or sexism in their workplaces or during events. These negative experiences can create discomfort, hinder professional growth, and discourage women from fully participating or expressing themselves in the industry.

Despite these challenges, it's important to note that many talented and successful female music photographers have overcome these obstacles and made significant contributions to the industry.

I've found the benefit exists not in my gender but in my ability to create a connection with the artists. Being personable and friendly has gotten me further than being a female in the industry.

Why is music important?

It's the universal language and it transcends barriers, both physical and mental. Music has the power to evoke a wide range of emotions, such as joy, sadness, nostalgia, or excitement. This emotional resonance can bring people together, allowing them to connect and bond over their shared feelings.

Regardless of one's background or native language, the universal language of music can be understood and appreciated by people from diverse backgrounds.

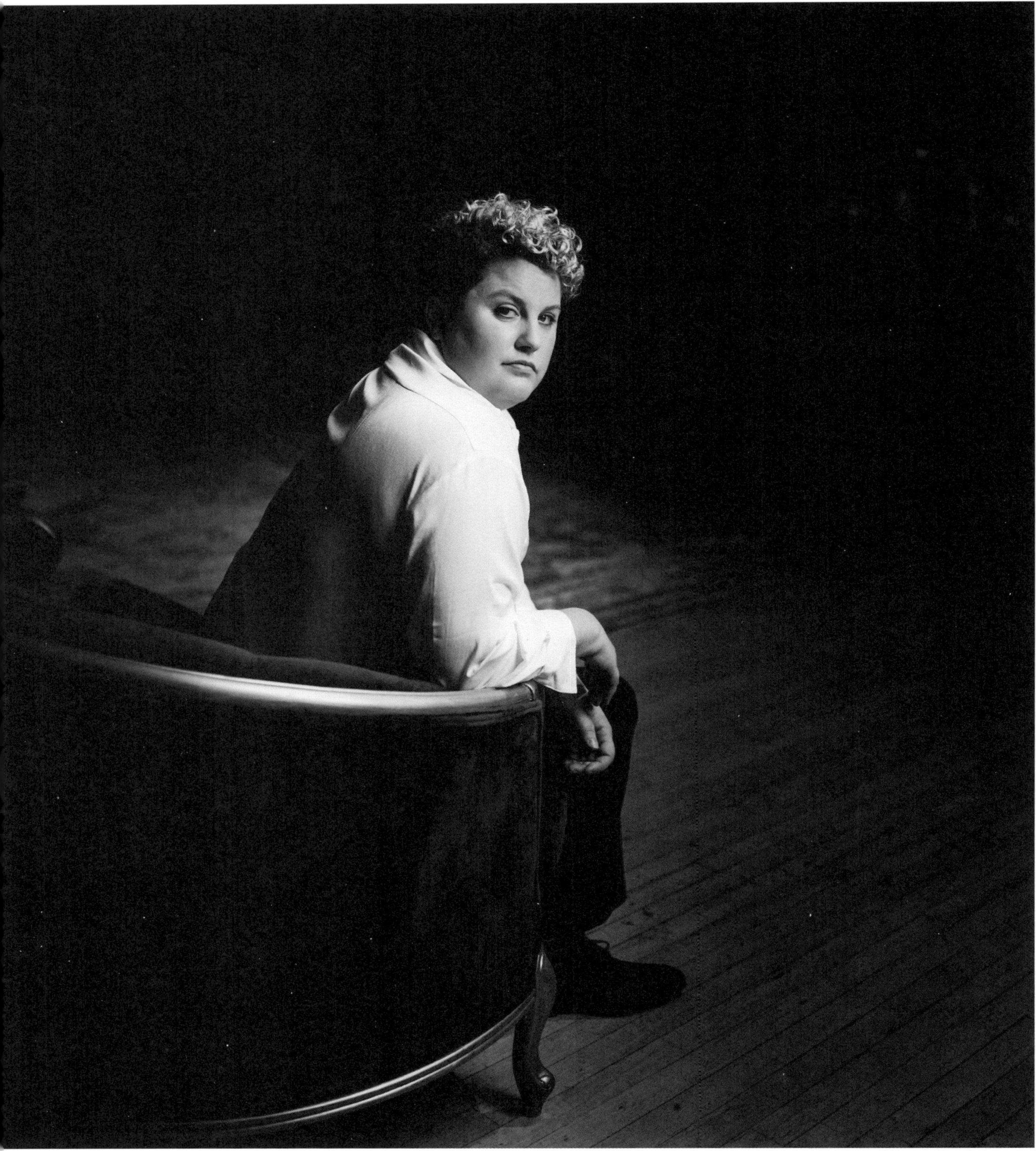

Kellie Loder

Singer and Songwriter

"I chose everything else, but music chose me."

What is your first memory of music?

My first memories of music take place in the church I grew up attending twice every Sunday. I remember the colour of the drums. They were transparent with a light blue tint. I always watched the drummer. I wanted to be like him. I would bring two pencils with me to services and bang on the top of the pew, trying to match what he was doing.

When did you realize that music was your path?

I've always had a deep knowing that music was my path, except I spent a lot of my time choosing everything else. I was nominated for a JUNO award while I was attending nursing school. I remember doing my first CBC interview in the hallway of the hospital on a lunch break.

I was pulled in a lot of different directions until I stopped letting my fear win that tug-of-war. I was afraid of the so-called *impractical* or *unrealistic* dreams I knew I would inevitably end up pursuing. I chose everything else, but music chose me.

You were born and raised in Newfoundland. How does this place inspire you as an artist and a person?

I grew up in a small town called Badger, right in the middle of the island. We got the hottest days in the summer and the coldest ones in the winter. I still can't make sense of that. I lived life on my dad's ATV, what we call a quad, or his Ski-Doo.

In 2018, I moved to Toronto to further my music career and build connections. When the *ol'* virus came to town in 2020, I came home to St. John's, where I lived before I moved to Toronto, and I've been here ever since.

There's something beautifully untouched about the landscape and overall energy of Newfoundland culture. There's a permission to be silly, to be yourself, and an innocence that lives here that I would protect at all costs. It's as if this place I call home hasn't been penetrated or infected by the symbolic needle of a more complicated life: war, status, hatred, greed, and power. At our core, we are people united with one beating heart. It's as if the air is breathable gold, and I get to enjoy it for nothing in return. Beware of Newfoundland. It might swallow you whole and never spit you out.

Tell us about the first time you performed in front of a live audience.

I've been performing for as long as I can remember. The beginnings were probably in front of the church congregation. Between playing drums, playing guitar, and singing, I was successfully playing my first unpaid gigs.

If I was born into the world a
boy but I felt the girl inside

Would you ridicule my choices
or undress me with your eyes

Would you march within the hate
parade or stand and hold a sign

That says there's only hate for me
and that I should take my life

"MOLDED LIKE A MONSTER"

Let's talk about "Molded Like A Monster," for which you received a 2021 ECMA win. You captured the emotion, fear, hatred, and hope into one of the most beautiful and important songs I've heard in a long while. Tell me more about putting all of this into a song. I imagine it was cathartic on many levels.

To be honest, this verse is about me. I switched the genders to *keep my secret*, but hey, I'm kind of over it now. Did I fool anyone? Probably not. I came out as non-binary/transgender in March 2022.

I had just seen the movie *American Sniper* at the theatre in St. John's. The next day, I was driving down Pitts Memorial Drive and feeling *shook* to my core by one of the scenes in the film. There was a little Iraqi boy, maybe eight years old, coming out of a building on the ground level. He picked up a large gun and pointed it at the American troops. The Sniper in the hills was begging the boy under his breath to drop the gun. Otherwise, he'd have to take his life. This scene put me into a spin. It dawned on me that we really don't get to choose the mould, the family, or the culture we're born into and that each of us appears to be or has the potential to be a monster to somebody else.

On that drive, the verses fell into my lap, and I sang them out. The chorus came to me in a bathtub when I was visiting my parents in Badger on a weekend. I called out to my mom, "Please bring my phone in, I need to record something." She jimmied the door open, held out the phone on record, and "Molded Like A Monster" had life as I sang and banged along like a church drummer on my naked knees.

Lyrics as storytelling: What does this mean for you as an artist?

If you put ten listeners in a room and ask them to listen to a song, I guarantee they won't all have the same interpretation. The magic happens when they take words that have nothing to do with them and apply them to their own lives based on their own perspectives. We don't just listen with our ears. We listen with our eyes too. Some of them even get to hear my story, but some of them hear their own, and that's okay.

A song that moves you. Every. Single. Time.

"Black Sheep" by MILCK.

You have an impressive and long list of stellar achievements. Your 2019 single, "Fearless," was chosen as the soundtrack behind the CBC's 2021 Tokyo Olympics coverage, and you were awarded first runner-up on the 2022 season of *Canada's Got Talent*. Congratulations! How have these experiences inspired you as an artist?

I've been an independent artist this whole time. Anything I've ever achieved was planted in the soil of my own effort, with different mentors, family, and friends inside and outside the industry watering my roots as they pass by. My mom and I applied for the JUNO award in her kitchen. I sent my song to the CBC on a whim with hopes they'd like it. I applied for *Canada's Got Talent* on the last day to apply, working part-time as a carpenter. I'm so appreciative of the career I've built and the boldness I believe I was born with. That doesn't mean I've never been rejected. It means I never gave up, even when I was. Anything is possible. It really is.

What do you need to be creative and productive?

Desire and time. For example, I didn't have to discipline myself to learn the guitar. I loved it so much. It's all I wanted to do, but without time, I was doing something else. It was only when I made room for my creativity to grow that it flourished. Writing comes fairly easy for me, but I believe in a healthy amount of discipline to keep writing and expressing, exercising the muscle, and listening to other music that will subconsciously inspire. Producing is a new passion. I think I'm good at it, but it's a hard one to accept for some reason.

I suffer a little from imposter syndrome. This year was the first time my name was in the bigger letters on a festival poster, and I grappled with that, if I'm honest. Whenever I'm performing now, I'm constantly telling myself "You deserve to be here. You're amazing. You've got this. Let them hear you. Let them be enamoured."

Do you have a dream venue where you'd like to perform, and a dream collaboration?

When I imagine myself performing at a dream venue, I've never really seen an arena. I've always seen a massive theatre, maybe a Massey or a Royal Albert Hall. If Adele heard my music, liked it, and wanted to write with me, I wouldn't say no. Adele's voice with something we created together: now that's a dream.

> I'm so appreciative of the career I've built and the boldness I believe I was born with. That doesn't mean I've never been rejected. It means I never gave up even when I was. Anything is possible. It really is.

Why is music important?

Music makes us feel things. It creates space for us to cry, dance, laugh, get angry, get sad, and so on. We're connected by our spirits like roots in the ground. We can be different trees in the way we look, sway, struggle, shed our leaves, and grow new ones. We can be different all while communicating, sharing nutrients, grafting under the surface, and helping each other be strong. I reach people through music. I'm just a small part of it all.

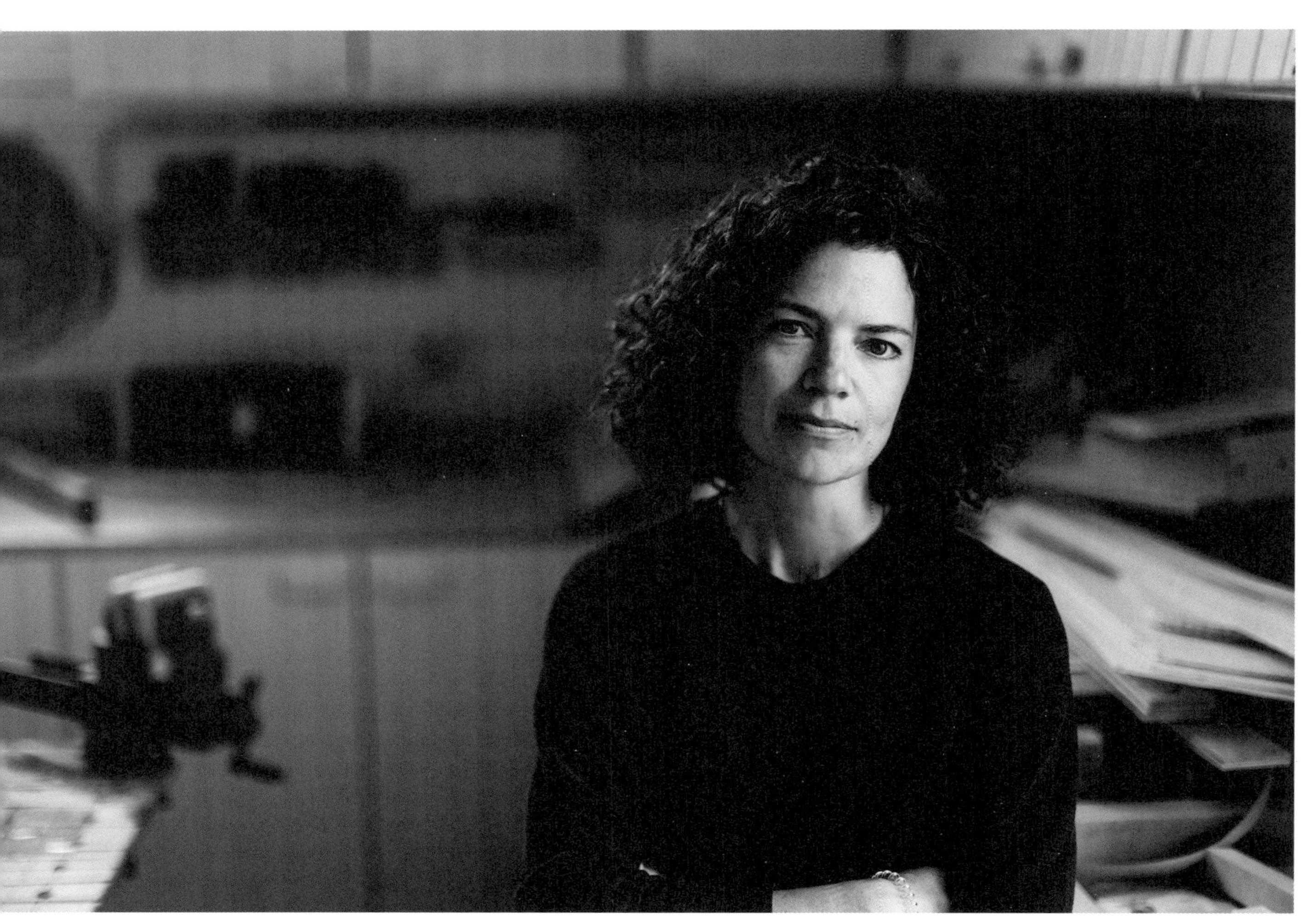

Katrina Tompkins

Furniture Designer, Maker, and Educator

"Design and fabrication are interdependent. The better one knows the materials, the better a designer one will be."

What is an early memory of using your hands to build something?

There hasn't been a thread of making throughout my life. I must have participated in the usual crafting and things at school, but none of those objects or experiences are with me still today.

The making I loved growing up was making camp! I grew up going to summer camp and loved canoe-tripping immensely. What lit me up then and still does today is portaging treks out into the wilderness, sleeping in tents, cooking over the fire, and singing and paddling my heart out.

Where did you grow up? How did this place shape you as a person and a designer?

Growing up, my mom was a real estate agent, and I wandered through tons of houses with her in my formative years. I'm certain that these experiences contributed to my interest in furniture design. I observed the differences in the quality of materials and the quality of work. I heard what she liked and formed my own opinions.

I've never felt very proud of or connected to where I grew up, which was in Oakville, Ontario. As a whole, my perception of the community's values didn't align with mine. It felt very homogenous in my neighbourhood: white, rich, and heteronormative. Maybe it's changed. Maybe there are diverse, queer, artistic corners of it that I never got to see. Regardless, it launched me on a lifelong search for belonging and knowing where I want to be.

Was art and creativity encouraged in your family?

The short answer is no. My parents didn't encourage creativity in their children necessarily; they were more focused on our development of a strong work ethic. They did, however, appreciate design and craftsmanship. My dad could spend all day admiring a dry-stone wall or an antique hutch, marvelling at the skill involved in their fabrication. My dad always longed to develop those skills himself, and his desire for this likely propelled me to explore making domestic objects. My parents are incredibly supportive now of my creativity and career in furniture.

At what stage of life did you know that furniture design would be your professional path?

When I was twenty-six, I got serious about figuring out a career path. I knew I wanted to do something creative and was drawn to furniture for its function and purpose. I was ready to commit to furniture. I worked really hard, and I excelled, finally. Perhaps it is that commitment that has helped me find the belonging that I was seeking, because I feel it in craft, and I believe that craft is rooted in community. There is accountability in both.

You studied at the New Brunswick College of Craft and Design, Sheridan College, and OCAD University. How did these programs prepare you for your craft?

Both Sheridan and OCAD U shaped my interests within craft and I'm so grateful for these opportunities to learn, though I did at times feel like a duck out of water as a self-identifying craftsperson in a graduate program. However, I realize how much I thrive when there's a research component to a project now, and I have my time in graduate studies at OCAD U to thank for that!

What motivated the move to Fogo Island? Do you feel a sense of belonging there?

I wasn't looking for a new opportunity. I had just finished my master's degree and was launching my new practice in Prince Edward County when I heard that Fogo Island Workshops (FIW) was hiring. I had to apply! I've always admired the work of FIW and their approach to place-based design. I was offered the position, and shortly after COVID-19 hit, my partner Michelle and I loaded up our pets and a trailer and made our way across the country. Michelle was very trusting and a great sport, having never been to Newfoundland before. We both love Fogo Island and all of Newfoundland tremendously, and we feel a sense of belonging, which is in part attributed to how welcoming the community has been.

Your company, Finefolk Furniture, operates in Prince Edward County and Fogo Island. What are the benefits and challenges of operating in two different places?

My business is always evolving and now, as I face a new challenge with woodworking, I have to be creative with how I shape my career. I have developed a sensitivity to sawdust, which is a pretty serious hurdle for a furniture maker.

Successfully splitting life between two places feels like it would take many years to master—we're in the early phases! What works so far is that Michelle and I have a healthy, independent relationship and we are able to spend long periods of time away from each other. So, if one of us needs to be somewhere and the other somewhere else, we divide and conquer, then blissfully reunite.

What does your studio space look like? What do you require to create?

In Newfoundland, I have a 14 × 26 foot *shed shop*, as I like to call it. It's sparsely equipped, heated with a pellet stove and clings to the edge of the sea. When we bought the property, the seller included his collection of several hundred vintage snapback caps, all local to Newfoundland and Labrador, acquired on his life's journey. They decorate the shed shop, hanging from nails in the rafters, exactly as we found them.

I have trimmed my working equipment down to next-to-nothing at my little shed shop. In Ontario, I have quite the opposite arrangement with all sorts of stationary woodworking equipment. Ironically, I've always been more comfortable with heavy machinery than hand tools, but now, I'm entering my hand tool years.

If the shop was left a mess, it has to be cleaned before I can focus on the work to be done. I love a tidy shop.

Who, where, and what inspires you?

I love digging into regional histories, materials, and culture and how these things came together to create the local vernacular. That's, in part, why I'm so taken with Newfoundland. I deeply respect the resourcefulness required of outport life and how folks made their furniture, toys, and domestic objects with the materials at hand, with limited tools or experience.

I'm inspired by my mentors and friends in woodworking. Heidi Earnshaw, Mike Paterson, and Chris Schwarz are all the real deal: skilled, committed, creative makers who have built a life around their craft practice. I think for all of us, furniture making is much more than a job.

I also have to circle back to Sheridan College for one more round of praise. The faculty were exemplary furniture educators. They really kept me on my toes then, all those years ago, and are still encouraging and supporting me now.

Dream place to explore and adventure to.

I am drawn to the north. I hope to see the Torngat Mountains someday. I might even have a case of the arctic fever. My favourite stuffed toy growing up was a polar bear. Think there could be a connection?

You've done a few apprenticeships. What are the benefits of apprenticeship, especially for women embarking upon a new profession?

My experiences apprenticing with professional furniture makers were not only beneficial in learning their ways of making but also, since I was staying on their properties, I saw how they lived.

Apprenticing was immensely helpful in envisioning how I could try to make it work for myself and helped shape the life I wanted to create. Both my apprenticeships were three weeks unpaid, with food and housing provided. Long enough to learn, give back, and make some lifelong memories.

For a creative discipline, there is a lot of responsibility in this work. I love the challenge.

What is unique about being a woodworker and an educator?

When creating furniture, there is quite a checklist of what it needs to be. At the base level, it has to carry a dynamic load, be comfortable, endure human and animal abuses, and look great. If you really care, then it also has to last, be timeless, original, sustainable, healthy, accessible, ethical, meaningful, local, and help others. My point is, for a creative discipline, there is a lot of responsibility in this work. I love the challenge.

As an educator, I want to convey the value of that scope of criteria. When teaching, my message is this: design and fabrication are interdependent. The better one knows the materials, the better a designer one will be.

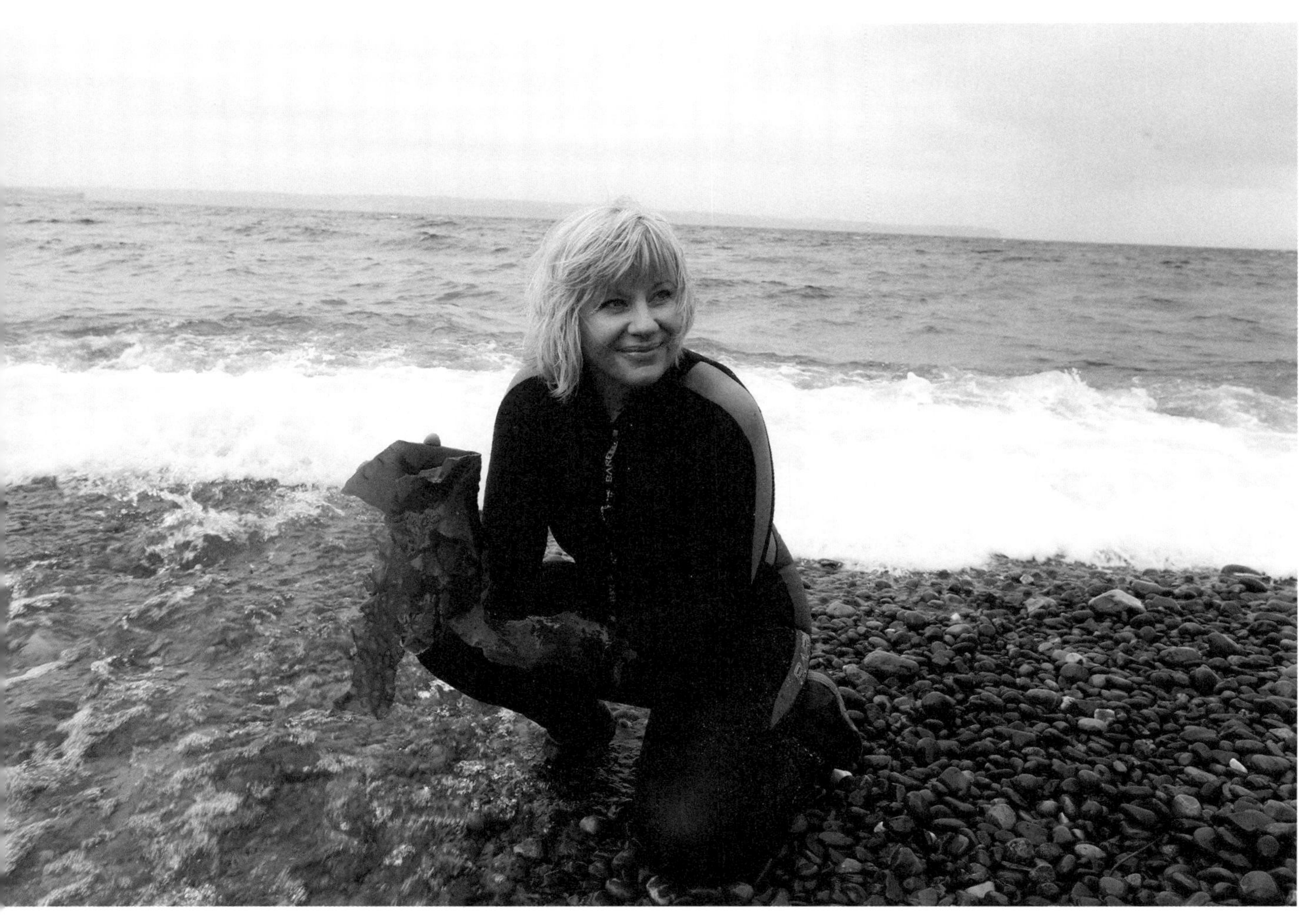

Lisa Walsh

Founder, Island Skincare

"We are a woman-owned and woman-led business. Everything we do revolves around our feminine energy. It has been a journey to find what works for me as an owner and a woman."

You were born and raised in Newfoundland—a unique and stunning landscape. What's an early memory of exploring its natural beauty?

The barrens surrounding my hometown of Bay de Verde have such a fragrant aroma from summer to late fall. It is a heady, fresh aroma of the ground, berries, flowers, and bushes. I just love it there—it's my happy place.

"I founded Island Skincare to create products made in harmony with the seasons. Luxurious, sustainable, award winning skincare from botanical ingredients native to the island. I was, and still am, continuously inspired by this island." How does this mindset inspire?

It is the little things in life that bring me the most joy. Fergus, my partner, and I love feeding the birds around our property and enjoy ocean walks. We're also amateur landscape photographers. It is like *National Geographic* every day here. The ocean and beaches are my favourite places to visit. Labrador has the most stunning beaches of any I have visited in the world. We have been to almost every nook and cranny on this majestic island for work and play.

You shared that you experienced a range of health issues that in part motivated the development of products that you could safely use and benefit from. How so?

I became a hair designer in 1985. I loved every minute of this creative trade. Back then, chemicals were not understood or spoken about. No one knew the damage that hair colour, hair sprays, and perms had on hairstylists and people working in salons. I owned three salons and business was booming, but my health, not so much. At the age of thirty-six, I was advised by my doctor and a specialist to change careers. I was always sick with lung infections, bronchitis, and head colds, and I had acne from the chemicals. I then realized I could not have children due to my career choice. It was devastating. I set out a course of action to create a healthy, safe, naturally derived brand that puts people's health first.

"I am happiest when near the ocean, her strength and beauty inspire me to live my best life." Please tell me more about how this applies to the story of Island Skincare.

Island Skincare was founded in a place surrounded by water, on an ancient subcontinent called Avalonia. When a brand designer asked me about what was most important to our ethos, the ocean and all her bounty and animals kept coming to mind. The ocean's colours are beautiful, and they are reflected in our branding. Everything about the North Atlantic is mystical and I cannot imagine not seeing her every day.

Before starting a botanical skincare line, you had another career. How did it prepare you for your current role with Island Skincare?

I've had several: hair designer, makeup artist, salon and spa owner, and high school and post-secondary teacher.

From an early age, I worked with my mother at the General Store in Bay de Verde. It was here that I learned from her how to merchandise retail items, order stock, and converse with buyers. They loved her because she was straightforward, courteous, and had an eye for what would sell. I also worked at the production plants in Bay de Verde as a student. That experience prepared me more than anything for this business.

I've worked as a Career Development Officer with the Government of Newfoundland, helping apprentices attain their Red Seal. I've volunteered with Skills Canada and taught cosmetology and esthetics at several public and private schools on the island. These jobs gave me more insight into creating a brand that would resonate with people and helped me put systems in place that run smoothly.

What year did Island Skincare officially open?

I started in 2009, incorporated in 2011, and quit my full-time job in 2012 to manage ISC full time.

You have a unique way of running Island Skincare.

We are a woman-owned and woman-led business. Everything we do revolves around our feminine energy. It has been a journey to find what works for me as an owner and a woman. Putting health and happiness first has improved the business more than any other single change we have made. Our staff workday starts anywhere between 9:30 AM and 10 AM and finishes between 2:30 PM and 4 PM depending on the staff's personal preference.

No one is stressed, everyone feels appreciated, and Fridays off are amazing. We are all on the same page when it comes to the company's growth and strategy plan. My partner Fergus retired from Bell and has spent his time improving our production processes. He is supportive and always considerate. Being a home-based business has given me the ability to look after my staff and business better than if I had to leave home. There is no commute, which gives me more time to enjoy my life with Fergus and our family.

The ocean's colours are beautiful, and they are reflected in our branding. Everything about the North Atlantic is mystical and I cannot imagine not seeing her every day.

Balance. How does this word resonate?

Balance is everything. Looking after myself is #1. This year I decided to make a radical change. With the aftermath of the pandemic creating staffing issues, I had to make a decision to outsource my production or change the way I did business. I chose to become a Solopreneur and embrace the parts of my business I enjoy most.

On a personal level, I journal every morning, meditate, and practice rituals that create calmness and confidence. Through COVID-19, I had so much anxiety from not knowing what was going to happen to my business. I've learned to take it day by day.

Are there any brick-and-mortar shops that carry the brand? Do you see the possibility for an Island Skincare retail shop in the future?

Online is our main store. In 2016 Island Skincare entered grocery stores in Atlantic Canada in Sobeys, and since then, we have been getting into more stores throughout the Atlantic, Canada, and abroad. We are also the amenity supplier of Fogo Island Inn, Battle Harbour Historic Trust, and Hodge Premises Inn. These are the three top-tier tourism destinations in the province. It makes me happy to be aligned with like-minded businesses and social enterprises.

All Island Skincare products are made in Newfoundland. Incredible! What are the benefits and challenges of this?

The challenge now is I can only make so much to maintain the quality I won't compromise on. I would say our research and development could measure up to Chanel or La Mer. I spent the first five years focusing on native botanical R&D. It's not about creating mass products; it's about carefully curating limited luxurious collections that are pleasurable to apply and treat your skin to an amazing experience. Creating in my own lab, foraging in the summer, and marketing my business is a big list.

Any new products or services we can look forward to?

Yes. I am currently creating an online formulating course.

My girlfriend Gail Morgan and I just launched *50+ The Luxe Life Podcast* to enjoy and celebrate our life and age. Just having a little fun with this!

And... there is a book in the works! I am so excited to share my experiences here on the island with the business over the last fifteen years. It is a book featuring foraging and the landscape through all four seasons.

What do you hope for the future of Island Skincare?

To stay in good health, continue to enjoy creating and formulating, and have the packaging evolve to as close to zero waste as possible.

To focus on the science and formulation that puts Island Skincare in a category of its own in the natural formulating space. This is so important to me.

Having our own supply chain and extracts is something very few brands can achieve; that is my legacy. Rare botanical extracts that improve aging, sensitive skin, and acne are the foundation of Island Skincare.

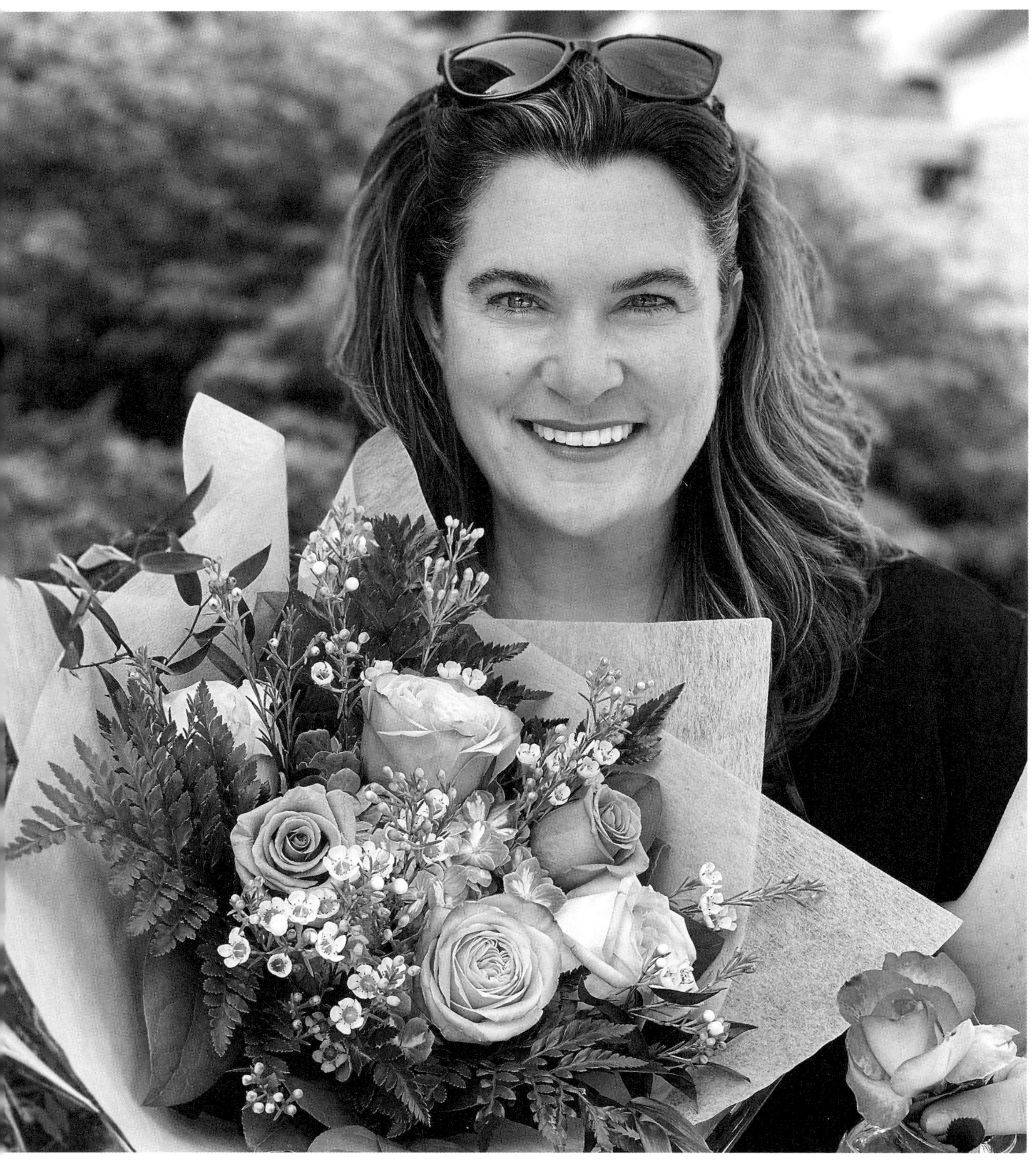

Sarah Keaveny Vos

Journalist, CBC

"In a world that can sometimes feel pretty dark, stories that offer lightness can be a beacon of hope."

What is your first memory of words?

My first memory of words was in elementary school. I'd written a story in which the main character was a little button on a shirt. The story was written from the button's perspective and point of view. It started with the button trying to get the reader's attention: "Hi there... Hello...? Look down... way down here, it's me, your button!"

I remember the day a teacher stopped me in the hallway and told me that the teachers had chosen my story to be published in the school yearbook.

I remember feeling thrilled and quietly proud. My story touched someone. It was going to be put into print and preserved in the school yearbook. It was the first time I felt like I might have a talent for writing. It was a real vote of confidence, and that empowering feeling has never left me. In fact, it has encouraged me all my life.

You were born and raised in PEI.

I am so grateful to have been born on Prince Edward Island. It is truly a place of kindness, caring, and beauty. Beauty, not just in its landscape, but in its people. This is a place where people slow down for each other.

My husband and I were working and living in South Florida when our first child was born. We'd been there a few years and enjoyed the lifestyle, but it had never felt like home. We knew in our hearts that we wanted to raise our family in Canada, close to our family, friends, and a community that cared about us. After raising our three children in PEI for the last twenty-three years, I can honestly say we made the right decision.

Professionally, I find the richness of the stories here as deep and beautiful as our famous red soil. The people I meet and interview inspire me. In a world that can sometimes feel pretty dark, stories that offer lightness can be a beacon of hope.

Journalism was not your first post-secondary degree.

One day, while sitting in my classroom at UPEI, I had an epiphany. I was halfway through my education degree and had made some really great friends. Those friends were just lit up by what we were learning and excited to get into the classroom and meet their students. They were passionate about teaching.

As much as I enjoyed it, teaching was not my passion. Students deserve to be taught by passionate teachers.

My husband was a newly minted RCMP officer, and we were stationed in a small town north of Saskatoon. I wanted to get out and meet people, so I went to the local cable station to see if I could volunteer. I pitched an idea for a show called *The Bright*

Side of the Road, which would focus on positive things happening in the community.

They gave me the green light and paired me with a great guy who became my co-producer, cameraman, and friend. That experience helped me find my passion for storytelling. I applied to the University of King's College journalism program and felt like I was finally on the right path.

When I look back, I am in awe of the people I have met over the years and the stories they have trusted me with. Stories that move and uplift, that resonate and make a difference. It has been an honour to share these stories and I am so grateful for it.

As I get older, I see there are many paths towards a happy life. From time to time, I've thought, *what if I had stayed on one path instead of searching further down the trail for another?* I think it is the human condition to ask *what if,* but I also believe that new opportunities are out there if you are open to them.

What's unique about your type of storytelling?

I describe my work as stories about humanity. Stories that shine a light on people doing good things in the world. Things that matter and lift others up. The people I speak to are folks you might pass on the street, smile at, and just keep walking by.

Until you hear their story. Until you hear how they are doing something special that is impacting others in a great way.

I feel these stories are important because they give us something our spirits need: hope, a belief in the goodness of others, and the inspiration to try and make the world a little better, in your own way. These types of stories help create connections and remind us that when we lift each other up, we all rise together.

I have always felt that these human stories—ones that some people might consider the "smaller stories"—can often have the biggest impact. Stories about kindness, courage, strength, and at the heart of it, our love for one another. That is where humanity is. That is where meaning is. That is where the soul is.

What you pay attention to grows. I choose to pay attention to and seek out stories that are about the goodness in the world. Bringing stories like these to our audience may help more goodness grow in our world. Or at least, remind us that goodness is here.

What are the benefits and challenges of seeking out stories that move the human spirit?

I can honestly say that every person I have ever done a story on has stayed with me. When I look into their eyes and ask questions about their life, a connection is formed. I carry that connection as I begin to form their story. I want the audience to feel that connection, and I really want the person who shared their story with me to feel like I got it right.

The kinds of stories I share are not the ones that lead the nightly news. But maybe one day they will be. The media is realizing more and more that people need to hear news that uplifts and inspires as much as they need to hear news that informs and explains. Of course, we need to have insights and explanations into how our world is running. But we also need a counterbalance.

As I get older, I see there are many paths towards a happy life. From time to time, I've thought, *what if I had stayed on one path instead of searching further down the trail for another?* I think it is the human condition to ask *what if*, but I also believe that new opportunities are out there if you are open to them.

Please tell me about the Gabriel Award and the moving story behind it.

Winning a Gabriel Award is one of the greatest honours of my life. But I didn't win it alone. I won it alongside the amazing children in Mrs. O'Keefe's kindergarten class in Souris, PEI. Five years ago, I saw a letter to the editor written by substitute teacher Marie McGaugh. Marie had witnessed a sweet act of kindness one morning during circle time and was so touched by it that she wanted to share it.

One of the little girls in the circle had accidentally put her shirt on backwards that morning. Her friend noticed the mistake and gently told her. The little girl was embarrassed and hung her head. Marie, knowing the friend never meant to hurt her classmate's feelings, used the situation as a teaching moment and explained that sometimes we can embarrass someone accidentally and hurt their feelings.

As Marie spoke, she saw the little girl who mentioned the mistake slowly take her arm out of her sleeve and turn her own shirt around. Then, one by one, each child in the circle did the same until they were all wearing their shirts backwards.

Marie was so moved by the children's empathy that she wrote a letter to the editor of our provincial newspaper, *The Guardian*. I read that letter and immediately reached out to Marie and the school to see if I could come and interview the kids about their beautiful gesture.

I called that story "The Kindness of Kids," and it won the 2019 Gabriel Award for Single News Story—Local or National. It was an amazing experience flying to St. Petersburg, Florida and attending an awards gala.

As soon as I got home, I made a beeline for those kids, who were by that point in grade one. I wanted them to hold the award, to feel the weight of it, and to know that they had earned it.

These little kids from a little town in a little province in Canada made a big impact because they did a big thing.

The future of storytelling.

I think the future of storytelling is waiting to be written. It's exciting to think of the new way stories will be told using state-of-the-art tools and technologies. Already, drones are giving us fascinating, fresh perspectives, and social media is bursting with creativity and imagination.

But we have to decide what matters to us. What's important; what's meaningful? What do we want to give our attention to? What do we want to grow?

Stories of strength, perseverance, and overcoming challenges? Stories of empathy, generosity, and caring? Stories that help us look at each other with a little more understanding and compassion? It's up to us to decide.

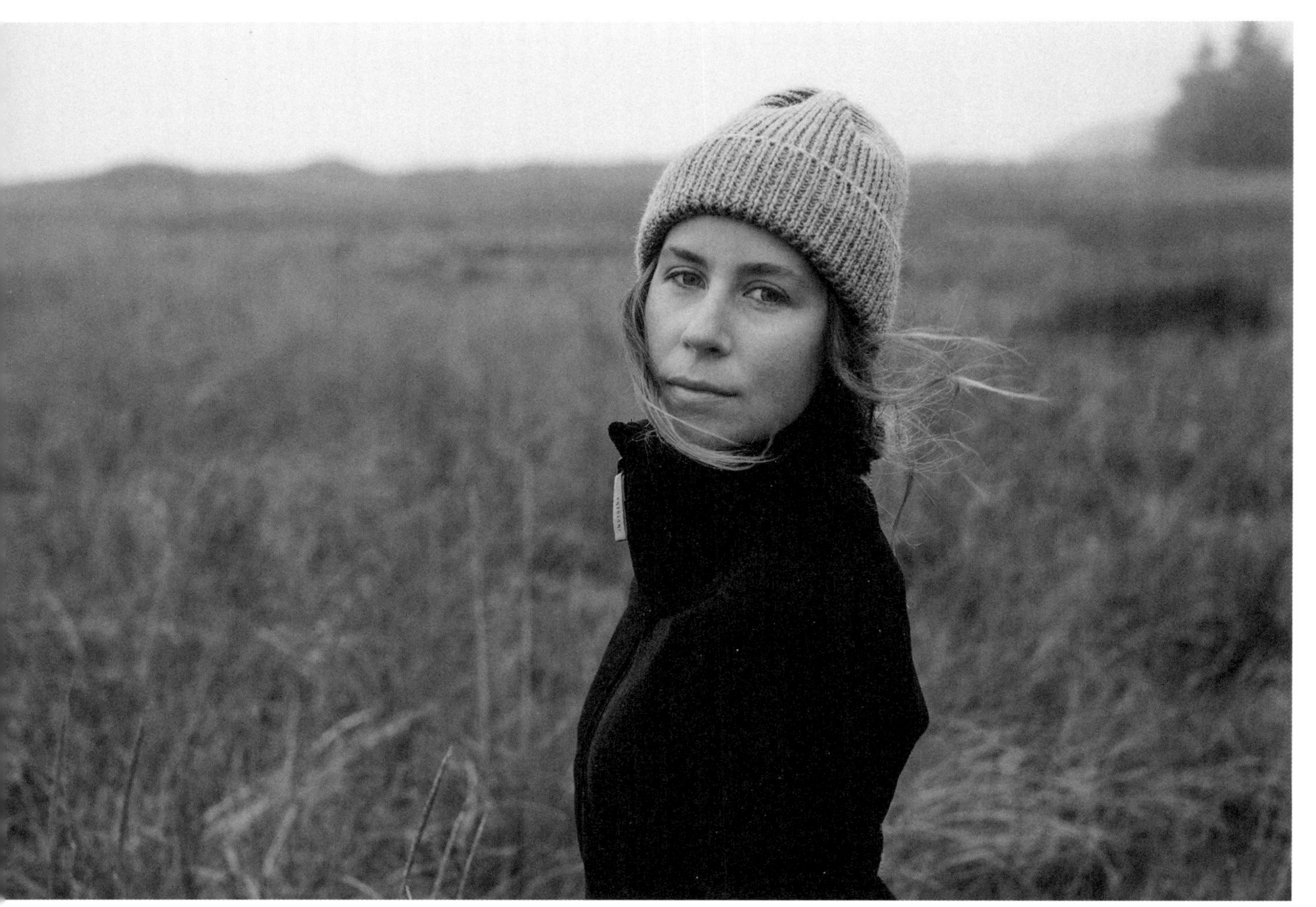

Catherine Bernier

Photographer and Artist

"Through photography, I pay attention to every detail that surrounds me. It's like walking with a magnifying glass or binoculars."

What is your first memory of a photo that moved you?

My mom took lots of photos of my two younger sisters and I with her 35mm camera: the laughs and moments when we were absorbed by our new hobbies, as well as the dynamic between the three of us. These photos allowed me to see how I felt surrounded by different environments, and how I love making art for hours, or playing outside near the water or in the field with my sisters. My mom had a lot of photos of her and my dad when they were younger, as well as some of my grandparents. These photos mesmerized me. At that moment, I was able to travel back into the past and learn more about my family.

Can you remember the first time you picked up a camera?

It took me a while before I decided to become a photographer. Where I'm from, there were no examples of people making a living from their art.

I studied for and earned a master's degree in career counselling. I worked for a few years in this field but didn't make a career as a counsellor. Something was missing.

My creativity was calling. I quit my well-paying, stable job and started to work as an assistant for a photographer and filmmaker. At twenty-five, I bought my first digital camera. My first subjects were flowers and red carpets. I brought my new camera along on a trip with my partner for his work to the Toronto International Film Festival. I got a few shots of Jake Gyllenhaal and Denis Villeneuve, and I was like, "Wow, this is cool." I then started doing commercial shoots, but it didn't feel right. I didn't quit my humanitarian career to shoot for brands that don't care for people or the environment. Now that I was able to use a camera and a program to edit photos, I needed to discover my niche, my identity as a photographer.

You're originally from the stunning Gaspésie region of Québec. How did this environment shape and inspire you?

I am lucky to have grown up by the St. Lawrence River, where the river becomes an open sea. The coastal landscapes and vernacular architecture definitely shaped my vision as a photographer. I feel very privileged to have cohabited with clear horizons. No buildings to obstruct the views; only the sea, the golden fields, a few small houses, barns, fishermen, and farmers blending into the environment. I believe the vast wilderness shaped my sense of aesthetic.

You now live in Nova Scotia. What motivated the move east?

My partner introduced me to surfing ten years ago, and we travelled a lot in South America and Maine, in the USA, to pursue our passion. After university, many of my friends were moving west to snowboard, but I decided to go further east to get closer to the Atlantic Ocean to surf. I moved by myself in the middle of winter before my partner could join me. I was surfing throughout the winter, acclimating myself to the cold conditions and my new community, which I fell in love with. After being landlocked for many years during my studies, it was profoundly rejuvenating to get back to my roots: living the coastal life that shaped my personality. I felt at home. In 2017, my partner and I bought the property of our dreams facing the Atlantic Ocean in rural Nova Scotia, where we've been able to slow down our pace, living with the flow of the tides.

How have your new surroundings inspired your approach to photography?

I feel incredibly lucky to live where we do: our parcel of land is home to a rich ecosystem. Through photography, I pay attention to every detail that surrounds me. It's like walking with a magnifying glass or binoculars. I've learned a lot about my new habitat that way and still have so much to learn. I decided to make our parcel of land my outdoor studio, where I can shoot for brands that are aligned with my values. On-site, biophilic textures are endless: a field of beachgrass, a loud ocean, a sky of many shades, a dynamic beach, a forest, a saltwater pond, a cliff of red clay, dunes, and birds—so much natural beauty.

How would you describe your shooting style?

I like harmony between people and the elements; that's why I like to showcase humans in grace with Mother Nature or a landscape without a single trace of humans. I have always been eco-anxious, so shooting a world that reflects a certain sense of harmony may be a coping mechanism for me to face a sad reality. From an aesthetic perspective, I like faded lights and low contrast, so colours and elements are not separated from each other; they live together peacefully.

What do you hope people feel when viewing your images?

We live in a very noisy world submerged by a shitload of information, so I hope the purity of the landscape I shoot opens up spaces in people's minds. It's all about the space between things. That's the beauty of perception. We, as humans, can play with it. I hope people sense the gratitude I have for the environment I'm surrounded by, and feel inspired by the humble people I like to interview and shoot.

How do you grow as a photographer? I imagine that your ideas, inspirations, and motivations evolve as you do?

At the beginning of my career as a freelance photographer and later as a writer, I've been fortunate enough to work with *BESIDE* magazine. For the first time, my creativity is serving a noble mission: my words and photos highlight stories of people who care for the world we live in. My collaboration with this publication is very fulfilling. Working with a team of creative directors, editors, translators, and illustrators gives me helpful feedback on how to improve my work, both as a photographer and writer. As I didn't formally study photography or writing, evolving with *BESIDE*'s team was a really supportive experience.

In 2022, I bought my first film camera. I was inspired by the new generation of photographers who have returned to a more rooted way of taking photos. I see it as an act of rebellion against the democratization of photography on phones. My goal is to shoot more on film. Using film requires one to trust their instinct, the present moment, and one's abilities.

Photography is a great medium, but I'm curious to try different ones. I believe that when we allow ourselves to experience the world in a different way, it can positively influence our art.

Who, what, and where inspires you?

Surf culture inspires me in terms of the unique relationship between the ocean and a surfer—the specific time and space when one is floating on a wave. It's a form of expression.

Currently, I'm inspired by Ty Williams's illustrations, Jasmine Parsia's collages, Cristina Gareau's coastal film photographs, Poppy Jones's photographs on suede canvas, and Ross Williams's beautiful surfboards. Recently, I discovered *EMOCEAN*, an inclusive surf magazine that champions diverse perspectives, radical creativity, relatability, and empowerment, with a focus on narratives by women, BIPOC, and LGBTQ+ surfers. It's refreshing to see this shift in surf media, which was, for a long time, focused on mostly white men. It's time to focus on different types of people and different viewpoints of the world.

You have a rather new endeavour, The Parcelles—Studio & Stay, which is described as an inclusive space by the ocean where creativity meets regeneration. What inspired this?

We renovated and lived in a cabin by the water that came with the property for a while before moving into the main house, which was being rented. The shack has served as an escape from our busy life in Québec City and as a creative retreat for me to write during the pandemic. The cabin sits on a private beach, facing the Atlantic Ocean. I wanted to share it with other artists, so I developed self-directed art residency opportunities at an affordable price during the low season. The Parcelles—Studio & Stay was born. We've hosted art residencies with artists from all over Canada. I ensure they have everything they need to achieve their goals. I can connect them to other artists during their week or art suppliers. During their week, we pick a moment for a photo shoot together, which gives them material of their process and portraits that they can use for their portfolio. It's not about the money but all about sharing my beautiful place with others.

> I believe that when we allow ourselves to experience the world in a different way, it can positively influence our art.

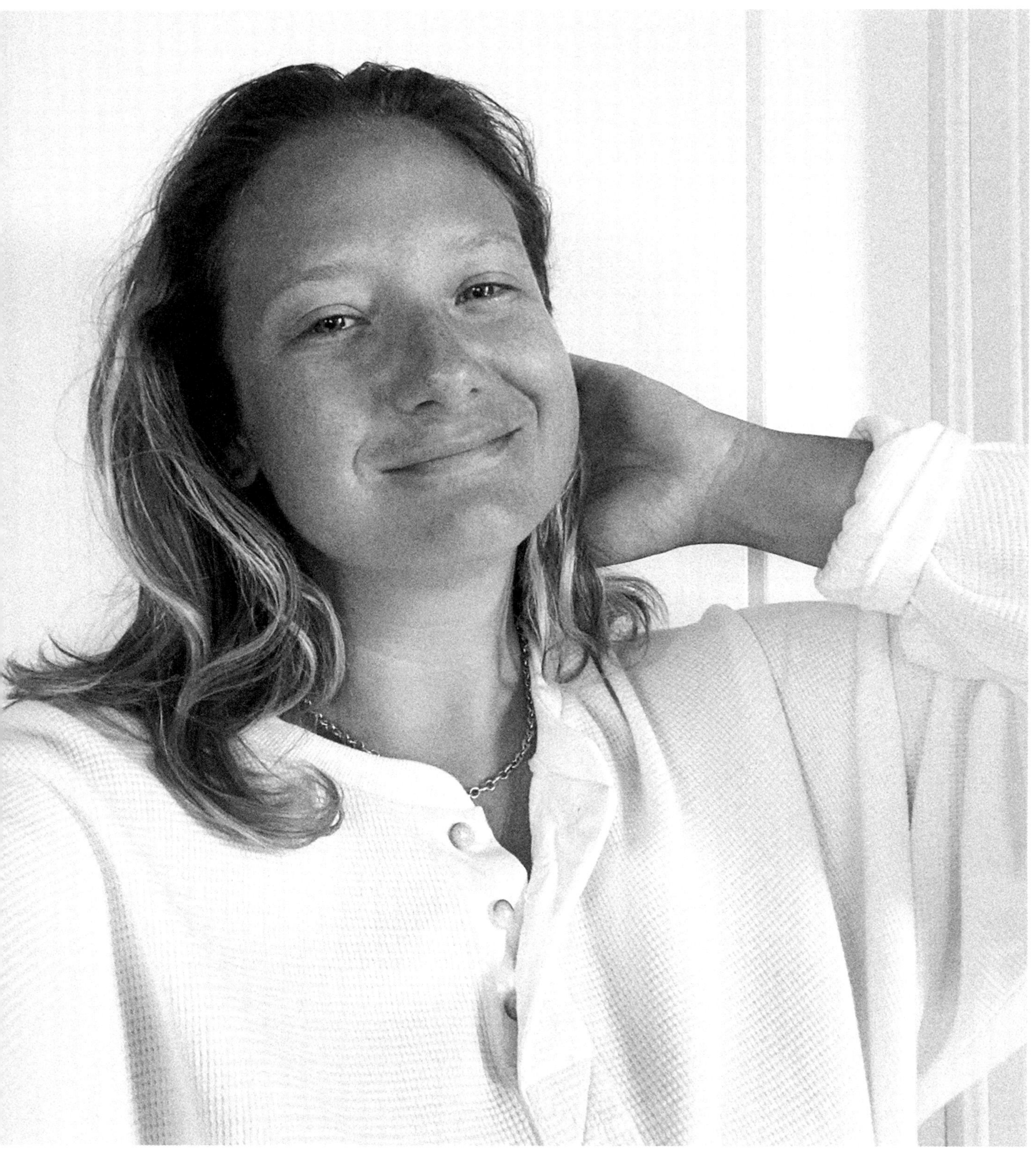

Anna Gilkerson

Designer and Co-owner,
Ana + Zac

"With gender labels, we are separating people. This is not necessary. We can all share the same styles. It's about how you want to wear it."

Can you recall a favourite piece of clothing?
When I was thirteen, my best friend's sister gave me a pair of jeans that she thrifted and no longer wore. Dark purple Levi's orange tab. I wore them to death and so did all my friends. There was a waitlist for those jeans.

You trained in fashion design at both FIT and Polimoda. How did these two different institutions prepare you for life in the fashion industry?
FIT was very business-forward. It was about learning skills we could take into the real world. My initial portfolio consisted of loosely painted watercolour fashion drawings. I did not get accepted, but I found a way to get a meeting with the top illustration professor, Steven Stipelman, and he showed me how to draw an acceptable croquis. He said, "Apply for patternmaking, and you can get in that way." I got in. It was a highly technical program and less artsy. Once I was there for a semester, I transferred over to fashion design. Stipelman really helped me. I will never forget him; he was a fabulous instructor with incredible stories.

In Italy, we got more into the conceptual process of design. The courses were intensive. I was fortunate to access the many resources around me, from art to architecture to street style. We would make the prettiest collection of books for our design classes. I have kept most of them. I can't throw them out! Every day, I would ride my bike to school alongside whizzing Vespas amongst trees and ancient sculptures—a far cry from New York's subway. Polimoda has a huge library dedicated to fashion. We had access to all the trend forecasting books and programs. This is where I first read about sustainable fashion. I had no idea about this concept before.

My studies in Italy helped me learn how to see the future by analyzing the past and present.

Prior to starting Ana + Zac, what kind of work experience did you have?
After school, I worked for a few years at Chabanel in Montréal in the fashion industry. I gained overseas communication skills working for David Bitton, and I learned to create detailed tech packs at a private label firm. I dabbled in film doing costumes and wardrobe. I always wanted to be my own boss. I've had a few different brands and businesses. I've learned a lot along the way, mostly about people. I always had this big vision for the world and how I could help save it, but it was always the big picture. The little picture matters, too. I've learned to be more understanding, patient, and flexible. In the long run, being kind

> I always had this big vision for the world and how I could help save it, but it was always the big picture. The little picture matters, too. I've learned to be more understanding, patient, and flexible. In the long run, being kind in any business will help your business, not hurt it. Looking out for others in a world where we are all connected is important.

in any business will help your business, not hurt it. Looking out for others in a world where we are all connected is important.

Ana + Zac is designed in Nova Scotia and made in Peru. How do you ensure that the brand maintains ethical and sustainability standards?

We did our homework prior to working with our manufacturer. They used to make fast fashion and became quite unhappy, but when their clients left for cheaper wages and faster lead times, it broke them in a good way. It is much better for everyone's mental health. Now, they only work with small boutique brands with a focus on quality. They work with us to ensure our products are well-made and durable. We are grateful to work with this team of highly skilled technicians, many of whom are women.

We produce our clothing through a short, vertically integrated supply chain; all managed in one area after our yarns are acquired. We primarily source GOTS-certified organic Pima cotton yarns from distinguished distributors like Bergman Rivera. The dye house that we work with uses low-impact dyes, and we ship using less plastic, re-using everything we can. Our packaging is minimal, and we now use compostable mailers. We are starting a re-sell and buy-back community program this fall, and we are working on a line of native cotton sleepwear that helps protect and strengthen biodiversity in Peru.

All these decisions build up to something that can make a big difference. There is always room for us to improve and transparency is key.

Did you set out with the intention of a design focus on sustainability?

There was no other option.

"We are inspired by our habit of sharing clothing and living a slower lifestyle." How has this inspired what you do at Ana + Zac?

My husband, Zac and I often share the same stuff. I think, initially, that was the inspiration behind the brand. On a larger scale, our ideas of gender are changing. It's less about a label and more about the individual. Our world is still very divisive, but humans, in general, are becoming more accepting of differences. In this society, we are very complicated, so we crave simplicity. There are so many distractions. Living with less makes us feel happy and free.

What does a slower lifestyle look like for you?

It's a journey. We've left the city and are spending less time driving and more time walking. We've decluttered. However, I still have a lot of clothing. There is a chair in the bedroom, and it houses a permanent rotation of samples, current collections, and old gems. I love thrifting. I am a clotheshorse! I like letting things go too. It's cathartic.

We have recently moved Ana + Zac solely to e-com. Simplifying our business model has given me more time to be creative and focus on projects.

You use a variety of people to model Ana + Zac.
I love that this is becoming the norm for many brands. Representation is fundamental to include many people in our design process and marketing. We all want to see ourselves in the products we purchase.

You mentioned the lost art of longevity in clothing. Are we seeing a shift in consumers' desire to purchase quality over quantity?
Making stuff that lasts is a weird concept for an industry built on obsolescence. It's a positive challenge. We want our customers to love our clothing for a long time, but we still need to sell clothing every season. Technically, we are supposed to be growing, and growing, but that's not sustainable if we are trying to make and consume less!

Success for me is a customer telling us that they have had the same garment forever, that it's their favourite, they wear it all the time, and it still looks the same as when they bought it.

We are looking for long-term relationships. Our customers are our extended family.

You're the parent of a child, Elly, who identifies as trans. I imagine the design and creative process at Ana + Zac, which focuses on offering a quality, non-gendered line of clothing, is fuelled by love.
Having a child who is trans has certainly pushed me to learn more about gender and identity, and that has been incredibly helpful in so many ways.

We went this route because not only did Zac and I want to create an inclusive space within our brand, but we also wanted to produce less. It goes hand in hand with sustainability. With gender labels, we are separating people. This isn't necessary. We can all share the same styles. It's about how we want to wear it.

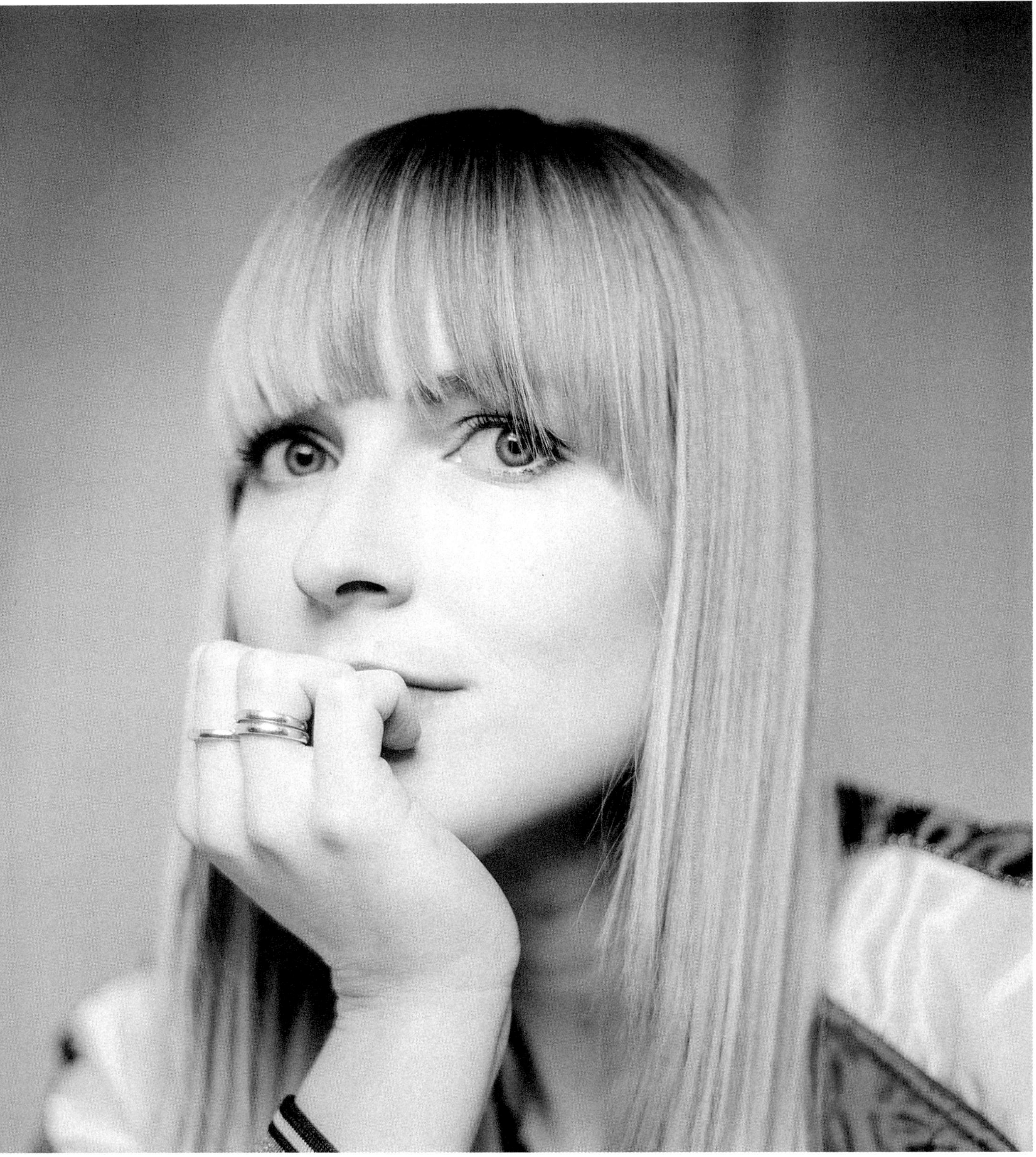

Breagh Isabel

Singer, Songwriter, and Producer

"Growing up surrounded by a music culture helped instill the fun and joyful aspects of making music, which made me fall in love with it."

What is your first memory of music?

I have a great photo on the desk in my studio of my father playing the piano. In the photo, I'm sitting on his lap, watching the keys; I'm less than a year old. I started to play as soon as I was big enough to reach the keys, so music was always a part of my life growing up. One of my earliest memories of music is being gathered in our living room, singing Christmas carols with all the family during the holidays.

You shared that music was a central part of family life growing up. How did being immersed and surrounded in this creative space move you towards a musical path?

My father played music growing up. He was in a rock band in the 70s with his twin brother who toured Canada; they were called The Brothers and One. He left the band to go to university, but there was always music at home, either him playing to us or my parents playing records.

I remember my brothers and I constantly begging my parents to get cable television. Looking back, I'm thankful my folks never gave in because, instead, we all gravitated to music! Listening to LPs on the record player, joining high school garage bands, and playing the family piano were big parts of my childhood.

You now live in Halifax but were born and raised in Cape Breton. How did this place shape and inspire you as a person and an artist?

I grew up when the Celtic music scene was reaching the world stage and had a broad definition, including everyone from Natalie MacMaster to The Rankin Family and Ashley MacIsaac. Seeing so many musicians from such a small area and niche musical tradition breaking through into larger markets had a big impact. Cape Bretoners are proud of their musical traditions and of the people keeping those traditions alive. Even though the music I make is far from the traditional music of Cape Breton, I was definitely influenced by it, especially the strong songwriter tradition that is a part of Celtic music.

Cape Breton Island was a great place to grow up because music was a big part of being social. Many musicians I studied with grew up playing music in a more formal or solitary setting. I think growing up surrounded by a music culture helped instill the fun and joyful aspects of making music, which made me fall in love with it.

What are a few early musical influences?

One of my first favourite bands was Paul McCartney and Wings. My parents had a record player in the living room, and I remember loving the albums *Ram* and *Band on the Run*. Later, as a pre-teen, I recall hearing my mom's copy of *Blue* playing on our stereo. As a pre-teen, Joni Mitchell's lyrics spoke to emotions I hadn't yet felt, but somehow, her words pulled me into the experiences she described. Listening to *Blue* was like fast-forwarding to future love, heartbreak, travel, and adventure! Her songwriting still inspires me to this day.

At what age and stage of life did you realize that music would be your professional path?

In grade 12, I had an amazing music teacher who encouraged me to begin songwriting (Monica MacNeil at Riverview High School). I had always played music, but once I began writing songs, I had the bug. When it came time to decide what to do after graduation, I knew I wanted to pursue music in a more serious way, so I auditioned for the music program at St. Francis Xavier University. I completed a Bachelor of Music degree in Jazz Piano Performance. However, many of the most talented songwriters and producers I've worked with have no formal music training, so I don't think it's a necessity for everyone.

How would you describe your musical style?

I am inspired by pop music, but I would describe my musical style as singer-songwriter. I think if there is any theme to the music I write, it's trying to be as honest as possible. I try not to think about what other people want to hear, or what will make me sound interesting or cool, and focus on telling stories about my life experiences in the clearest way possible, hoping people can relate.

How do you approach each role?

Performing, writing, and producing are all pieces of a whole, but each is like flexing slightly different creative muscles. Performing is about connecting with an audience and experiencing the excitement of making music in a live setting. Songwriting and production are like a slowed-down version of performance. There are moments of inspiration, but it's about taking your time and creating in a thoughtful and deliberate way.

A song that moves you. Every. Single. Time. You. Hear. It.

"A Case of You" by Joni Mitchell. I have listened to this song so many times over so many years that it almost serves as a time-travel device.

Who, where, and what inspires you?

I have a note on my phone where I constantly write down words, sentences, or ideas that could be the start of a song. Whether it's a conversation with a friend or something overheard on the street from a stranger, I try to keep my ears open for ideas. Lately I have been finding inspiration from reading. I'm part of a monthly book club with a few close friends, and we pick out our favourite quotes from every book we read. Now, I am always on the lookout while reading—it has helped inspire a few songs.

What do you need to be creative and productive?

I have a small home studio where I do most of my music-making these days. It has become my favourite creative space. I have my keyboards, guitars, and computer for recording and production.

Nashville plays a pivotal role in your path. Please share more about this place and its impact on you and your work as an artist.

I went on my first writing trip to Nashville ten years ago and it's had a big impact on my path in the creative world. At the time, I had been part of a songwriting camp organized by Gordie Sampson and then had the opportunity to go there with my band at the time, Port Cities. Learning about the Nashville style of co-writing opened up a new way of writing music and collaborating with others that really solidified my love of songwriting.

I have done several writing trips there over the years, but in 2019, I completed a production internship that really grew my skills in music production and allowed me to plant some roots in the city. The music scene in Nashville is truly world-class, and through that internship I met artists, writers, and producers who've become partners and collaborators.

"I had no firm intention of delving into a solo artist project when I wrote 'Girlfriends,' but the song easily became the most honest thing I had ever written. I started to feel like I had something to say that might resonate." A powerful and very personal statement. What motivated you to step outside your comfort zone and begin exploring more personal experiences in your music?

I think a lot of the music I write comes from personal experiences. I believe that by telling a story in an honest way, people will be able to find a piece of themselves in it, even if it's something they have never experienced.

Your debut single, "Girlfriends," is about a specific type of heartbreak.

The song is ultimately me wearing my heart on my sleeve. Working my way in reverse through the experience of having a crush on a friend in high school but not knowing how to categorize or acknowledge that.

I believe that by telling a story in an honest way, people will be able to find a piece of themselves in it, even if it's something they have never experienced.

It's about little, and sometimes big, moments and thoughts I did not know what to do with at the time, but now realize were just expressions of me figuring out who I was. I know it's still not universal, sadly, but I think a lot of younger people now have access to language and role models on the internet or around them that normalize being queer.

What's a career highlight of yours?

One of my all-time performance highlights was at home here in Nova Scotia. My former band, Port Cities, opened for k.d. lang at the Halifax show of her *Ingenue Redux* tour. It was our first time playing an arena, so that was amazing. I've also been a huge fan of k.d. and her music since I was a teenager. She was one of the first openly queer Canadian artists I had heard of, so she was a huge inspiration.

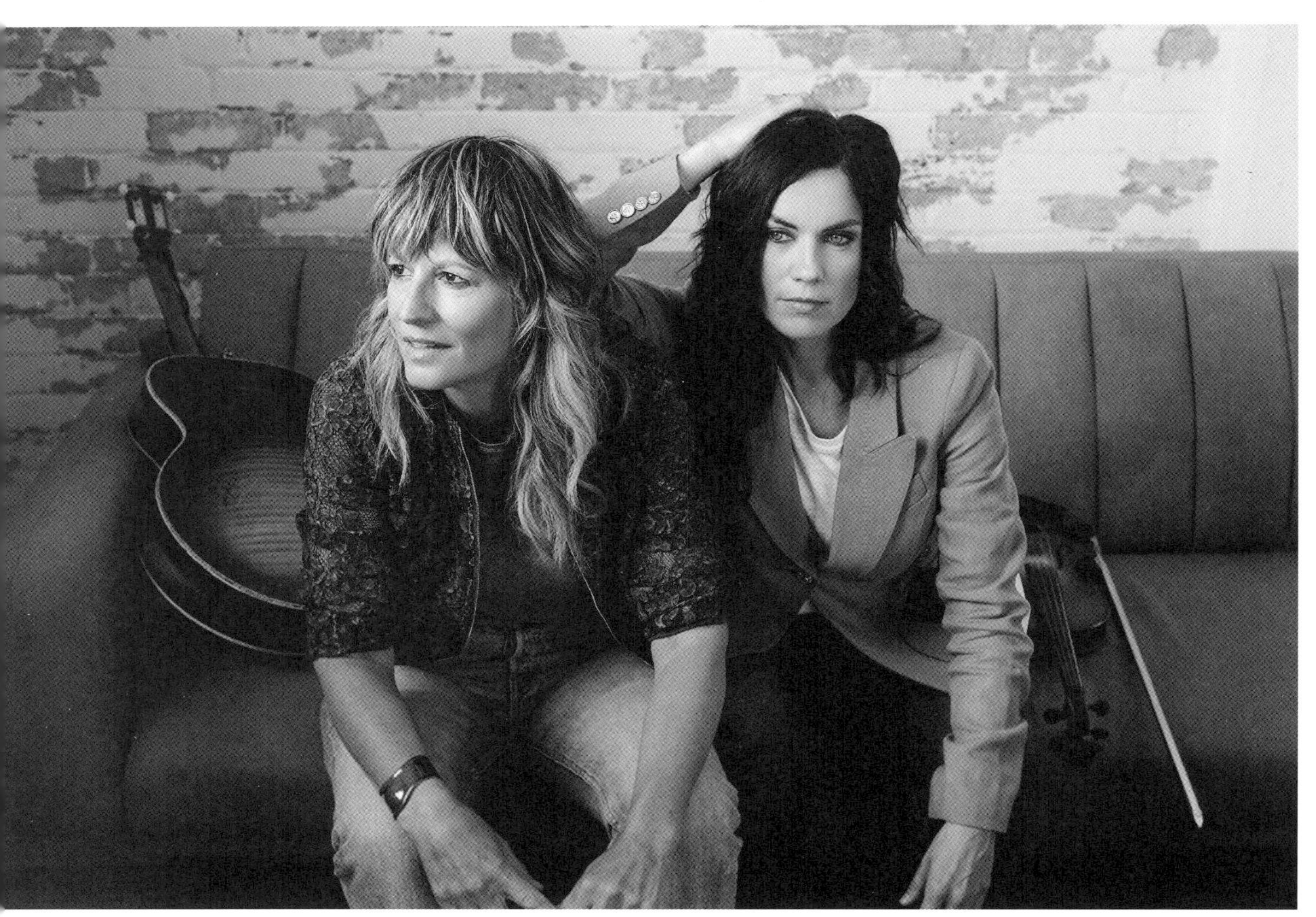

Brenley MacEachern & Lisa MacIsaac

JUNO-nominated Multi-Instrumentalist and Harmonizing Duo, Madison Violet

"When I felt like getting out of my own head was impossible, I would pick up my guitar, and all my problems seemed to slip away."

BRENLEY

"In the end, we are storytellers who weave our messages with acoustic guitars, fiddle, and loads of harmonies."

LISA

What is your first memory of music?

Lisa: It's of my father, playing the fiddle in our kitchen. He was a beautiful player, and there was always a tune or a cassette blasting in the background of a concert he had recorded. I also have vivid memories of the epic house parties that my mom and dad would throw in our basement. Fiddlers, piano players, and step dancers from Cape Breton and the mainland would come and play into the wee hours. I didn't realize how lucky I was until I became an adult, having the gift of music around me all the time.

Brenley: My earliest feeling of music was when I was around eight or nine, when I heard "Old Man." My father is one of sixteen children, so when we went back to Cape Breton every summer, all the aunts, uncles, and cousins would return to the island for family reunion, and we would throw large bonfires down on the beach in front of my grandmother's house. There was always music. Everyone would sing. There would be fiddlers and guitar players. One night, my cousin Bradley took out his guitar and started singing "Old Man." I remember just walking closer and closer to him, being sucked in by the song.

Tell me more about how Cape Breton has inspired and influenced you as individuals and musicians?

Lisa: I grew up in a tiny, rural community called Creignish, just a short jaunt from where Brenley's family is from. There was not a lot to do aside from playing baseball, hiding in the forest, or learning music. My best friends and I sang in the church choir, went to fiddle lessons together, and would sit on the school bus singing three-part harmonies to The Rankins songs. Music was ingrained in our DNA. So many professional musicians came out of that small area for such a small population. And you can hear the grit in our style of fiddle playing, likely from the salt water that surrounded us.

Brenley: My parents' idea of a family vacation was packing four kids, either in to the back of a beat-up Ford Mercury or a pickup, with a truck-bed camper on the back and heading straight east to Cape Breton every summer for 2–3 weeks. I didn't live in Cape Breton, but I would venture to say I did a fair share of growing up there. Flat tires, sleeping in mall parking lots when the campgrounds were too full, laying on my elbows on the huge bed staring out the window, darkened with privacy film, above my parents, who were below driving the truck. Completely illegal, but man, I sure loved doing things against the rules. I feel like breaking rules and improvising when you need to, and sitting out when you just feel like listening, encapsulate the way I feel about the music and the culture in Cape Breton. There's no plan, really. It just flows.

When did you realize that music was your path?
Lisa: I never thought that I would end up playing music professionally. I didn't really know it was an option. I earned a fairly decent living playing the fiddle solo and in folk bands in high school while my friends were babysitting. I was going to study pharmacy at Dalhousie University, but then I was asked to tour in the musical comedy show *The Cape Breton Summertime Revue*. That's when I really got the touring bug. I left school a month early, faxed my work to my teachers, and graduated. I never looked back. When I met Brenley, I didn't know how to play the guitar. She taught me a few chords a couple of decades ago, and here we are.

Brenley: I got my first guitar as a high school graduation present from my parents. A twelve-string Norman. I learned every Tracy Chapman song there was to learn; The Eagles, Rolling Stones. I loved playing and singing, but I was quite shy, so it never occurred to me that I would ever or that I could even do this for a living. When I felt like getting out of my own head was impossible, I would pick up my guitar, and all my problems seemed to slip away. I tried private lessons for a minute and went through a few teachers, but I just wasn't good at learning in a formal sense. I learned from my cousins and from watching people play.

First time you performed live with an audience?
Lisa: My first performance on stage as a fiddle player was a group performance with all of Stan Chapman's students. I had decided that I would attempt to freak out the aging audience as a nine-year-old and begin my performance left-handed. Midway through the set of tunes, I switched it over and played right-handed. I don't think they had ever seen anything like that before. But I could see the shock in their eyes. The disbelief. And I liked it. I liked that I was able to draw in an audience, and lock eyes with people, just by playing an instrument.

Brenley: I was in a cover band called Gadzoox! I started belting out "You Can't Always Get What You Want" by the Rolling Stones, and the reaction from the audience felt like I'd died and gone to funland. My first live gig was at a dive bar in Huntsville, jam-packed, and I'm there on stage in a dirty t-shirt and a pair of jeans. I knew I had to find a way to do this as a full-time job.

The band's name is Madison Violet. What is the inspiration behind it?
Lisa: When Brenley and I met, we bought an old '88 GMC Vandura camper van and ran away to the US to start writing our first album together. We were a couple, in the closet at the time, and just needed the freedom to be who we were without the fear and consequences of being found out. We drove straight down to New Orleans and across to Malibu. The only stipulation on that trip was that we had to search each town for campgrounds with hot springs or hot tubs after many hours of driving. We landed in New Mexico. Both lost time in the natural hot spring. Not sure exactly how much. Our watches stopped. The clock on the van stopped working. The laptop wouldn't turn on. We had no idea how much time we were unconscious in the water. I won't get into all the details, as it's basically out of an *X-Files* episode, but the woman's name, who checked us into the campground with her many cats with no tails, was Violet. It was an absolutely *Mad* experience. Hence, *Mad Violet*. Over the years, it eventually morphed into *Madison*, and the rest is history. Or, rather, a mystery.

"We are East Coast musicians [who] began creating music together that had roots firmly planted in their past, but with contemporary and modern elements generously overlaid." Please explain.
Lisa: There's a rich history of Gaelic and Scottish music in Cape Breton. I barely knew a pop song or an

electronic instrument until I was fifteen. It was only when I met Brenley that I found myself listening to more genres. Connecting the old world of traditional music with acoustic instruments and more modern electronic sounds. Our most recent album, which we produced ourselves, falls under the folk umbrella, with hints of pop and electronic elements. But in the end, we are storytellers who weave our messages with acoustic guitars, fiddle, and loads of harmonies. We play everything from clubs to theatres, folk festivals, kitchens, and because we cross a few genres and can bring out a bigger electric sound when needed, we can cater to the environment in which we're playing.

What has it been like working together?

Lisa: I had lived in black and white for a long time. I needed everything to be perfect. Every word and note aligned without much room for error or creative mistakes. I didn't have the capacity for happy accidents that could sometimes turn into something even more beautiful. Working with Brenley has allowed me to colour outside the lines and work in the grey. Producing together in the Airstream came with a lot of hesitation and fear, but we were able to give each other space, allow both of our voices and ideas to be heard, and never once disagreed about the music. It was not nearly as challenging as I had anticipated.

Brenley: Lisa and I were almost ten years in a romantic relationship. I'm surprised that the last few didn't completely tear us apart. We went through so much trauma together in those last three years together. My brother was murdered. We had a miscarriage just entering the second trimester while we were out on a European tour, and yet we knew we had a bond that would hold us close no matter the obstacle. Three months after the miscarriage, we both simultaneously met *someone new* and *boom*, that was that. We didn't talk much about it. It just kind of happened. Although it was mutual, we had a few turbulent years of touring following the break-up. We wrote an album called *The Good in Goodbye*, but we weren't really ready to reveal ourselves or the real struggles within the band, not wholly. We've come a long way with how we treat one another and how we talk to one another, but sometimes those bad habits, the buttons we push, and the past dynamics reappear, and they can be quite painful. I've learned so much about Lisa over the last few years by learning more about myself and turning the telescope around.

A song that moves you. Every. Single. Time.

Lisa: "Look at Miss Ohio" by Gillian Welch.

Brenley: "Seventeen" by Sharon Van Etten.

You toured with Canadian icon Chantal Kreviazuk in 2021.

Lisa: We got pretty tight on that tour. We opened up about our lives and our personal experiences. Laughed a ton! For me, performing on stage is something I feel very lucky to do. But it's all of the behind-the-scenes moments, the deep conversations, the cheesy jokes, the sharing of food; that is what makes touring a joy for me.

Brenley: Chantal is hilarious. We hit it off right away and became fast friends driving from Québec City back to Toronto. She wanted to do the drive right after the show, but we were like, "No, we are staying and making that seven-hour drive tomorrow!" She's fierce behind the wheel. We had a ball on that tour, and her audience is fantastically loyal and supportive. So, to get in front of a crowd like this, after not having played for so long, was a gift.

Music brings people together.

Brenley: Music is the one language we can all speak. A song comes on and you have your own unique experience with it, a memory maybe, and in that moment, there can be healing.

Lisa: I really couldn't say it any better. It's like she was in my head when she wrote that, which happens often after twenty-three years of performing together.

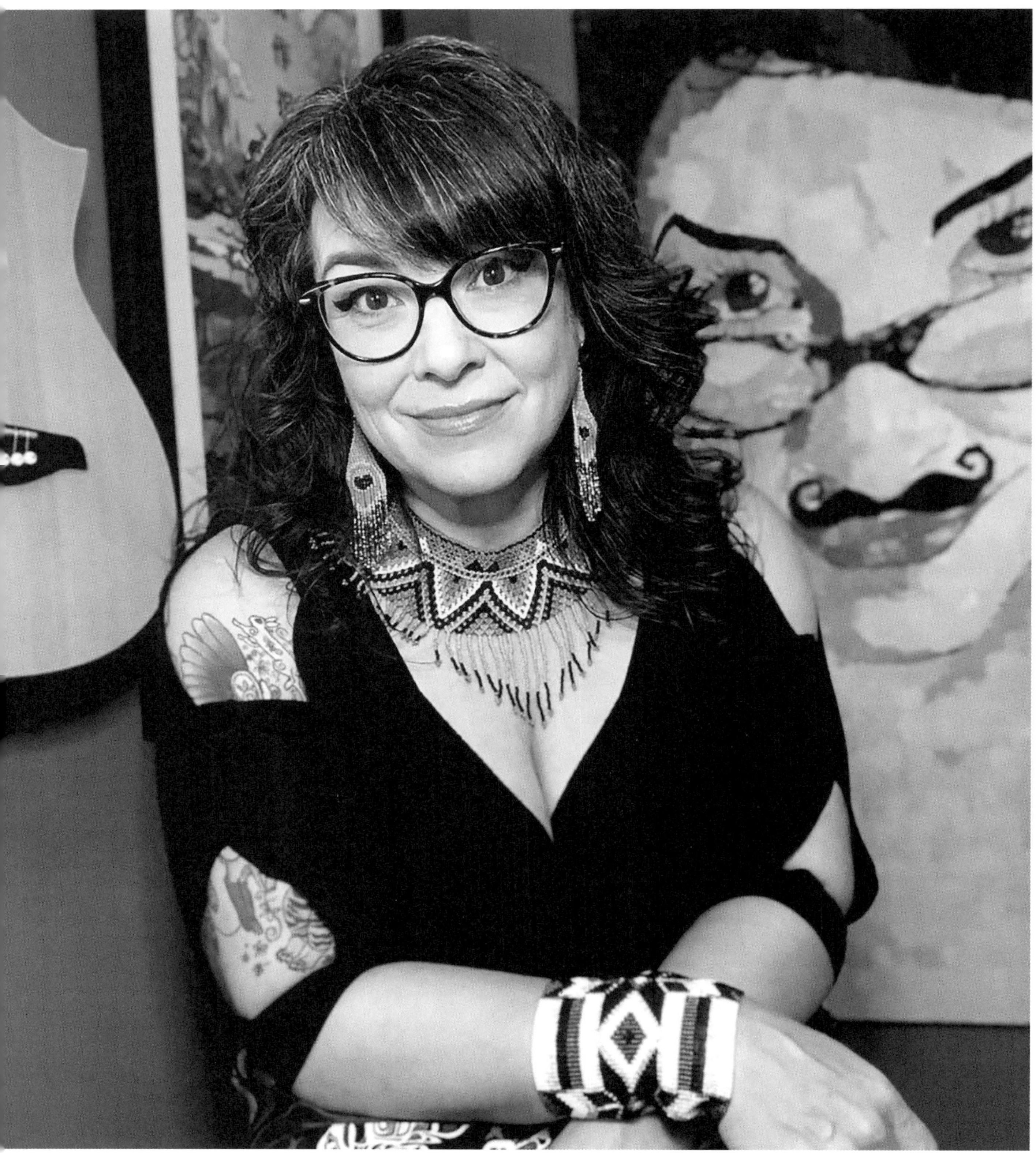

Tara Audibert

Indie Filmmaker, Illustrator, Comic Artist and Owner/ Producer/Director, Moxy Fox Studio

"For female Indigenous voices to be heard, they can't be filtered through a male colonial lens."

What is your first memory of creating art?

My first memory was being punished for drawing windows on the wallpaper in my bedroom. When I was two, I got in trouble for using dark blue permanent marker and *E.T.* puffy stickers on the side of my doll's crib to create a dramatic scene. My punishment was to try to remove the permanent marker with soap and water, but this did not deter me from continuing to create art with disruptive results.

At what age and stage of life did you realize that animation would be your professional path?

In high school, when asked what I wanted to go to college for, I said *art*, of course! "Well, you've heard of a starving artist, haven't you?" Said my parents. "Maybe you should choose something where you can make money and do art as a hobby?" This made sense to me, as the thought of starving was not something I wanted to experience. So, I decided I would be a marine biologist because I loved swimming and dolphins; I could work at SeaWorld.

Thankfully, I never ended up torturing seals and dolphins. I failed out of the Bachelor of Science program and the Bachelor of Arts. I told my parents, "I tried it your way. Now I'm going to do it my way." I graduated with Principal's Honours and am pleased to report I have not starved a day as an artist.

A cartoon series that sparked your interest in this genre?

Scooby-Doo, Where Are You! was one of my favourite cartoons growing up. *The Flintstones* was another favourite, which also got me in trouble. I wanted to draw the Flintstones and tried in my sketchbook, but the proportions were all wrong, and I couldn't draw fast enough while I was watching the show. This was before the internet and Google. I recorded an episode on the VCR so I could pause the tape on a spot where it wasn't all squiggly. Then, I taped saran wrap over the tube TV and used a black permanent marker to trace Wilma, Fred, Betty, Barney, and Dino, so I had an accurate reference for my drawings. I would have gotten away with it. If only the permanent marker hadn't marked through the saran wrap and onto the TV.

Your resume is a fascinating timeline that reflects hard work, lifelong learning, and a passion for your craft.

There is a Japanese proverb I learned in judo: "Fall down seven times, get up eight" ("nanakorobi yaoki"). This applies to my artistic career as well.

After animation college, I worked at an animation studio in Halifax, creating broadcast animation.

I had applied to be an animator but was hired in the clean-up department. As I worked cleaning up all sorts of talented animators' work, I was able to see and trace off frame-by-frame animation and see what made something look good and what made it look great.

I had considered being hired for clean-up a failure, but it became a huge success for me later on as I surpassed animators who had started in animation when I was in clean-up. I am very thankful for being in clean-up and learning from all the animators, though I was not very happy about it at the time.

I applied to another show to be an animator and was told that I was too valuable now in the clean-up department and they couldn't move me to the animation department. Fail. This was a real wake-up on how the industry worked. It was not based on merit. They hired a male animator, and I was unimpressed that the quality of his work I cleaned up was far below my own animation skill level. I went to the director and said if I wasn't hired for animation, I would be seeking employment elsewhere. After that meeting, I was hired as an animator on the production team. Success!

You work in a predominantly male industry.

I started working at age sixteen as a part-time reservist in the Canadian Armed Forces. One of the first things I learned in my GMT (General Military Training), besides how to do a push-up, was that as a woman, I had to work twice as hard to get half the recognition of my male counterparts. Was this fair? No.

I could work for a large studio and get lots of fun credits working on other people's shows, but I choose to do it myself, have my own studio, and be a producer, director, writer, and artist. For female Indigenous voices to be heard, they can't be filtered through a male colonial lens. There are many things I can do independently that I would have never been able to do had I followed a typical path in animation.

"Representing female and Indigenous characters in the zeitgeist."

I was sitting in the backseat of my parents' Pontiac on my way to my *Me-me's* house. I looked out the window and New Brunswick, in the fall, had the same look of the plains. It reminded me of the terrible, scary *Indians* I had seen on TV. I cried out "I'm afraid of Indians!" There was a pause in the car, then everyone laughed and one of my aunts said, "Well, you're in a car full of em!"

"NO! Not us kind of Indians, the BAD Indians!" I corrected. They all laughed again. "We are the only Indians here."

The adult version of me creates stories and characters for the child version of me who was afraid of *Indians* so that she doesn't have to be afraid and can be proud of her culture and heritage. Not just the warriors fighting to defy colonialism, but the love and humour that I feel define Indigenous culture.

One thing I'm committed to in my career is adding female characters to positions of power in stories. I also include non-binary characters and look to represent Two-Spirit people who are my friends and family and a large part of my life.

Practice failure and you'll be really good at it. As an artist and entrepreneur, failure is an everyday occurrence. If you aren't ready for that, you'll spend a lot of time crying over things that don't deserve a second thought.

"The importance of failure."

Practice failure and you'll be really good at it. As an artist and entrepreneur, failure is an everyday occurrence. If you aren't ready for that, you'll spend a lot of time crying over things that don't deserve a second thought. For my last short film, *I am the Warrior*, I applied to more than 100 film festivals, and every day for months, I got a rejection email. But I kept applying, and several selected my film and made it an award-winning Best Animated Short! I have always played the numbers game with everything in life, and it has yet to fail me. If I apply for 100 film festivals, it's bound to get in to some. If I apply to forty jobs, one is bound to hire me. If I have 100 ideas, one has got to be good!

I was diagnosed with ADHD in my forties and started taking medication a few years ago. I was wary because my doctor said it would take away my "superpowers." What I think he was referring to were my "coping strategies." I have had ADHD all my life, thus I had to come up with ways to work around or work with my brain. I'm really organized and can manage many people along with myself now after forty years of using multiple calendars, piles of post it notes, notebooks, magnet boards, and several other excessive forms of organization simultaneously. All this stems from anxiety I have about being late, not finishing an assignment, or forgetting an appointment. Having general anxiety disorder and ADHD have hindered me in many ways—but they also make me a great producer and an even better entrepreneur. It is great for someone like me who gets bored easily as I can move from job to job with interest and enthusiasm as each new job is a diversion from the last thing I was doing. Eventually I need to make my way back, but soon that first thing will become a distraction from something else, and over time many things get done.

You practice yoga, judo, and jiu-jitsu.

Yoga plays a pivotal role in my constant striving for relaxation. I have been practicing yoga for more than twenty-five years. I've been training in judo and jiu-jitsu for several years now to regularly practice failure. I initially joined judo to exercise and learn self-defence, but I found so much more in my practice. It takes a lot of courage to just show up. They say a black belt is just a white belt who kept showing up. The purpose of my yoga is now flexibility for judo; I do jiu-jitsu to be better at judo. I create artworks based on judo. My dojo is the place I go to relax. There's a meditative aspect to martial arts that gives me some relief from my overactive brain.

The importance of storytelling...

Storytelling shapes children's lives and influences who they become. The stories they hear need to be ones with positive messages for the future. Sharing our stories allows those who come after us to follow our path. I hope my stories will help shape others the way they shaped me.

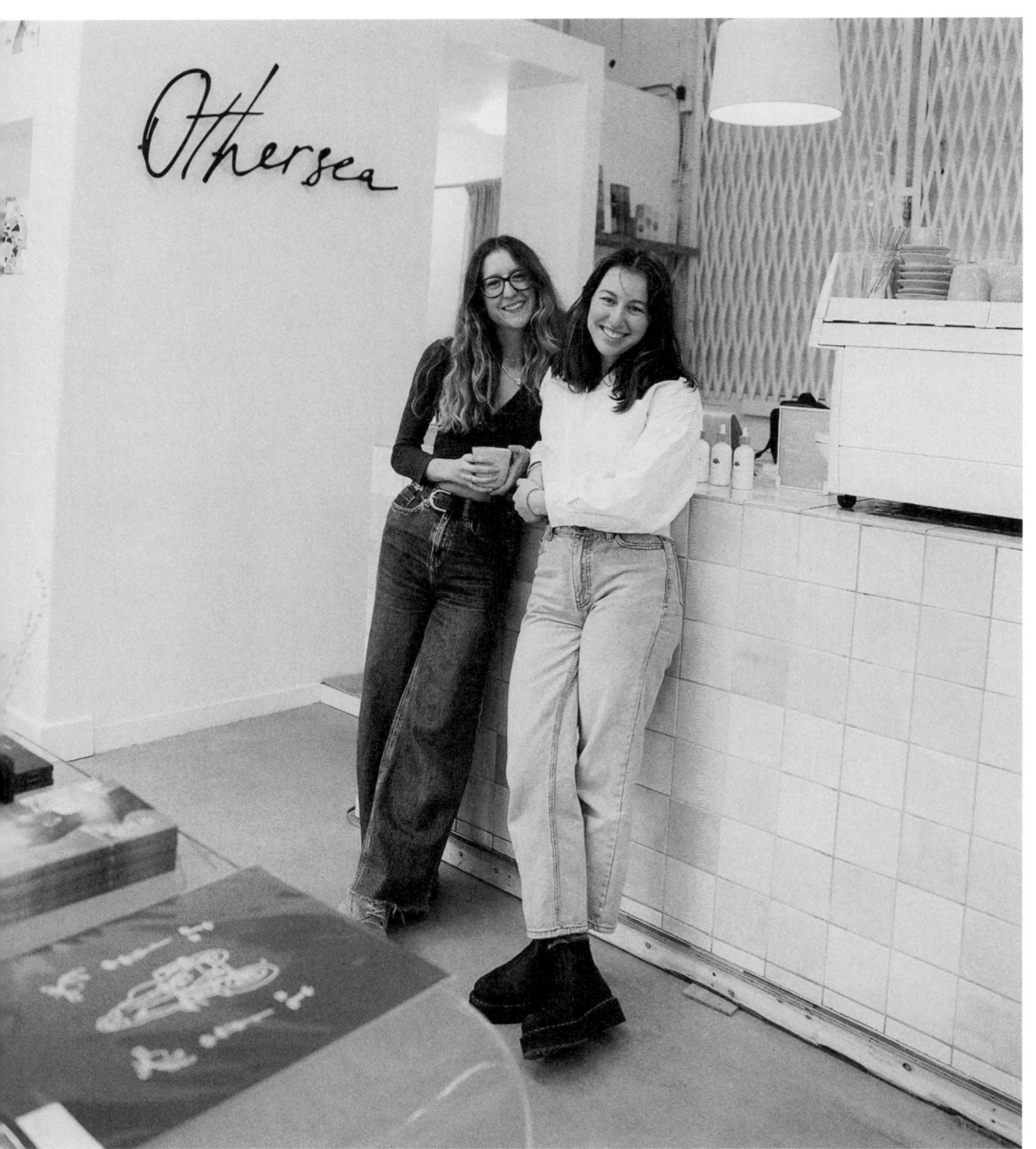
Othersea

Joëlle Landry-Bergeron & Marie-Laurence Desaulniers

Co-founders, Othersea Bikini

"My family spent summers travelling on a boat between Québec and Florida. Water was my playground."

JOËLLE (JOJO)

"Saltwater, wherever in the world, is where I feel my best, both in my mind and body. It's where I feel most alive."

MARIE-LAURENCE (MARLO)

You both grew up in Québec. How did the geography shape you?

Jojo: I grew up in Saint-Nicolas, on the south side of Québec City. I was lucky to live by the St. Lawrence River. My house was literally in front of a beach where my brother and I spent our summers playing. My family spent summers travelling on a boat between Québec and Florida. Water was my playground. I was young, I didn't feel a strong connection to my birthplace and told my parents that I wasn't meant to live in Québec. I wanted instead to live by the sea and the palm trees. Now, I appreciate all that Québec nature has given me—my passions, well-being, awareness, and goals.

Marlo: I was born in Rimouski and raised there for most of my youth. I was living in the Bic, which is close to where the St. Lawrence River becomes saltwater. It has a very chill vibe, with mostly open-minded, artistic people. When I think of my youth, it's the smell of saltwater that comes to mind. In Rimouski, what I loved doing most was going on adventures with my parents anywhere to see the sunset, no matter the season. When I go back to Rimouski, I feel at peace. That place made me. Saltwater, wherever in the world, is where I feel my best, both in my mind and body. It's where I feel most alive.

What inspired you to start Othersea Bikini in 2016? Were you two friends before becoming business partners?

Marlo: Joëlle and I met in CEGEP. It was love at first sight. From day one, we've been best friends. We both went to fashion marketing school without knowing what we wanted to do with it, but we knew we wanted to do our own thing.

After two years in the program, we started talking seriously about our dream job and were both on the same page. We just went for it.

We love making bikinis and clothes that comfortably fit the female form. Our main mission is to shift the way the fashion industry works. Jojo and I asked ourselves, *what is our purpose?* We questioned whether we wanted to pursue this path, given the circumstances. We came to the conclusion that we would only move forward if our brand could help initiate change in a positive direction.

Our main mission is to shift the way the fashion industry works. Jojo and I asked ourselves, what is our purpose? . . . We came to the conclusion that we would only move forward if our brand could help initiate change in a positive direction.

What attracted you to beach culture?

Jojo: Growing up in the cold and travelling on a boat for most of my childhood, beach culture appealed. After watching the surf movie *Blue Crush* a thousand times, I dreamed of being a professional surfer or living someplace near the ocean, happily married to some surfer dude. During my internship at college, I selected a Californian surf shop and decided to spend the summer there. With Marlo visiting for a couple of weeks that summer, we decided that we would buy future homes near a beach and start a swim company, which we did! The mindset of being somewhere warm and slow living was important for us. I think many people have the same kind of nostalgia for the sun and beach culture.

Marlo: We both love to travel and discover unique shops around the world. This inspired us to recreate that vibe in our hometown. Allow people to be transported to another place and travel to their own city when they enter our tropical space.

Othersea designs are timeless with a twist. Who, where, and what inspires you?

Jojo: Our community inspires us, as do the people we meet while travelling and the places we dream of exploring one day.

Our customers have shared with us that they wish to take the minimum with them on their travels. They want to have versatile, long-lasting experiences with a piece of clothing they can travel with around the world. We want our pieces to carry the stories and memories of a certain trip.

Marlo: How we live and experience the world inspires what we create at Othersea.

"Our greatest wish is that every woman accepts herself in all her facets and can proudly wear a bikini that she feels beautiful and confident in." Love this. There's been a long overdue shift in our perception and acceptance that all bodies are beautiful. Why is this important?

Marlo: My mother always told me, *t'es belle, t'es bonne, t'es capable*! (You are beautiful, you are talented, you can do it!) These words gave me so much confidence. I want to do the same for others. At Othersea, we don't work with models but create and show clothing styles that can easily work with all shapes and sizes.

What has been the customer response to Othersea Bikini?

Jojo: It has been great since the very beginning. We have a beautiful community of people here in Québec City who are returning customers and who share their love of our brand with friends, what we call *le bouche-à-oreille* here in Québec.

A beach experience that left a lasting impression?

Jojo: It would have to be my very first solo trip experience. I had just turned eighteen and was discovering the world and the woman I wanted to become in this world. I went to Costa Rica and then to California, where I learned new languages. I met people who inspired and encouraged me to travel and experience new things. This is when I decided I would eventually start my own brand.

Marlo: Joëlle and I bought a van, branded it with Othersea logos, furnished it in a couple days and took off for two months driving around the USA. Although this trip was not the most exotic place I've been to, what I loved most about this trip is that every day was different. We never knew what was going to happen and had no plan except to chase the sunsets and create memories. It's similar to how I feel running a business. We still have a lot to learn. We have plans and goals but never really know what will happen next.

What are the benefits and challenges of creating a sustainable brand?

Jojo & Marlo: Local fabric manufacturers or distributors are hard to find. When we find one, we want to build a long-term relationship. We select ones that offer ethical products or that work with natural fibres. We try to work with certified fabrics that our customers know and trust—no bullshit in terms of ecological solutions for the fabric. We want to create a feeling of trust with our customers, and the certifications give us the warranty that our products are made equitably. When we speak of production, it's a big challenge to keep it all in our hands and produce everything locally. Employees, rental spaces, and equipment are costly, and we try to keep our prices as low as possible. The quality and the fact that it's all handmade here in Québec makes for a quality product within a reasonable price point.

You've collaborated with several other brands. What is special about the collaborative experience?

Jojo & Marlo: We have met such beautiful and inspiring people doing these collaborations, and it's one of the things we love most about our work. We have an opportunity to share our knowledge, and pull together our strengths, and creativity to create a unique and meaningful object that will last.

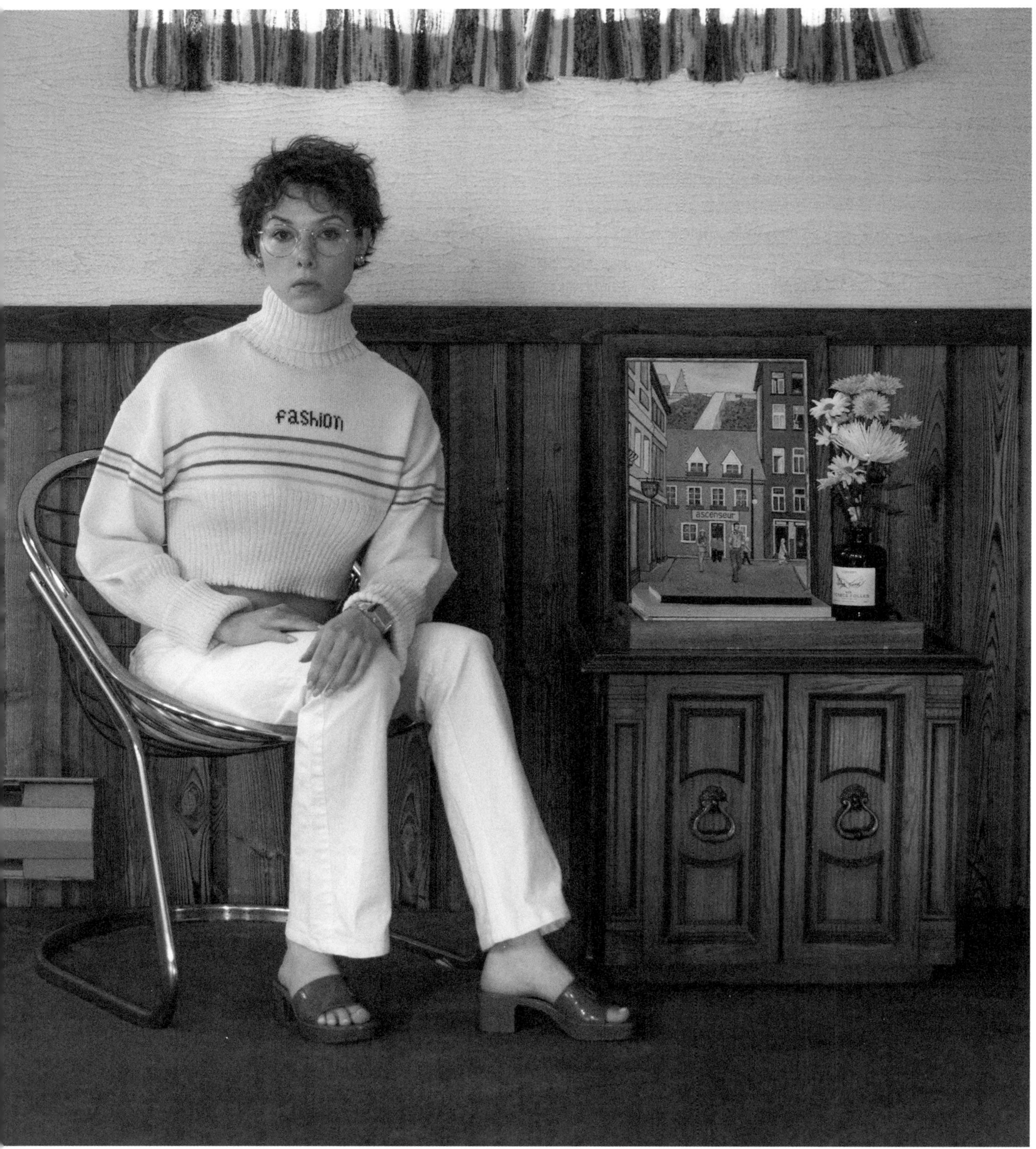
fashion
ascenseur

Leah Legault

Knitter and Knitwear Designer, Caulis Knitwear

"I'm making knitwear for someone who enjoys wearing a conversation piece, who appreciates the quality and quirkiness of something homemade, and who likes to know who makes the product they purchase."

Your first favourite piece of clothing?

A blue nightgown from Costco with *The Little Mermaid* on it. There wasn't anything special about it, but I remember asking my mom to buy it for me. When she said no, I decided to buy it *myself* with money I had received for my birthday. It was my first clothing purchase. I was six years old.

How would you describe your personal style?

I love clothes and dressing up. Every outfit is an opportunity to present myself as whoever I want to be, or be seen as, on any given day. My style can range from contemporary, clean, and professional, to an eclectic mix of handmade knits and grungy vintage pieces.

At what age did you realize that fashion would be your future?

I started sewing around age six, learning how to mend holes, and began knitting at thirteen or fourteen. My mom taught me the basics, and I learned everything else through books or online. I never thought of fashion as my future. I initially wanted to be a visual artist and studied studio arts. Knitting was a hobby. It was a way to enjoy a creative and meditative practice.

In art school, I learned about textiles in my fibre art classes. After graduation, it became clear that fashion would be my path.

Before starting Caulis, you had a career in retail.

Although I have fond memories of my retail days, the experience has been invaluable in terms of learning about the business side of fashion. Jobs in customer service and sales can be hit or miss. Like many entrepreneurs, I grew tired of working for someone else and felt I could take all I had learned to start my own brand.

What inspired you to begin Caulis?

I started Caulis with a rebellious spirit. Working in retail, I saw that there was a customer for everything, and truly anything could be sold. I saw a lot of overpriced, poorly made items fly off the shelves, and I knew I could offer something better.

I had a few glasses of wine one night and registered my business online. At the time, I was managing a small boutique in Westmount. I used the money I earned working there to fund my knitting project.

My first business purchase was a 1980s retro knitting machine I found on Kijiji for $500 that I still knit on today. It would, I believed, be a good side project that would give me the opportunity to be creative and run a business independently, where I could enjoy being creative and let the brand grow slowly, organically, via word-of-mouth.

There was a lot of trial and error in the first year of prototyping and a certain level of getting comfortable with what I don't know compared to what I'm good at.

The inspiration behind the brand name?

So, fun story. I was initially going to use my name, Leah Legault, but it was November 2018, and Québec's François Legault had just been elected Premier. I wasn't a fan, but politics aside, with us coincidentally sharing the same last name, I didn't want people to think it was some type of Ivanka Trump scenario.

I started searching the origins of Legault and pulled up an old French dictionary that said the word *Gault* comes from the Latin word *caulis,* a botanical term for the stalk of a plant. I liked that it had a plant-based definition, reflecting my preference for natural materials. Mistakenly, I thought it was pronounced *co-lee,* a homonym for the French word for package, *colis*, which also worked because I'm an e-commerce brand and my products are shipped. It turns out it's actually pronounced *co-liss,* a homonym for the Québécois swear word, *câlisse.* Whoops.

Sweaters. Vests. Scarves. Beanies. Toques. All in a beautiful, bold, block colour palette. What inspires you?

When I started Caulis, I was writing for an indie magazine. I was inspired by the designers I had met here in Montréal, along with my mentors and peers.

A piece is made when I feel the itch to make something I wish I had but can't find. I recently made a rule for myself: *don't make something if it's already easy to find elsewhere.*

I create knitwear for someone who enjoys wearing a conversation piece, who appreciates the quality and quirkiness of something homemade, and who likes to know who makes the product they purchase.

You're also a mom. How has this changed you as a designer and a person?

Becoming a parent made me realize how fast days go by and that taking care of my family, community, and self, along with the pursuit of goals and self-actualization, takes time and effort. To maintain them all requires a level of task management I didn't know I was capable of. It does not leave room for wasting time, and to maximize the hours I have, I've cut out aimlessly consuming media. I used to think if I wasn't constantly plugged in, I might become irrelevant and uncultured, but I've found myself to be more confident and imaginative since spending more time with my own thoughts rather than everyone else's.

Parenthood also has me feeling like the future is full of unknown possibilities. I used to think becoming a mom would make me rigid and boring, as mothers in the media are often portrayed, but I've never felt more adaptable and easygoing.

"I prefer to work alone, my lifestyle, my dreams of escaping the corporate world..."

To maximize the hours I have, I've cut out aimlessly consuming media. I used to think if I wasn't constantly plugged in, I might become irrelevant and uncultured, but I've found myself to be more confident and imaginative since spending more time with my own thoughts rather than everyone else's.

I'm a bit of a hermit and have a strong preference for analog technology and working with my hands. Something about the peace and quiet of solitude and working on a physical task makes way for independent thought. As much as I love teamwork in different contexts, I began Caulis to be 100 percent independent, without partners or employees. I want to run Caulis exactly as I want without having to compromise my vision or balance other people's expectations with my own.

How do you apply the principles of sustainability at Caulis? How can we make slow, sustainable fashion accessible to more people?

It is a key factor, although I have mixed feelings about advertising my brand as such. Sustainability was initially my main focus when developing my brand. I knew knitwear was a great option because garments can be knit directly into their shape rather than cut from a larger cloth, which generates a lot of wasted offcuts. All the yarns I've used to date are 100 percent natural fibres only, like wool, linen, hemp, and cotton, which don't cause microfiber plastic pollution, and I can't honestly promote my brand as *eco* or *green* with everything I know about what goes into fashion production. All I can do is be transparent about how I make my products to equip my customers with as much information as possible to decide what they are buying.

The truth is that nothing new that is made and sold is environmentally friendly or sustainable because the production of goods inevitably takes a toll on the environment.

In terms of accessibility, the more sustainably something is produced, the more expensive it is to make, which makes it less accessible to the majority of people. The most sustainable fashion everyone has access to are the clothes that are already in our closets. Opting to buy quality pieces we intend to love for a long time, spending a little more on individual pieces and shopping less.

The future of fashion?

I'd love to see a future that focuses more on individual style rather than trendy items, which would encourage people to find new ways to wear and play with the clothes they already have. When people do buy new, it would be from independent studios and artisans, who are making things slowly to support themselves rather than accumulate wealth for their shareholders. I hope luxury customers begin to realize the value in buying custom, small batch, or made-to-order pieces from local tailors, dressmakers, or artisans rather than mass-produced fashion from high-end brands.

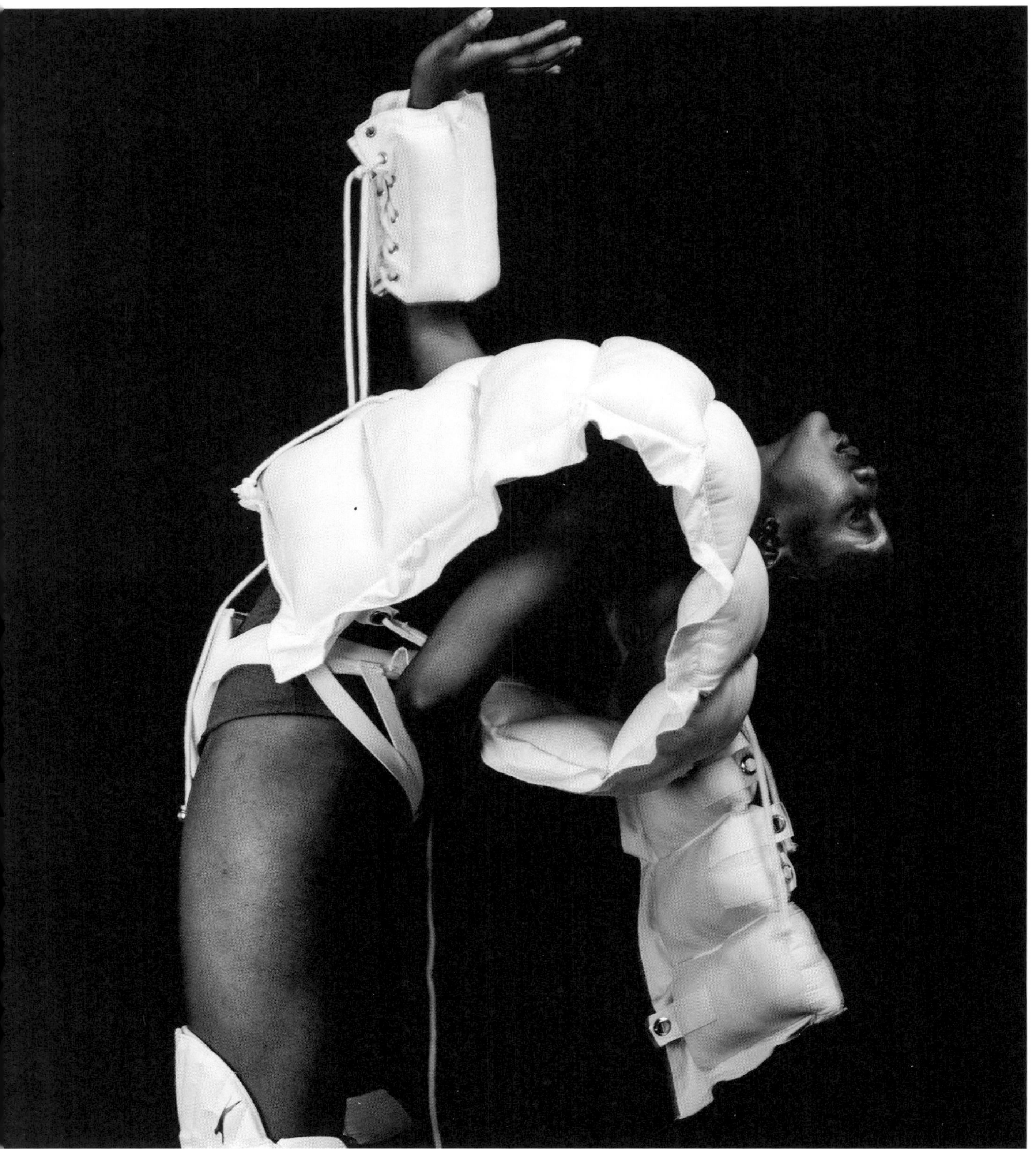

Maycie-Ann St-Louis

Movement Artist, Director, Freelance Model, and Co-founder, Black Montréal Creatives

"I understood that my passion and love for modelling was greater than the limitations the industry then placed on me."

What is your first memory of movement?

It's of me racing other kids in my elementary school yard. I received requests before recess to race my classmates, and most kids bet on me winning. These requests often came from boys thinking they couldn't get beaten by a girl. On occasion, I would also get requests from students in older grades. I quickly realized that I had the ability to run faster than the average kid. The sense of control that I felt in my body is one I can still kinetically tap into today. Running made me feel like I could move through anything, like a human version of flying!

Did you participate in any specific sport?

My main sport growing up was track and field.

In sixth grade, I was approached by a track coach who ran the municipal track team. They asked if I would be interested in taking my track career to the next level. I was a sprinter and a good one at that.

I ran competitively until 10th grade. I loved running, but the competition aspect was too much. It demanded a lot of mental strength.

My Olympic dreams eventually became something unachievable. As I made peace with that, dance appeared, taking the number one spot!

My dance journey began at church performing Praise dance, which serves to praise God in the form of movement. The movements are embellished with beautiful ribbons, flags, and long, twirling skirts. It was something special I did on Sundays.

My little sister and I were given the opportunity to enrol at a local dance studio in partnership with our school. They offered us a tuition-free six-month apprenticeship. Starting dance at age fifteen in a studio was unusual, as most of the students there had been dancing since they were toddlers. But I had a natural dance ability. Years of dancing in my basement with my siblings and copying the moves of dancers in music videos on BET had served me well.

Have you always been creative?

The performing arts intrigued me, and I found myself craving the idea of having the power to *move* an audience. I was involved with anything that sparked the opportunity to express my personality and talent. In elementary school, I participated in talent shows, school musicals, improv, and joined the school band, where I played the clarinet. When I graduated from elementary school, I was awarded the Nimfa Ekbote Performing Arts Award, which was awarded to one student who exemplified great artistic potential in several fields. I was twelve years old at the time and didn't understand why I was the one chosen for this award; I didn't feel worthy of it, but in that moment, I understood that people around me saw more than I could see within myself, and so I carried that revelation with me to high school and vowed to pursue my passion for the arts.

In high school, I joined the strings program and picked up the viola. My best friend and I bonded over our love for performing and pushed one another to keep striving for and extending our creative identities. We managed the Glee club together, joined a string quartet and senior symphony orchestra and participated in a school board-wide talent show called TOPS. It was important to surround myself with other creative people as it validated what I was doing while some people viewed my interests as something for "losers." The arts were for me, a way of life.

You were born and raised in Montréal. How did the city shape and inspire you?

Until the age of sixteen, my day-to-day life took place in the suburb of West Island. It's a primarily anglophone, family, and community-oriented area.

Being raised in that community encouraged me to naturally gravitate towards communal initiatives. I volunteered at a retirement home, as a peer tutor and also at the West Island Black Association. At my high school graduation, I was awarded the YMCA award, the Leadership award and the Lindsay Place High School Alumni award. These merits spoke to the impact I had both inside and outside of school, and remains at the core of who I am. I love to serve and help others, a principle I carry through my artistic practices.

After high school, I commuted daily to Downtown Montréal, where I was accepted into a CEGEP at Dawson College in the Community Recreational and Leadership Training program. While living in West Island, it was hard for me to picture myself in a *big city*, but once I was there, I saw Montréal in a completely new light.

The city landscape was overwhelming and sometimes felt suffocating compared to the spacious and serene energy of West Island. Being in Montréal allowed me to discover all the city had to offer culturally and artistically. I enjoyed exploring museums, festivals, and dance studios, and connecting with other creatives through various events and networking opportunities. Maximizing my time and efforts in a space where more people and opportunities reside allowed me to create a strong, creative identity.

"I call myself a movement artist . . ."

I feel this term is limiting knowing all I want to offer the world creatively. However, it sums up what I do at the present moment. I use movement as a driving force to draw the best out of myself in my various art practices, whether it's dance, movement direction, or modelling. I feel things are always better understood through action, and I encourage others to examine themselves when they are *doing* things.

My dance background gives me a good understanding of my body, which means posing is similar to freezing dance movements in real time and playing with angles in relation to myself and the lens. I also understand how to tap into different states of being and emotions.

Dance and modelling have allowed me to better understand the experience of the subject in front of the lens.

> I use movement as a driving force to draw the best out of myself in my various art practices, whether dance, movement direction, or modelling. I feel things are always better understood through action, and I encourage others to examine themselves when they are doing things.

My preferred approach references inner child's play and organic movement. Nothing should be forced, but rather felt from a place of understanding which can be drawn from a previously lived experience.

Why is art important?

Art allows us to compartmentalize spaces, experiences, feelings, emotions, moments, and ideas. It gives us the opportunity to live limitlessly through time and space.

You also have an extensive modelling portfolio.

I started modelling at seventeen. People would often remark on my tall, slim build and suggest modelling as a path to explore, but I never felt *beautiful* enough to venture into that cutthroat world. Once I switched my attention from track and field to dance, I became more comfortable with my femininity.

A lady at my church was organizing Montréal's Africa Fashion Week and was looking to cast models. She asked me to audition. I successfully smashed the casting call as my dance abilities were easily transferable to the runway.

After doing Africa Fashion Week, my name circled around, and designers asked me to walk their shows. A year later, I expanded my portfolio to include photoshoots. I reached out to local photographers on Instagram, offering up my modelling services on a collaborative exchange to build my portfolio with the goal of a modelling agency signing me. The hard truth is that I was rejected by all the agencies I applied to.

I pursued modelling as a freelancer and still have not signed to an agency, yet managed to get myself to work with some of the biggest brands in the business.

What have you learned about yourself through modelling?

One challenge for me was navigating the industry as a Black body in predominantly white spaces. I found myself being the only Black body cast on several shoots. I've experienced many instances where the makeup artist did not know how to do makeup on my dark complexion, or the hairstylist had never worked on coiled hair before, which made me feel like I was a burden and was not as worthy as my non-Black counterparts. But I didn't let that stop me! I understood that my passion and love for modelling was greater than the limitations the industry then placed on me.

You relocated from Montréal to London during the pandemic.

Although I was successful in Montréal, things felt a little too predictable. I needed to make a change for my career, but most importantly, for my personal growth.

It's not about location, but more about the vision and mindset. London presented me with a more international scene.

More creatives, more opportunities, more spaces in which to express oneself creatively, as well as a more diverse talent pool. This specifically is what allows London to have the strong creative identity that it does.

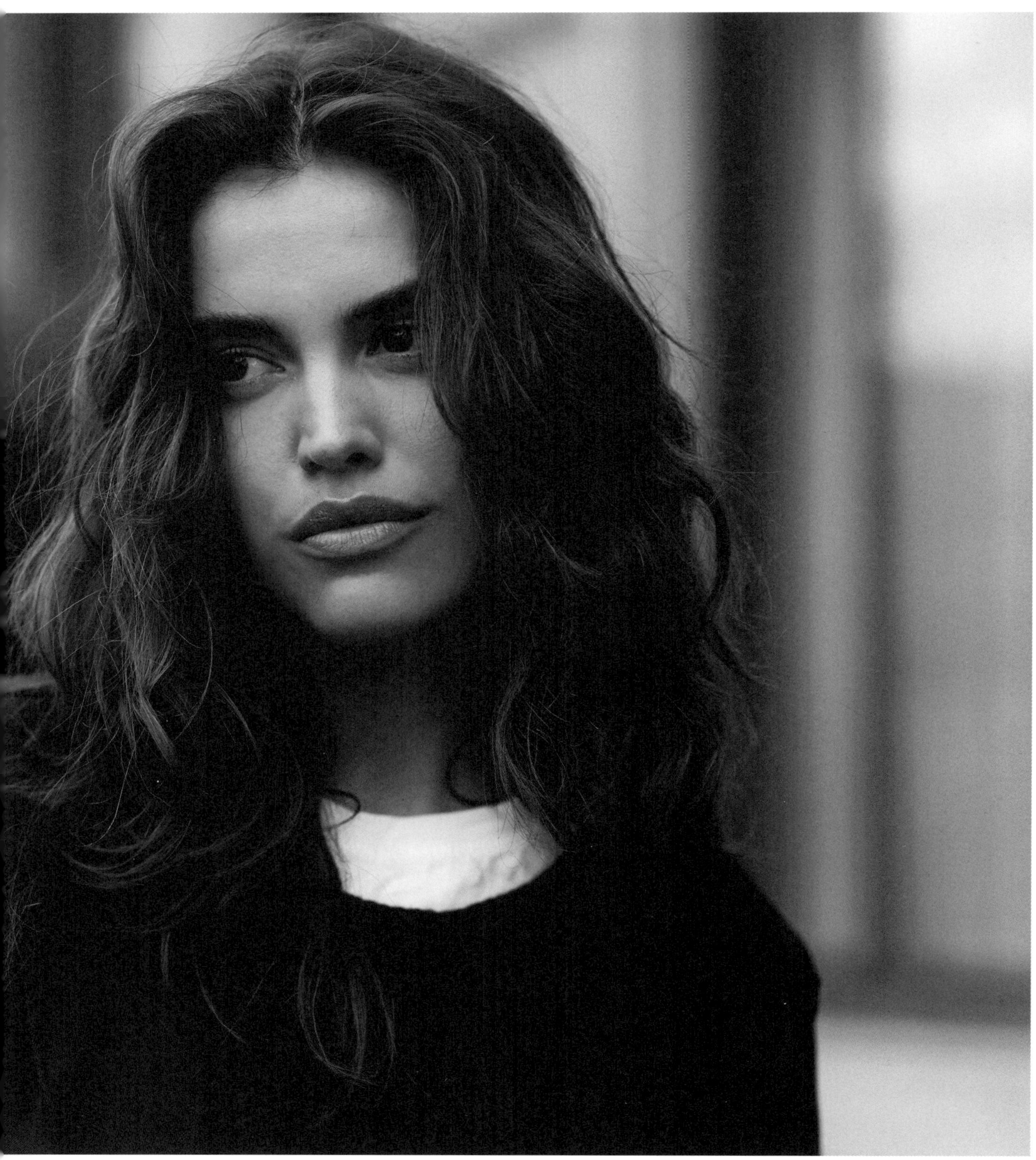

Britt Bergmeister

Model and Sustainability Activist

"Instead of relying on the importance of *what* kind of job I have, I now appreciate that it doesn't matter what I do but *how* I do it."

How amazing that we are doing this interview fifteen years after first meeting each other—you were a student in my ninth-grade English class at the American School in Japan. Watching you mature into a passionate, creative young woman has been an honour. Let's begin with your first recollection of being aware of and interested in sustainability.

It's rare to share a connection like we have, living in Japan and experiencing a complete shock, in all the best ways, to our systems. As two Canadians in a sea of foreigners, I felt a special bond between us that was familiar and comforting. Thank you for always being so supportive and staying in touch.

Growing up, my parents and I would discuss trash and recycling, wondering where our *stuff* went, especially in a city like Tokyo, where no litter was accumulating in the streets.

In 2017, after five years of modelling in New York City, I met up with a group of models (we call ourselves the *Model Mafia*) to discuss how we could support one another and improve our environmental impact. This group would later go on to attend women's marches in New York and climate marches in Washington, DC, all using our influence and voice to inspire one another and our community members to form better habits. For me, this meant starting my own website and platform, *On Duty Citizen (ODC),* to promote sustainable and ethical fashion. From there, my passion for sustainability really took off.

How did the experience of living in Japan shape you?

I moved to Japan when I was twelve and stayed until I was eighteen. While Toronto is an eclectic melting pot of distinctive cultures and customs, I attribute much of my empathy and appreciation of how others live to growing up in Japan during these formative years of my life.

A lot of my job today requires showing up on set and working with new individuals. I can attribute an openness to putting myself out there and collaborating with so many unique personalities to growing up in a foreign country.

Was modelling a profession you dreamed about pursuing?

It was definitely something I was passionate about from a very young age. From seeing photos of my mom modelling in Paris to the influence of shows like *America's Next Top Model*, I liked the idea of transforming myself into different characters, travelling the world and wearing amazing outfits.

I remember one pivotal moment in Japan when a male friend, who was modelling as well, and I shared photos from one of our most recent photoshoots. I had a *very* big crush on him, and when he told me he really liked my pictures, there was a realization that images of me in my hair, makeup, and a beautiful outfit was attractive to him and could potentially make him like me more. It feels scary to admit that. That was a moment when I realized *sex sells*.

For that very reason, I'm so glad I only modelled part-time at such a young age. I started modelling full-time when I turned eighteen, still very young but mature enough to realize the industry had so much to offer beyond taking pretty pictures. Modelling has since evolved for me. It is a privilege to have a voice and a platform with thousands of followers. I try to share sustainability initiatives as well as have a space to have important discussions with my followers, friends, and family.

Your passion for sustainability expanded a few years ago when you founded *On Duty Citizen*. Tell us more about what inspired this venture.

I love learning, and having my own company has shaped so much of who I am today and who I continue to evolve into. It has led to incredible conversations with brands about innovative tools they're using to adapt to the sustainability crisis. It has given me a platform to host events for models to discuss the importance of supporting one another within our industry. It has allowed me to collaborate with my community members and chat about projects they're working on within sustainability, our impending social justice crises, the MeToo Movement and beyond. While modelling is my main source of income, ODC has led to many incredible conversations that help me learn and grow.

How has your career evolved over time?

People always ask me *what's next?* I used to think I had to be successful at so many other things beyond modelling to feel worthy. I understand where people are coming from; modelling is an extremely volatile industry. It took a lot of time for me to realize it's okay to strive for longevity in this career as long as I'm still happy.

I'd love to say my confidence has evolved over time, though sadly, it's still hard to face rejection. It is difficult because oftentimes, there is little to no feedback, so I end up critiquing myself. That said, I used to let my anxiety control me, but I've become good at using tools like therapy, meditation, and even admitting to myself I needed to go on anti-anxiety medicine. As an eighteen-year-old in this industry, I used to feel voiceless. Now, at thirty, I realize I have power as a model, and I have so much more to contribute to each job beyond the clothes I am wearing.

I realize I have power as a model, and I have so much more to contribute to each job beyond the clothes I am wearing.

The life of a model involves a lot of travel, time alone, competition, and rejection, yet you appear to move through it with grace.

I'm lucky to have a supportive husband and family, and I truly believe I couldn't have sustained a career this long without them. My mom and stepdad have supported me in many ways. One fashion week, my mom flew to Milan to be by my side when I was feeling lonely. She dropped everything to be there with me, and that's something I'll never forget.

My husband has had to deal with me missing nearly every anniversary, birthday, and vacation. While I'm sure it's incredibly frustrating to deal with the *last-minuteness* of my job, he wholeheartedly accepts it without showing any annoyance. We've gone through long distance three times, living between Toronto and New York, and while it has been challenging, he always accepts that sometimes I have to prioritize work. It always works out how it's meant to when we go with the flow of life.

Does a brand's commitment to sustainability factor into your decision to work with them?

It absolutely does! From the food I eat to the products I wear, I try to be conscious. I've been introduced to many incredible brands through modelling and *ODC*, so if I shop new, I always try to support a company that is transparent about their practices. However, buying second hand, renting my clothes, or hosting clothing swap parties is my first choice to alleviate waste that ends up in landfills.

I've also become much more aware of the companies I'm modelling for. I'd love to say that I only work with sustainable and ethical brands, but I wouldn't be able to sustain myself if I did. I do, however, see a progression in the last ten years of how many companies care about their impact.

I am very conscious of the companies I support, but I also try to not let it swallow me whole. Eco-anxiety is something I can relate to. I try to look at environmental crises with a lens of optimism and realize that I'm doing my best *most* of the time and that my impact matters.

"The pandemic years were when I experienced the most personal growth."

Through the grit, grind, and competition, New York City pushes you to excel within your career, which I wholeheartedly accept and admire, but COVID-19 made me realize there was beauty in the in-between, gentle moments that don't always have to contribute to career growth. Instead of relying on the importance of *what* kind of job I have, I now appreciate that it doesn't matter what I do but *how* I do it.

"I continue to find my voice in this industry and strive for longevity."

Longevity means accepting how I change every year and learning not to compare myself to others. To speak up when something doesn't feel right and to practice boundaries. If I'm worn thin, it's okay to take a break without feeling guilty. Most importantly, kindness and professionalism are key pillars in striving for longevity in this profession.

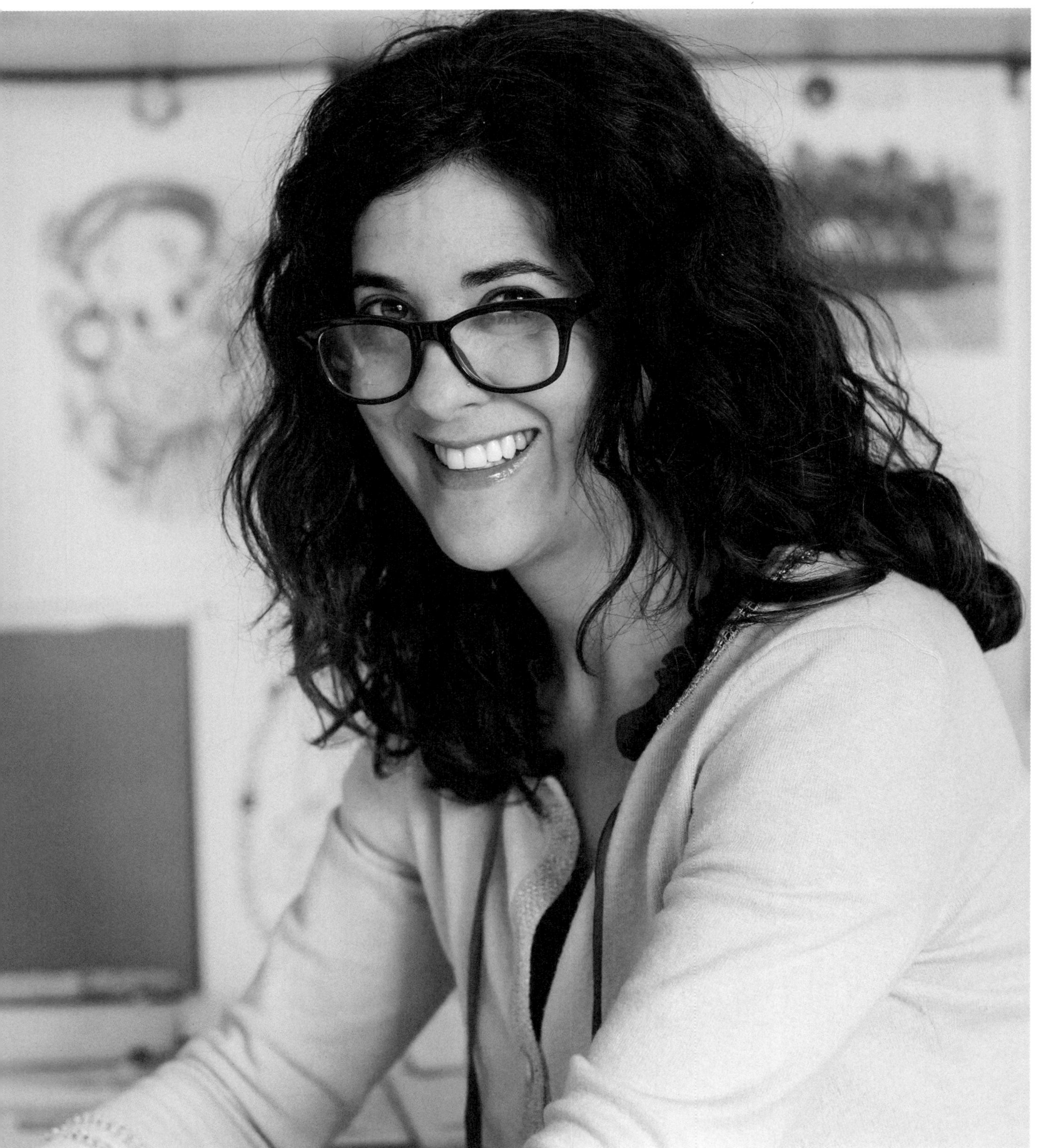

Carolyn Gavin

Painter, Designer, and Illustrator

"I paint the things I love and in that, I find inspiration."

What is your first memory of art?

I remember my mum and other family members always doing creative things. I think this rubbed off on me. I was fascinated by the process of putting pen or paint on paper and creating something from a blank sheet.

You describe yourself as "a flower child of the 60s." And you grew up in South Africa. How did the physical and cultural surroundings shape you personally and professionally?

I think definitely the warmth and sunshine had a lot to do with my unfiltered early perception of light and colour. It's inherently natural for me as an artist to go bright, and I have no inhibitions when it comes to colour. South Africa was a beautiful physical environment to grow up in, although politically it was and is completely rotten and corrupt. There was some trauma at a young age of feeling that things were unjust, but one was told to keep it to oneself!

But culturally, it was exotic and interesting with incredible music and a vibrancy I've not found anywhere else in my travels. I miss that.

When did you arrive in Canada? What was your first impression?

I left South Africa to travel to Israel for three months and live on a kibbutz. Then, onto Greece, Turkey, and then London, where I worked and lived for about a year. After that, in 1991, I joined my family in Toronto. My folks had always thought about leaving the crazy of South Africa and emigrating to Canada for a safer place for their kids and grandchildren. It was a huge sacrifice for them to leave everything they had known for a new and foreign place. I appreciate that so much now that I'm older. They paved the way for the younger generation to have a better, safer life. I arrived in Canada, not knowing anyone, and hated it on site! It grew on me after leaving several times for more travel and journeys back to Africa. I finally settled in 1993 and decided to get on with it and make it my home.

At what stage of life did you realize that pursuing art was your path?

At a very young age, I knew what I wanted to be. I had watched my graphic designer aunt make a poster by hand and I was hooked. I loved the arts, and my parents sent me to an amazing art teacher at the age of about nine. Nina Campbell-Quine taught me the basics, like gouache, watercolour, still life, pen and ink, papier mâché, etc. She was a brilliant, well-known artist herself and taught in the most fascinating way in an incredible, light-filled studio with easels and tons of natural light pouring in through huge glass windows.

She inspired me in her way of seeing the world and the strength and potential of an art career, especially as a woman.

Your work is vibrant and uplifting. How did you go about focusing on finding inspiration through travel, flowers, colour, and patterns? Was this intentional or something that developed over time?

I think it's been a progression of media and subject matter, and I've come full circle. I started off painting, then moved into graphic design and illustration, and now I'm mostly painting again. I paint the things I love, and in that, I find inspiration. Travel provides all of these things but with new eyes; that's why I love it so much. Same subjects, but new again.

Would you say travel is a big part of who you are? What is your favourite spot in the world and where would you like to go that you haven't been?

I would have to say Belize is my favourite spot as I go there to recharge and rejuvenate over the winter months. It provides the peace I need and the visual beauty and warmth that I crave over the darkest days and coldest nights.

I would love to go to Kenya, Zanzibar, Peru, Columbia, Japan, Cambodia, Thailand, Australia, and New Zealand.

You work in gouache, watercolour, and pen and ink. Why these particular mediums?

I love the fluidity of watercolour. I love the freedom it gives me as I'm working and letting the paint and water do its thing on the paper.

Gouache and acrylic require more physical brushstrokes, and conscious and unconscious play of paint and where to put it. All are wonderful and I constantly go back and forth between the two. I think this is a good mental exercise. Freedom and control, back-to-back, like weight training for the mind. Letting go and coming home. I use pen and ink mainly in the watercolour paintings to add detail and another element and dimension on top of the paint. Delicate lines of ink play with the shapes underneath. It's a nice contrast of thick and thin, soft and hard.

I constantly go back and forth between the two [mediums]. I think this is a good mental exercise. Freedom and control, back-to-back, like weight training for the mind. Letting go and coming home.

What do you need in order to create?

I need the energy and inspiration to do it. Once that is there, yes, good light is critical, and a pretty studio all helps. Often, I light incense and sometimes listen to music or a podcast.

Are there times when you're not inspired? How do you get through this?

It often happens. I try to take a break and then maybe play with paint—nothing too serious. I just sit down and paint something, anything. This does help.

What are your causes?

Animals, veganism, and the environment. I wish people could change their mindset to the fact that eating a cow, pig, sheep, or chicken is exactly the same as eating a dog or a cat. I think if more people could change to a plant-based diet, so many environmental catastrophes could be avoided.

I read somewhere, "Carolyn makes sure her life is filled with beauty and creativity." Love this. What specifically fills your life with beauty and creativity?

I'm happiest when I'm feeling good, and everybody around me is healthy. If all that is good, then things align, and I can fill my head with beauty. When life gets in the way, then it gets harder. Then, painting becomes a relief and an escape.

What is most precious to you?

Health above all.

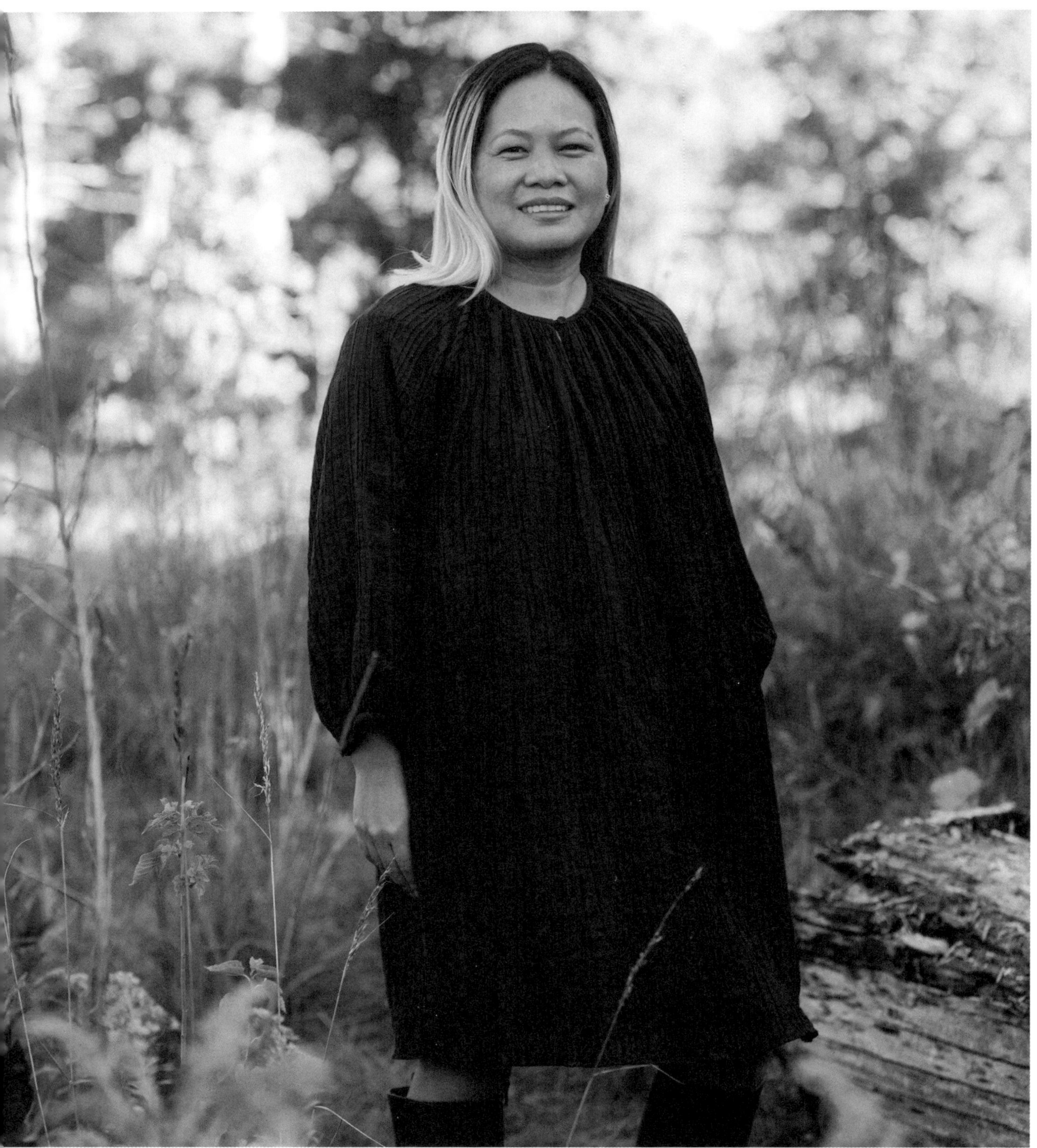

Truc Nguyen

Writer and Editor

"My work is always shifting and evolving, but I have found that I'm happiest when I am working on a wide variety of creative and editorial projects."

Can you remember the first thing you wrote? Do you feel you were destined to become a writer?
Even as a child, I was a voracious reader. In elementary school, I remember once reading something like 700 books in a summer, in part to win prizes from the local library's reading club. I even got a part-time job as a library page and even considered becoming a librarian, but never thought about pursuing writing as a career—it simply wasn't something that was presented as a possibility to me.

In middle school, I wrote some, in retrospect, pretty terrible op-ed pieces for the student newspaper. That was my first time writing for public consumption, and I guess I never really stopped!

At what age and stage of life did you realize that writing was your professional path?
It's funny, but after all these years, I still don't really identify as one because my career path has been anything but linear. While always writing, I've worked as a magazine editor, fashion stylist, editorial producer, brand consultant, and content strategist.

I briefly debated between English and fashion design for undergrad, but the latter program won by offering me a full scholarship! I also completed an MA in Communication and Culture and contributed to one of the student papers at university for a few years.

Where was your first official writing gig? First published story?
I used to be responsible for the shopping information or *credits* in the first few issues of American *Vogue Living*. I also had a few bylines as an intern at *Glow* magazine, which was thrilling!

You worked with Condé Nast in NYC. Please tell me more about this time and how it shaped your career. As well, life in Melbourne, Australia. What took you there?
I did a semester abroad in Melbourne in my third year of undergrad. It was an incredible, life-changing adventure—in fact, I met my now-husband at a barbecue for Canadian exchange students! Looking back, I think the positive experience I had in Australia made me feel more confident about pursuing an internship—and then, later, a career—in New York City after graduation.

For me, one summer interning in Manhattan led to a second summer internship, which, completely by pure luck, turned into a job at 4 Times Square. The three years on and off that I worked at Condé Nast weren't always easy, but it was an unrivalled opportunity to work with and learn from incredibly talented, dedicated editors and contributors. That experience, and some of those connections, opened many doors for me later in my career.

You're an avid traveller. How have these experiences inspired your work?

I love to travel, and I am so thankful whenever I get to do it for work. I've been to fashion weeks in New York, Milan, and London, worked backstage at the Soul Train Music Awards, and travelled everywhere from Los Angeles to St. Catharines, Ontario, for photoshoots. What I love most about many of these experiences is actually the many talented, creative people that I get to work with, interview, or simply meet at the destination.

Throughout your career as a writer, what inspired you to focus your time, energy, and expertise on lifestyle features?

Because of my education and industry experience, I focused on fashion writing for the first part of my career. It wasn't until I was on staff at *Flare* magazine that I started putting my hand up for other writing opportunities.

My work is always shifting and evolving, but I have found that I'm happiest when I am working on a wide variety of creative and editorial projects. On any typical week, I could be working on a shopping story for a fashion magazine, a long-form lifestyle feature for a newspaper, a short travel post for an online publication, *and* an entrepreneur profile for a business magazine.

You shared that choosing a creative career as a working-class immigrant was challenging. Have you been able to convince your parents that your work is valuable and sustainable?

My family immigrated to Canada when I was seven, in part so that my siblings and I could have an opportunity for a better life. My parents sacrificed a lot for us, and I think it was sometimes confusing for them that I wasn't interested in pursuing a stable, more *respectable* profession like law or architecture.

Thankfully, they've always been accepting of my educational and career choices, even when they didn't understand them. I think they always knew I would make things work and that they wouldn't have to worry about me.

My parents sacrificed a lot for us, and I think it was sometimes confusing for them that I wasn't interested in pursuing a stable, more *respectable* profession like law or architecture. Thankfully, they've always been accepting of my educational and career choices, even when they didn't understand them. I think they always knew I would make things work and that they wouldn't have to worry about me.

What are the joys and realities of having a multi-hyphenate career? It appears that many of us do this now more out of necessity than anything.

When I was in school, it was still very possible to be a fashion designer or a magazine editor for decades at a time. These days, stints are often much shorter and have high turnovers, as many industries have experienced disruptions. In fashion and lifestyle media, some full-time jobs still exist, but they may be lower paid than before. Today, whether you're an employee or a freelance worker, it's more important than ever to be agile and flexible in your career and pursue continuous learning.

A writer who has consistently wowed you with their work?

My friend, Isabel B. Slone, has written some great fashion and cultural zeitgeist pieces for publications like *The New York Times* and *Harper's Bazaar*.

A story that has stayed with you?

In 2019, I wrote a story about being part of the *sandwich generation* for *Elle Canada*. As my parents and my kids get older, and the challenges grow and evolve, it's a topic that I still think about often.

One of the best parts of my job is that whenever I am ruminating on something in my life, I can usually turn that curiosity, frustration, or concern into a story idea. Then, I get to learn more about the topic, access leading experts in the field, and have an opportunity to help others who might be in the same situation.

What is the future of storytelling?

The formats and conventions may change—after all, the medium is the message, as Marshall McLuhan famously wrote. But I think storytelling will always be important, and authority and credibility will continue to be important to audiences, especially when there is so much inaccuracy and misinformation online.

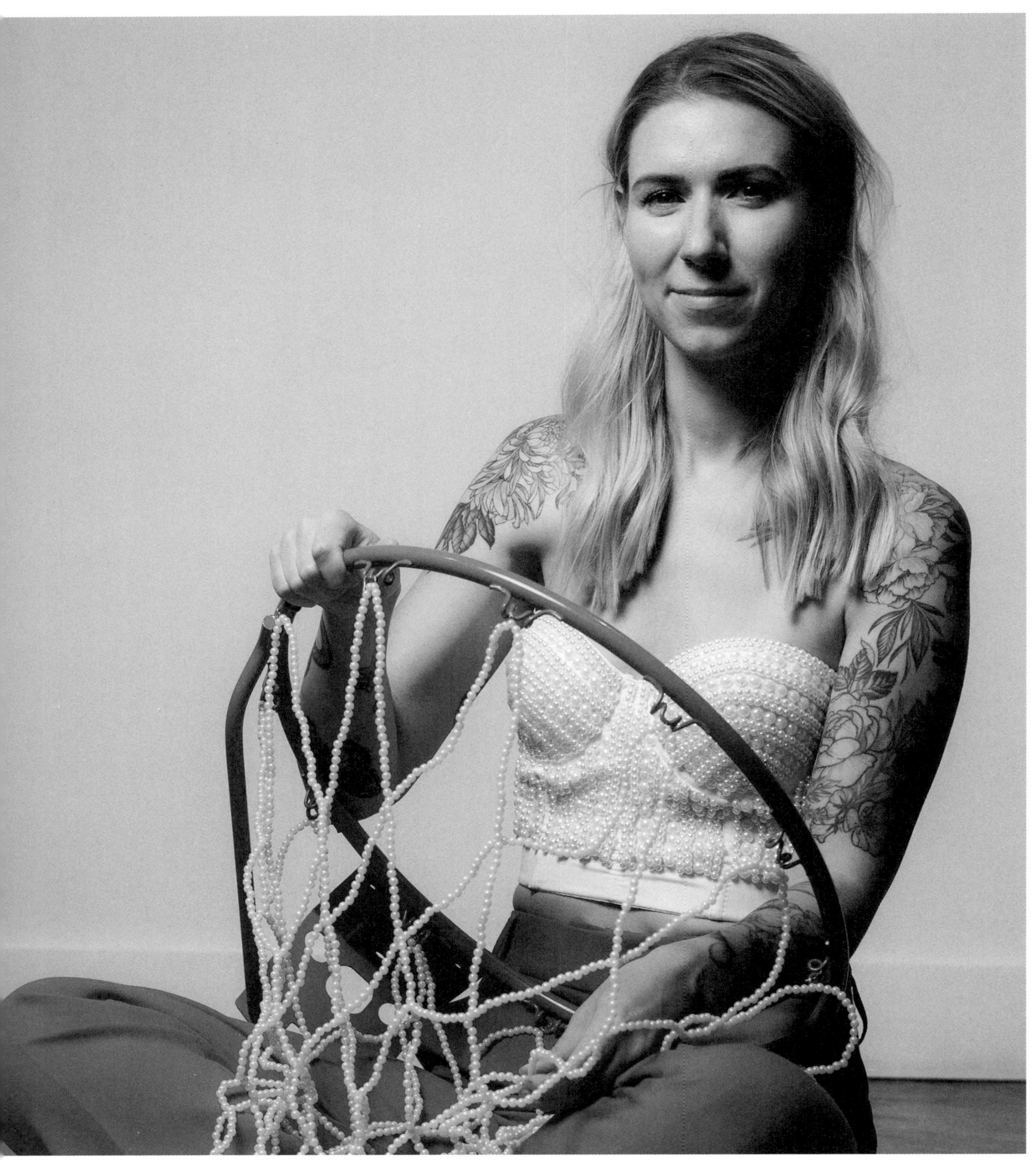

Mallory Tolcher

Visual Arts Athletic Artist

"I'm interested in challenging gender and sexuality stereotypes by creating work that balances softness and strength."

What is your first memory of art?

Growing up, my family and I would visit Thunder Bay and stop at my aunt's store, Silk & Cedar. Along with having beautiful, the back of her store was filled with walls of silk flowers. I was mesmerized by the sizes, shapes, and colours. I find myself leaning more into the feminine wonder I had as a kid in those specific environments.

Was creativity a pivotal part of your childhood?

To be honest, I wouldn't consider myself an artsy kid. I was born in Winnipeg and spent most of my time running around outside and hanging out at the park. My mom would be crocheting, cross-stitching, or embroidering, but it didn't interest me at the time. I remember being very young and watching a behind-the-scenes feature of a Betsey Johnson fashion show, where they were interviewing makeup artist Charlie Green. She talked about putting makeup on the models while they were lying down. I became obsessed with makeup and would apply it for hours at a time, lying on the floor with a mirror.

How does your fascination with all things fashion inspire the current themes in your work as an artist?

When the pandemic in 2020 caused everything to shut down, and nothing new was being made, I gravitated towards doing things that brought me joy—watching old fashion runway shows and reading books about designers. When government restrictions eased up, I signed up for sewing classes at a local sewing store and started to create sport-related items with high-end fabrics. For the first time in my art career, I felt like I was exploring themes and materials that feel authentic to who I am and what I love. In my studio, I have a photograph of myself as a young girl dressed in a dance recital costume while sitting on the floor of my living room. I often look at it while working and feel like I am honouring that little girl.

You describe yourself as an Athletic Artist.

When I first started making work about sports, the pieces weren't great in that they were simple, unrelatable, and uninspiring. In class critiques, both classmates and teachers had a hard time talking about my artwork, and the feedback I received was frustrating. I almost dropped out! I developed anxiety and started to think art wasn't my path. To cope, I would run on the track at the school's indoor gym. I started training to slam dunk a basketball. It wasn't until then that I started making connections between sports and myself as a white, cisgender female. I started to investigate sports through a specific lens, one that focused on my experiences and how they've led me to believe that certain kinds of bodies, behaviours, and attitudes are acceptable and sanctioned while others are excluded, repressed, or even punished.

You're also a teacher.

I never thought I would become a teacher. However, during my last years at university, I started visiting elementary and high school classes to do art workshops. I loved being in a fun and creative environment. Being an artist has helped me organize community projects, like painting Canada's largest sports court mural with my students with special needs. Being a teacher allowed me to learn about new technologies, artists, trends, and skills that I might not have otherwise.

You currently live and work in Guelph, Ontario. How do your surroundings inspire?

Guelph is known for being green, both physically and politically. Its greenery and trails have inspired me to fall in love with trail running. When I first moved here, I was successful in getting the Artist-in-Residence position and decided to make a series that I could install along the trails, encouraging viewers to see the exhibit in its entirety. The experience connected me with wonderful individuals and local businesses that also promote movement and sport.

Tell me more about your Nothing But Net series, a beautiful collection of hand-crafted basketball nets.

Basketball is a beautiful sport as it's a balance of power and grace; its artful improvisation within immutable structure is unparalleled.

My very first nets were made by knitting and crocheting yarn. The initial idea didn't generate much interest from my friends and colleagues. My friend Jeff believed in the project—he and I spent a lunch

By drawing inspiration from fashion and basketball culture, my work references the female form at its most powerful and vulnerable, giving strength to all aspects of what it means to be a woman.

break writing a proposal about mesh made of traditionally feminine materials that would be placed on public courts and documented over time. I submitted the proposal to the Ontario Arts Council, and it was successful. I then purchased beautiful materials from my aunt's store, and once the nets were constructed, I won over my colleagues and others who doubted the original idea. The community loved them, too! My social media blew up after posting images, and publications like *Frankie*, *The Torus*, and CBC *Arts* started to write about them. I'm grateful the work has received so much traction, but I also feel left out when I see all-male sports-related art shows. I'm hoping that sports publications, teams, athletes, and organizations start embracing females and the feminine in sports so that there are more inclusive collaborations in the future.

Many of your pieces use what we perceive as feminine materials (lace, flowers, chandelier-type glass pieces, leather, tulle, silk, pearls). Is this intentional?

Yes! I'm interested in challenging gender and sexuality stereotypes by creating work that balances softness and strength. By drawing inspiration from fashion and basketball culture, my work references the female form at its most powerful and vulnerable, giving strength to all aspects of what it means to be a woman.

Over time, we've seen an incredible rise in the number of female athletes. And we're celebrating it.

We are making the difference. Social media has been able to highlight, in real-time, the inequalities that females face in terms of facilities, transportation, and overall treatment in comparison to their male counterparts. Athletes, in general, have been fantastic at using their platforms to address these issues, and people are realising that female athletes have been the frontrunners when it comes to social activism.

Sculpture. Drawing. Public Art. How does the process differ for each?

When I create public work, the process is very much grounded in the specific space—who lives there, who visits there. Often, the project will turn into community art that is a participatory experience by and for the visitor. I like to pull people in, whether with a colourful sports court or by using delicate materials that are tempting to play with. Drawing is much more of a private and intimate process for me. While I used to focus on creating realistic portraits of athletes, my drawing has since been the driving force behind designing my sculptures and installations.

Please describe your creative process.

I carry around a small sketchbook in which I record thoughts and quotes, glue materials, and draw diagrams that I refer to while in my studio. I love to bounce ideas off my husband because he's not interested in art but loves sports. If he thinks it's a good idea, I feel like it's a winner. Once I feel confident about the piece, I like to be alone, in my space, with the door closed. I often have reality television playing in the background or Rihanna on repeat.

"I want to focus my work on being strong and female."

We named my daughter Jordan after Michael Jordan. For a long time, I fought against making work that would be considered *too feminine,* as I was scared to not fit into the current culture of the sport, which is hyper-masculine. Sport is marketed to us with big, bold colours, loud music, bright lights, and sex appeal. There aren't many moments of softness and quiet, of doubt, or of growth. Now that I have a daughter and see her running around with boys, I want her to always feel included. I want her to be seen as a strong female. But that doesn't mean she needs to be considered feminine, such as the ideals that have been pushed on female athletes for decades. I embrace the feminine in my work because it helps me develop more clarity in my own voice as an artist.

Why is art important?

Art is like breathing. A good day is when I have gone for a run and worked on some art. Giving myself that time makes me the best version of myself so that I can be the best mom, partner, friend, daughter, and teacher. Art is important because it's what we consume daily, whether it's through the TV we watch or the music we listen to, the colours and visuals we see in indoor and outdoor spaces. Art is important for everyone's mental health.

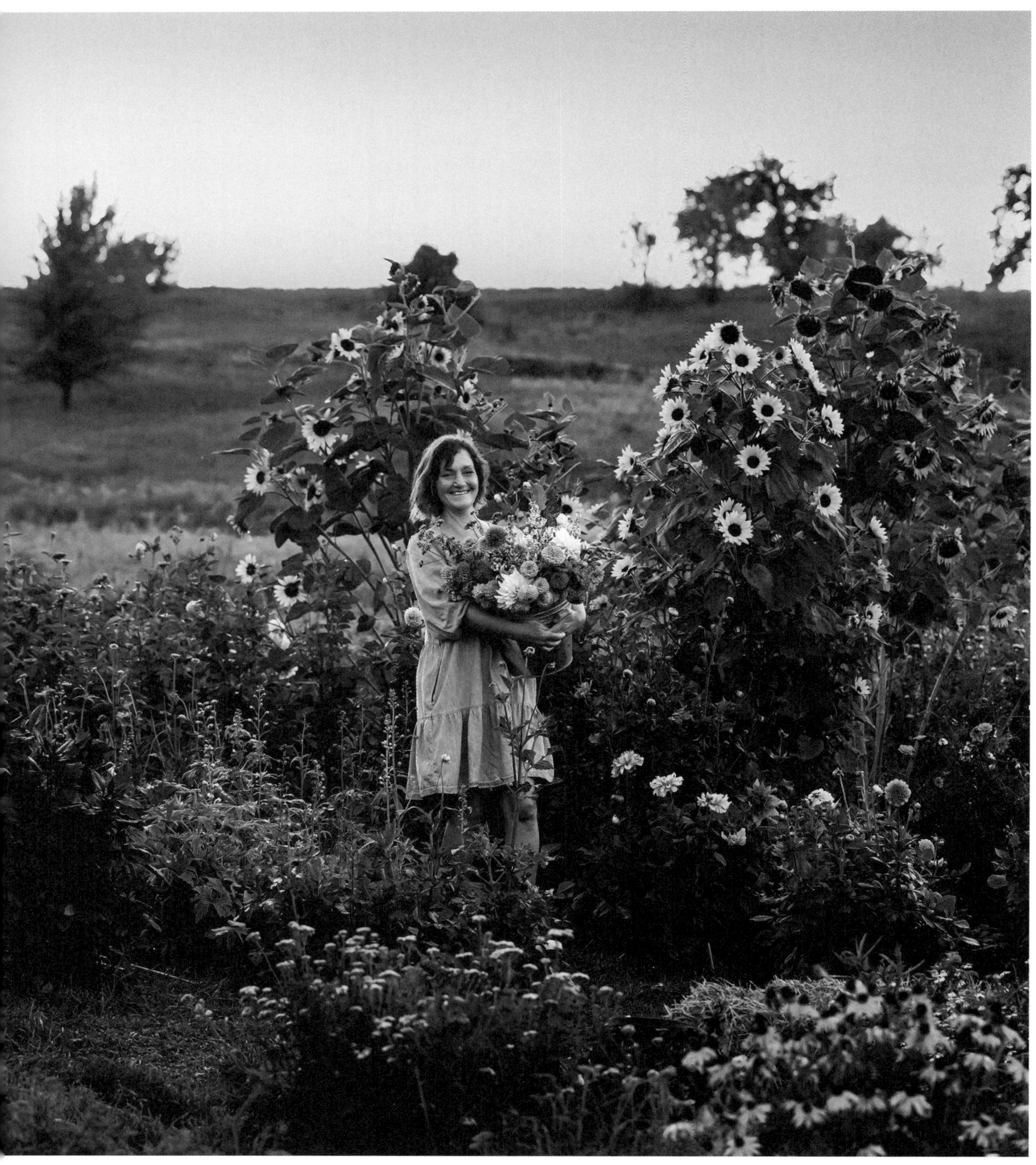

Janet Tuenschel

Owner and Flower Farmer, Country Cut Flowers

"I think we all have a responsibility to be kinder to the earth. I want to leave my little corner of the world a little better than I found it."

What is your first memory of flowers?

My grandmother's grove of lilacs behind my grandparents' farmhouse and the row of colourful hollyhocks along their old barn. My other grandparents had a one-acre garden behind their home, filled with an abundance of vegetables and flowers. I remember my grandmother's gorgeous peonies and the unreal portulaca. The third early memory is of the Royal Botanical Gardens in Burlington. I loved the rock gardens' beautiful winding trails and bridges, but my absolute favourite was the Lilac Dell. I remember running up and down the hills, breathing in the sweet scent of the lilacs.

"I stumbled my way into this business. I left office life in 2012, with very little planning . . . perhaps none. Knowing I'd always loved gardens and gardening, I started up a little gardening business." This is a brave path to follow. Any surprises once embarking upon starting Country Cut Flowers?

The gardening business and the farm overlapped for a year or two. As they both grew, I was overwhelmed, and as they were both full-time enterprises, I wound down the gardening business. It felt a little nuts to be closing the business that made money, but I was choosing the one that I loved. That first year, I was nervous about bringing in enough customers and revenue to justify the business. There was no need to worry because, in July, my farm was featured in one of the biggest Toronto blogs. It felt like Toronto had descended on me! The blog went live on a Saturday morning, and that day, I was already flooded by all the visitors. I tried my best to manage the crowds and flower supply but had to shut down the farm within a few days. We barricaded the driveway, and most times, when I left or came home, there were people waiting in their cars along the side of the road. I shed a few tears as I explained to people they had to leave or took phone calls from disappointed flower lovers. Over the next two weeks, I cleaned up the flower patches, the flowers regrew, and I started to sell tickets online. It gave me the control I needed over the number of visitors to the farm. The following few years, more cut-your-own flower farms started popping up, so I don't have to worry about the same crowds, and I don't always require tickets anymore. Later in the season, we now have drop-in days. There is plenty of room for all the flower farmers, and I love seeing more around.

You shared about not feeling confident but doing it anyway. What did you do to quiet the doubt? And persevere with your passion?

When there's something I'm really drawn to, I can visualize the fears being picked up and set aside. It's like they're sitting beside me. I may even have a conversation with the fears, but they must stay to the side—I can be forceful with them on occasion. I find it interesting because when I'm upset about something, I don't seem to have that same level of control. I think the passion perseveres because, at this point in my life, this is all I can see myself doing. It's like the pathways I loved at the RBG as a child have been transported to the pathways in my gardens. The feeling I had standing in my grandparents' gardens, I now feel in my own gardens. There's a connection to the earth and the flowers that I can't quite explain.

What have been the benefits and challenges of starting a flower farm from scratch? I imagine you're constantly learning.

Starting my flower farm from scratch has allowed me to choose my plantings so the flowers are the ones I really want. I've designed the layout of the gardens, too, although those have sometimes arisen simply because a pile of dirt killed the grass. I guess it's become a combination of planning and happenstance. Cultivating new land is challenging as we get the weeds under control. And there are some weeds that defy control, like bindweed, so we have to grow alongside it. I've taken farming, flower design, garden design, and horticulture courses. And there's always reading and online research and being a member of organizations like the Association of Specialty Cut Flower Growers.

"I grow all my flowers naturally, with sunshine, water from our property, compost, and a little love." Why is this important to you?

I think we all have a responsibility to be kinder to the earth. I want to leave my little corner of the world a

The feeling I had standing in my grandparents' gardens, I now feel in my own gardens. There's a connection to the earth and the flowers that I can't quite explain.

little better than I found it. We've planted thousands of trees to reforest most of our property. So far, we've found natural ways to deal with disease and insects. With healthy soil, some of those problems can sort themselves out. Sometimes, it simply means more work to do things naturally.

What is unique about Country Cut Flowers?

I want people to have peaceful experiences here. Rather than row after row of flowers, like most flower farms, we have small gardens and meandering areas to sit and rest. We also offer workshops with unique classes, picnics, and small weddings.

Cut-your-own flowers. What inspired this, and how have people responded?

When I started the farm, I sold my flowers at the Newmarket Farmers' Market. I put out buckets with loose flowers so people could choose their own flowers. I noticed how much people loved choosing the flowers and how much time and care they took. One late-season Friday, I contacted the market manager and told her I just couldn't get myself ready for the next day's market. I posted on Facebook that I would open for cut-your-own flowers that Saturday. I had visited a beautiful cut-your-own-flowers farm when my first son wasn't yet a year old, Wildflower Farm, owned by Miriam Goldberger. Her farm had stuck in my head and heart for years, and some part of me believed I might be able to run a cut-your-own-flowers operation too. I didn't have very many followers, but that first Saturday saw a steady stream of customers. I tried it again the following Saturday and had even more customers, and I was hooked.

Favourite flower and why? Not sure that's a fair question to ask . . .

Not fair! I think it's a category of flowers, the spring flowers—lilacs, daffodils, tulips, peonies, and lily of the valley. There's so much hope tied to spring flowers.

I imagine there is some level of stress in this industry. A few unknowns. How do you work through the more stressful moments?

There is a surprising amount of stress associated with farming. We're at the mercy of the weather, disease, and insects. When we have weeks without rain, there's only so much that I can do. When the Japanese beetles show up, I know we'll be sacrificing a lot of flowers to them. I'm constantly learning how to manage stress, and don't have it all figured out yet. But talking when I'm stressed helps. Keeping the stress bottled up leads to problems down the road. I stretch, meditate, and walk. I'm amazed constantly by what I can sort out when I go for a walk in the forest. I start the day with some quiet time before the *busyness* of the day begins. I try to journal as much as possible. But I think recognizing that it's a privilege to do what I do and accepting that stress is a part of it helps. There's no sense railing against the things I can't change, but rather I find a way to work with, or at least alongside, them.

What do you enjoy doing outside of the farm?

I love to read and hike and cross-country ski.

I like to think that people are generally paying attention to what make us smile, like the beauty of flowers. Have you seen a rise in sales since the pandemic?

Yes, there's been an increase in flower sales, particularly an interest in buying local. I think flowers are important because they bring joy. It's as simple as that. Whether they grow in your garden or are purchased from a local flower farmer, they provide happiness.

Where do you envision yourself and the business five years from now?

I want the farm to provide more opportunities for retreats and healing. I'm not sure yet how that will take shape, but as the population of our region grows and becomes busier, people will need more restful experiences, and opportunities for connection and community.

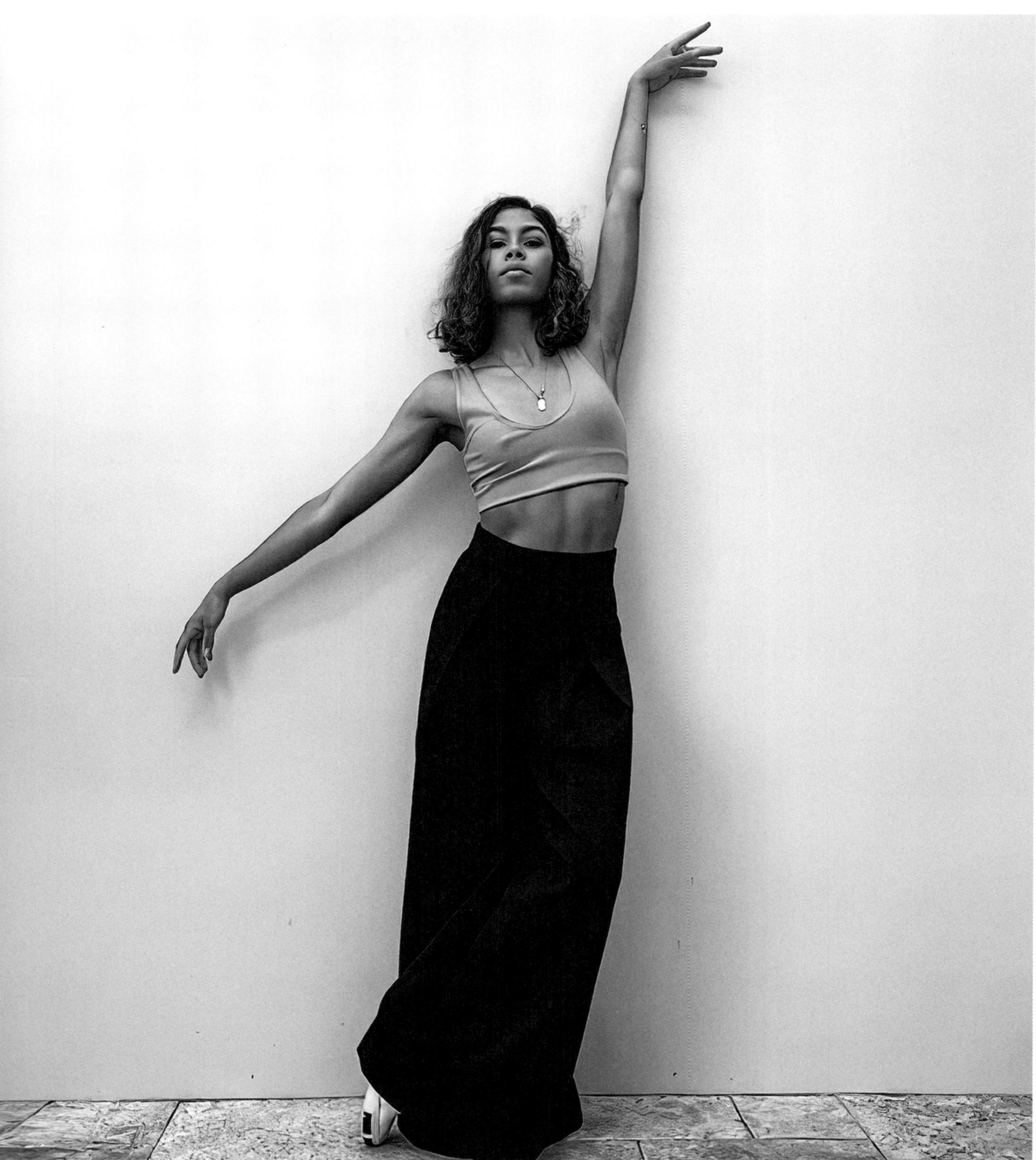

Tene Ward

Ballerina, National Ballet of Canada

"Watching a dancer bare their soul and create an entire world through movement is what makes our job so special; that is what makes this career so beautiful and my heart so full."

You were born and raised in Australia. How did this environment shape you?

I lived between Melbourne and Sydney. The Australian cultural landscape is extremely whitewashed, so a lot of what shaped me into the person I am today has been my Sri Lankan heritage. My family made a constant effort to surround me with Sri Lankan culture, food, and people who helped me embrace my individuality, especially in spaces where I have been told countless times that individuality will be the reason I won't succeed.

What is your first memory of dance?

I was around five years old in my first dance concert, performing a jazz routine. During the group dance, the other girls were doing the wrong steps and going the wrong way, so I tried to move them and stand in front to show the steps properly. This memory always makes me laugh as I continue to try to be a leader in the studio to this day. Not to mention that the feeling of being so excited and at home on the stage is the same feeling I have twenty years later.

Were you exposed to various forms of dance and movement growing up?

I always wanted and needed to be moving. I spent a lot of my early years learning multiple dance forms such as jazz, tap, and acro. It wasn't until I was eight that I started ballet. I also sang, acted, and enjoyed other sports, such as swimming, running, and netball. I believe dance stayed with me throughout it all because I could express myself; it wasn't just about the movement. As special and exciting as it may be, through dance, I could tell a story, relive a memory, or explore a different life, all within the studio.

At what stage of life did you realize that pursuing dance would be your professional path?

It wasn't until I was maybe sixteen that I learned about Misty Copeland. It was the first time I had heard of and seen representation in a major ballet company. She inspired me to push and work even harder to get to her level. I continued to train at a prestigious ballet school in Melbourne; however, during my time there, I was constantly told to quit or move into contemporary dance. During those moments, I was extremely lucky to have the support and wisdom of my *mum*, who never let me give up on myself. She constantly reminded me that, "No one is like you, you are unique, and that is a good thing."

As for training for professional life, there are things you learn through school, such as a training

> I believe dance stayed with me throughout it all because I could express myself; it wasn't just about the movement. As special and exciting as it may be, through dance, I could tell a story, relive a memory, or explore a different life all within the studio.

schedule for the gym or Pilates, but most of it I learnt within my first year of joining a company. I was extremely lucky that the dancers at the National Ballet of Canada were so generous.

A performance that moved you—one in particular that perhaps shaped your path or moved you towards a professional career in dance?
In fact, the past two days (May 2023) have been the most recent times a performance moved me. Second Soloist Tirion Law is a close friend and debuting as Juliet, and it brought me to tears to see her achieve her dream and do it so effortlessly and beautifully. I also watched a run through with First Soloist Chelsy Meiss and Principal Dancer Ben Rudisin in *Romeo & Juliet*. They were awe-inspiring, putting every ounce of love into the roles and completely embodying the characters in a way I hadn't seen before.

During my schooling, technique was made to feel like the be-all-end-all of a dancer. But since joining a company, that perception has changed for me, especially when I witness moments like the ones I mention above. They continue to remind me that technical proficiency is always phenomenal to see, but watching a dancer bare their soul and create an entire world through movement is what makes our job so special. That is what makes this career so beautiful and my heart so full.

What year did you join the National Ballet of Canada? Congratulations! First thoughts on Canada?
Thank you! I joined in August of 2018. I can't believe how time flies. Oh, my first thought was definitely about how I, an Aussie, was supposed to survive the winter. Immediately, I had to stock up on winter gear. The thin coats I had brought were not going to cut it, that's for sure. I do love Canada and love the life I have here; however, I am unsure if I will ever get used to the cold!

Prior to dancing with the National Ballet of Canada, where else have you worked?
I did a few short-term contracts with The Australian Ballet and trained in Amsterdam with the Dutch National Ballet Academy before moving to Toronto. I also spent my graduate year working as a bartender.

A choreographer, a dancer, or a type of dance that has inspired you over the years?
I would say Crystal Pite and Rena Butler have been extremely influential for me. Both female-identifying choreographers have broken many barriers to get to where they are today. They never let their egos take over and constantly push dancers to discover more within, to surprise and always believe in themselves. When it comes to dancers who inspire me, that is always changing. I feel fortunate to be surrounded by talented and dedicated colleagues, even in daily company classes. There are many times I look around and am inspired by the people standing beside me.

Within my own work, emotions or experiences are a major driving force. It can be so cathartic to leave it all out there on the dance floor, as they say. I especially draw from my family, who I love so dearly and who constantly support me. Knowing they are there for me allows me the freedom to delve deeper into who I am, who I want to be and where I want this unique journey of dance and life to take me.

I imagine that dance has brought you to some incredible places, spaces, and stages. Which one stands out and why? Hard to choose, I imagine.
Most recently, the company went on tour to New York with a triple bill. We performed at the City Center, which is a historic theatre. Being backstage and performing, knowing how many other companies and stars had been there too, was very thrilling. This was made extra special for me as it was the first time my mum would see me perform with the company since I joined in 2018. Having my biggest cheerleader, best friend, and lifelong inspiration in the audience made those shows unforgettable.

Your work is exceptionally physical and emotional. How do you ensure that you're performing and working in peak form?
Focusing on mental health and going to therapy has played a huge role in allowing me to mentally and emotionally show up for myself so I can perform to the best of my abilities. This job can focus extensively on the negative aspects of a person, as we are constantly trying to nitpick and find something to improve upon. Due to this, practicing gratitude has become key in my wellness regime. As for physical wellness, cross-training is vital in preparing a dancer for the stage. I will, however, point out that during shows, I am conscious of not overdoing it with the gym training as I am on stage for every performance, so finding time to rest during a busy season is a high priority, as well as finding time for recovery post-show or after a six-hour rehearsal day.

What does your life look like outside of the studio?
Busy! I am a big foodie and extremely social, so you'll often find me on the hunt for a new dinner spot with my friends. Otherwise, you'll find me at the gym or on a bike ride, enjoying the sun at the beach or in the park. However, once winter hits, I am a bit of a recluse, and you won't see me anywhere outside work except for right on my couch binge-watching reality TV.

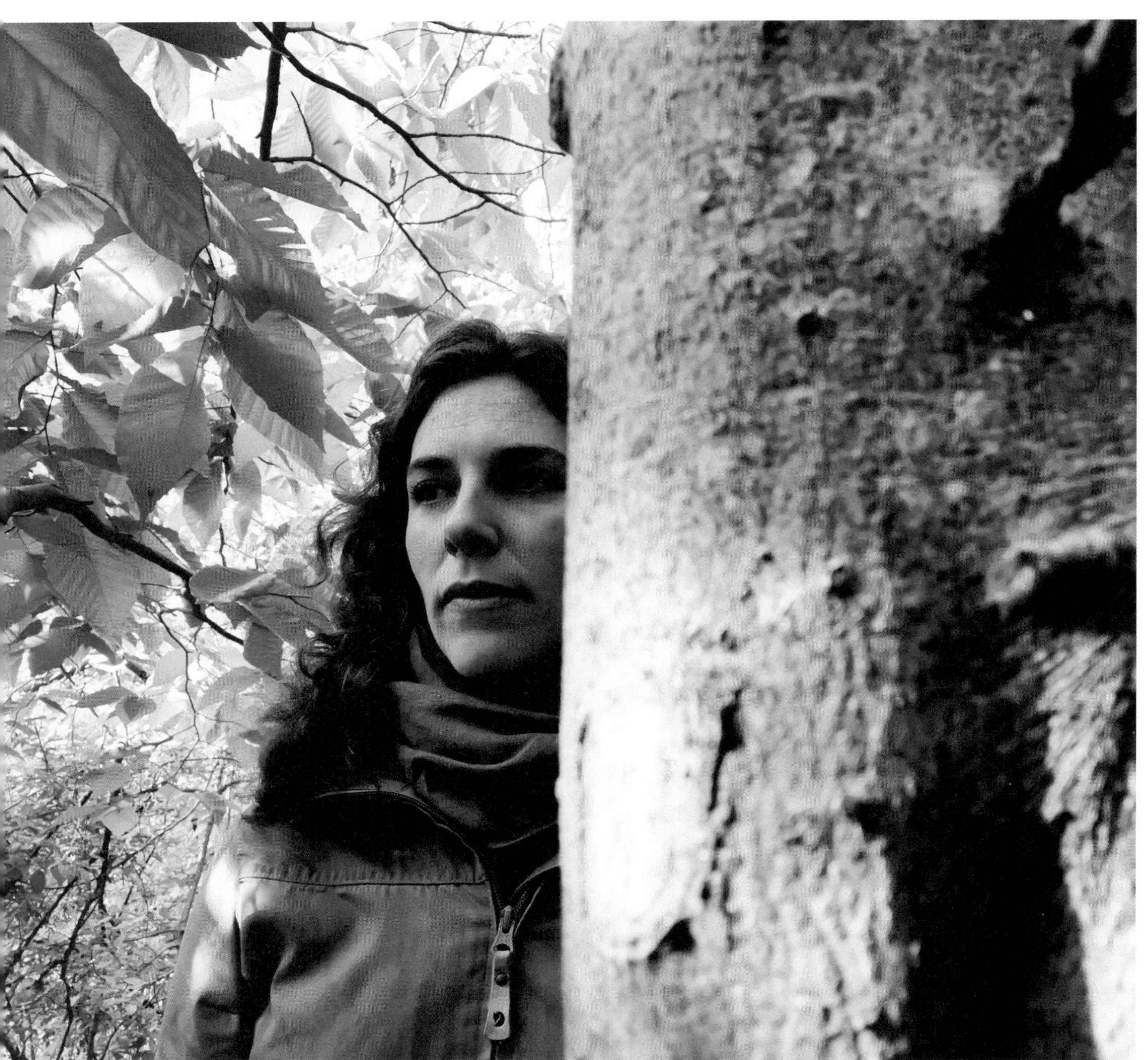

Anna Williams

Artist

"I hope that my art helps, in some small way, to provide my daughter with a more nuanced and equal place in a changing world."

What is your first memory of art?

My first memory of art is as a maker. I grew up in a very creative family—my mother is a potter, and my father, her biggest champion, is a doctor and lover of all things unexpected and creative. They both take great fascination and joy from beauty, eccentricity, mystery, and passion in all aspects of life and take great care to foster these traits in all their children. My earliest memories of making art are playing in her studio and loving the silky slip of cool clay through my hands, all the things to build from it, and the magic of the transformations with kilns and glazes.

You grew up in Ottawa and live there now with your wife and children. How does this environment inspire you?

Ottawa is the most generous, creative community I have ever been a part of. I have experienced immense support and loyalty from the artists of this region. Ottawa has a large number of extraordinarily high-calibre woman artists, gallerists, arts writers, and curators who continually go above and beyond to encourage, champion, and mentor other female artists. It is, without a doubt, one of the biggest reasons I am still making work.

At what age did you realize that pursuing art would be your professional path?

It was in my mid-twenties after I studied Fine Arts at Mount Allison University. I was invited to have a solo show at the L.A. Pai Gallery—everything launched from there. I never intentionally chose to be an artist professionally—I just kept making and making. One piece led to the next; one opportunity challenged me to look for other opportunities.

The critical skills I needed for life as a professional artist were touched upon in my fine arts program, but the meat of it was generously imparted to me by my arts community. It can be extraordinarily lonely and stressful to navigate all the work of running an art practice that is on top of the actual making of the work. However, it is so integral to the success of your practice, and that knowledge is so varied and so specific that only other artists can help you find your way.

Who, where, and what inspires you?

I am most inspired by the natural world and storytellers who explore that thread that connects women to our animality and the land from where we come. Artists and writers such as Kiki Smith, Mary Anne Barkhouse, Ali Smith, and Robin Wall Kimmerer fuel my investigation of how our relationship to nature, family history, identity, and mythologies of womanhood can intersect to offer alternative definitions of what it means to be female and the importance of re-establishing a partnership with the natural world as a means to reunite with our true selves.

"The relationship between the natural world and the female experience and how that impacts my art is pivotal." Please explain . . .

For the natural world and I, physical and psychological borders define our reality. The borders between feminine and unfeminine, human, and animal, tameness and wildness, savage and civilized—rules about what is natural and what isn't—have governed my life. As a woman, I have struggled and failed to fit traditional definitions of femininity—too male to be female and too female to be male. In my practice, I engage with what is considered appropriate female behaviour as I explore the physicality of making art, the construction and manipulation of female identity, and power relationships in contemporary society.

In my artwork, the historical narrative of the bronze material and the personal stories of female identity being represented come into conflict. Throughout history, bronze has been viewed as a masculine, technically challenging, and highly valued status symbol. As a queer female artist, I feel a unique need to take ownership of this history by using it to tell intimate tales of female vulnerability. In representing aspects of female identity previously used to classify, weaken, and shame women's bodies and psyches to subdue them within a patriarchal society in bronze, I am bringing together what was viewed as other, animal, mystic, and monumentalizing it as valued and immutable.

What is the impact of societal gender and family expectations, both positive and negative, on your creative productivity?

As I move through the chapters of my life, the transition that has been one of the most challenging to navigate has been that of motherhood. Western culture has a very defined construction of the notion of mother and what is considered appropriate maternal behaviour.

My primary artistic goal through my newest work is to broaden the definition of motherhood by breaking down what is considered acceptable maternal behaviour and thus offer narratives to support and nourish women on the margins. I want to encourage a sense of belonging, expand circles of trust, and foster a notion of the collective that offers acceptance and inclusion as the standard instead of integration. With the intention that mothers like myself, who have never felt like they belong, begin to see ourselves reflected in the culture that surrounds us.

What have been some barriers between creative success and financial success as an artist?

There is a pervasive and deeply flawed romantic notion that artists get such satisfaction from making their art pieces that financial reward, let alone fair pay, is not required and, even worse, perceived to cheapen the artwork to discuss or ask for it. Making art is nourishing in many respects, but you still need to buy groceries and pay for childcare! As an

I want to encourage a sense of belonging, expand circles of trust, and foster a notion of the collective that offers acceptance and inclusion as the standard instead of integration. With the intention that mothers like myself, who have never felt like they belong, begin to see ourselves reflected in the culture that surrounds us.

artist, I work at or below minimum wage, often even for free or at a loss—it is a deeply imbalanced power dynamic, where being in a perpetual state of sink or swim has meant that I have felt like I can never say no and am desperately trying to keep everyone happy and interested in my work. My most valuable asset as an artist is a good reputation. As Patti Smith says: "Build a good name. Keep your name clean."

You shared that you have depression.

My practice is the space where I process my pain and nourish the narratives and beauty I need to be able to find hope. We are the stories we tell ourselves, and in my studio, I can begin the process of writing a healing narrative. A creative brain is not a quiet, easy, or calm place, but it is never boring, and one has to learn how to ride the ups and downs of serotonin and cortisol to keep the ship right side right. However, as the years piled on, it has been the isolation, the financial stress, and the endless rejection letters that are part and parcel of running an artistic practice, not the brain chemistry, that have worn the hardest on my mental health.

Being a full-time artist is no longer what works for me, my mental health, my family and, in a rather humorous turn, my art. In a confluence of time, hard work, community, and luck, I have had the extraordinary honour of joining the Dominion Sculpture Team for the Government of Canada.

I feel liberated and supported to live a creative, healthy, happy, and balanced life. My studio is, for the first time in many years, again a place of exploration and creativity free from the negativity and stress of straining to keep a leaden ship afloat.

Why is art important?

It offers me a way to nourish those of us who find ourselves on the margins of what is considered societally acceptable. It provides a venue for me to envision new ways of seeing the world and my place in it. A space to create new narratives and realities to provoke and mediate a dialogue with individuals who don't see the world through my lens.

I hope that my art helps, in some small way, to provide my daughter with a more nuanced and equal place in a changing world.

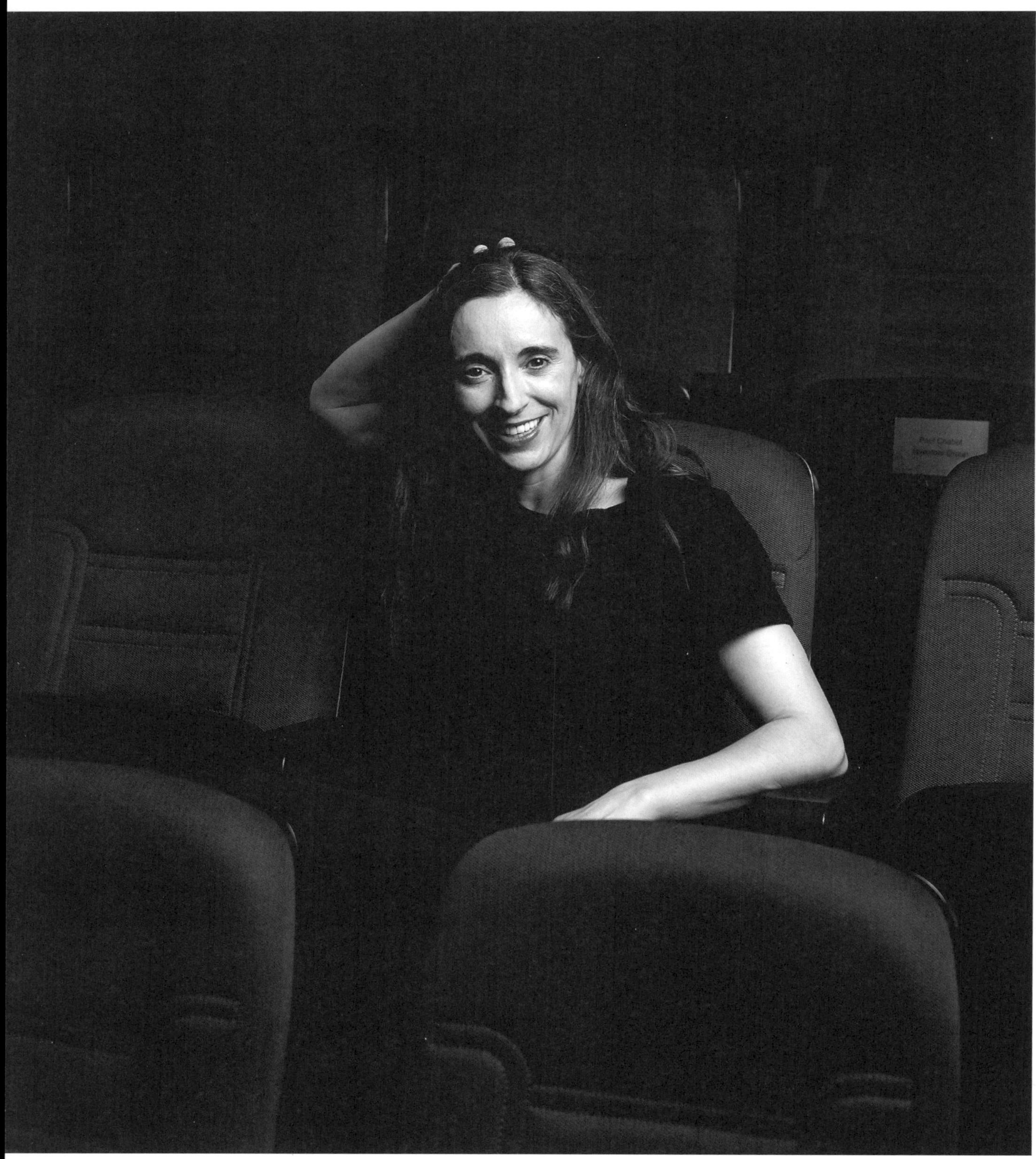

Jolene Bailie

Choreographer and Artistic Director, Winnipeg's Contemporary Dancers

"The funny thing about life is that you often do things you once said you would never do."

What is your first memory of dance?
Watching black and white Fred Astaire movies with my dad.

Your path to dance and choreography specifically was somewhat of a circuitous journey.
The funny thing about life is that you often do things you once said you would never do. I always wanted to be a dancer and part of an ensemble company. I never had a goal to be a choreographer or an artistic director. I just wanted to dance and be a dancer.

For many years, I performed full-length solo shows featuring choreography by others. After years of this, I suddenly felt that my own voice was not even in my own show, even though it was a solo show. It was a weird, awkward, and challenging fight-or-flight moment. I suddenly felt it was absolutely necessary to choreograph my own solo work and perform it in my show. This then grew to choreographing for an ensemble.

You grew up in Winnipeg, a city that, for its size, has an impressive range and access to culture and the arts. How has it shaped you?
The prairie landscape, with views of the sunset and large blankets of snow makes one realize every day how small they are in the world. I love to catch a bit of the sunset every day I can. I've been known to run across the street, even in my pyjamas, to get a better view some nights.

What is unique about being a choreographer and creative person in Winnipeg?
Something unique here is that you may have to provide more for the dancers in addition to the choreographic process, as there are few opportunities here for training at the professional level.

As for being a creative person, Winnipeg and prairie artists have a unique sensibility and humour. The logistics of working in Winnipeg are, perhaps, not for the faint of heart. Isolation, the very harsh winters, and the design of the city are all impactful. Then, there is the reality that there is arguably less funding for dance—all make navigating one's vision and reality a bit of a juggling act.

How does the physicality of dance and the creative energy of being a choreographer connect for you?
My focus shifted to choreography out of necessity. I like to compare choreography to writing. You are trying to summarize your deepest understandings, your deepest hopes, fears, and wishes for the world, in the most succinct and relevant means.

For me, as a choreographer, movement is like air. It allows me to breathe my fullest and deepest breaths, and it is in these deepest breaths that I am most connected to everything.

You've been the Artistic Director of Winnipeg's Contemporary Dancers since February 2019. Tell me more about this experience.

It's been a wild ride! I never envisioned myself as the Artistic Director of Winnipeg's Contemporary Dancers until I applied for the job. I had known the job was vacant, but it wasn't until I read the job posting and realized that I had all the skills and experience listed that I even considered applying.

It's a very full lifestyle. It's very intense, and the work is very hard but also very meaningful. I suspect most people have no idea how relentless the work is, but I know that for the art form and for the artists, this is vital and important work for dance.

You worked as a freelance dancer and choreographer for nineteen years. What are some major differences between being freelance and working with a company?

When you freelance, there is an opportunity to design your season in a very personal way. I had more flexibility as a freelance artist and a lot more time, but I also had fewer responsibilities. There is always a give-and-take, and I think both ways of working are highly valuable.

For me, the timing of freelance work was very critical. I worked freelance through two degrees, my teacher certification, three pregnancies and six and a half years of breastfeeding. The flexibility of freelance work allowed me to pursue a master's degree in another country and continue working in the studio, even with newborns. This would likely not have been possible if I was not working freelance.

Why contemporary? What draws you to this style of dance?

Funny thing, I started training in contemporary dance without really liking it all that much. I had come from a ballet, tap, jazz, and Irish dance background. I came into contemporary dance already working long hours as a dance teacher. I wanted to be in the studio all day and all night, and contemporary dance was a way to do that.

Needless to say, I very quickly grew to love contemporary dance. Don't get me wrong, it was a hard transition, but also an important and life-changing transition.

How has motherhood inspired and challenged you? Did becoming a mom alter the way in which you move and/or choreograph?

I have three kids. Each one is incredibly different from the other, and from me. I never knew I could love so much until I had kids. I also have a partner who I love just as much. For me, being both a caregiver and a partner, I am constantly hanging on and letting go. The act of letting go is really profound as you know you have to do it, and you know you have to do it before it's too late.

What does your life look like outside of the studio?

I don't have any hobbies. I mostly work. When you work in the arts, the work is never done. It can be really hard but also really meaningful.

In the spring, I bought a starter garden kit as part of a fundraiser for my kids' school, so we grew some vegetables and planted a few perennials for the very first time. Some seeds were more successful

For me, as a choreographer, movement is like air. It allows me to breathe my fullest and deepest breaths, and it is in these deepest breaths that I am most connected to everything.

than others. One day, I thought perhaps I had killed some as it had been blistering hot, and they were all limp and so incredibly wilted, but with a bit of water, everything perked up and did just fine. It was wildly reassuring and also profound how dead something could look and then come back to life. It gave me so much hope. I teared up when they all perked up.

Advice for someone looking to pursue a profession in dance?

Go to places where you feel valued. Try to be around people whose faces light up when they see you. Try to connect as well as you can with people, even when it's hard. Try to build reciprocal relationships, as without a *call-and-response*, there can't be meaningful connections. Above and beyond, teachers, schools, choreographers, and peers can be many things at once, including hard-working, talented, and kind. Always be yourself and try to trust yourself that you are enough.

Why are art and dance important? Especially at this particular moment in our history as a society?

Art and dance are so important because they are reflections of our humanity, our feelings, our thoughts, and our time. Reflection is necessary for the evolution of everything. This applies to science, dance, education, and pretty much everything else in the *thinking-feeling* world.

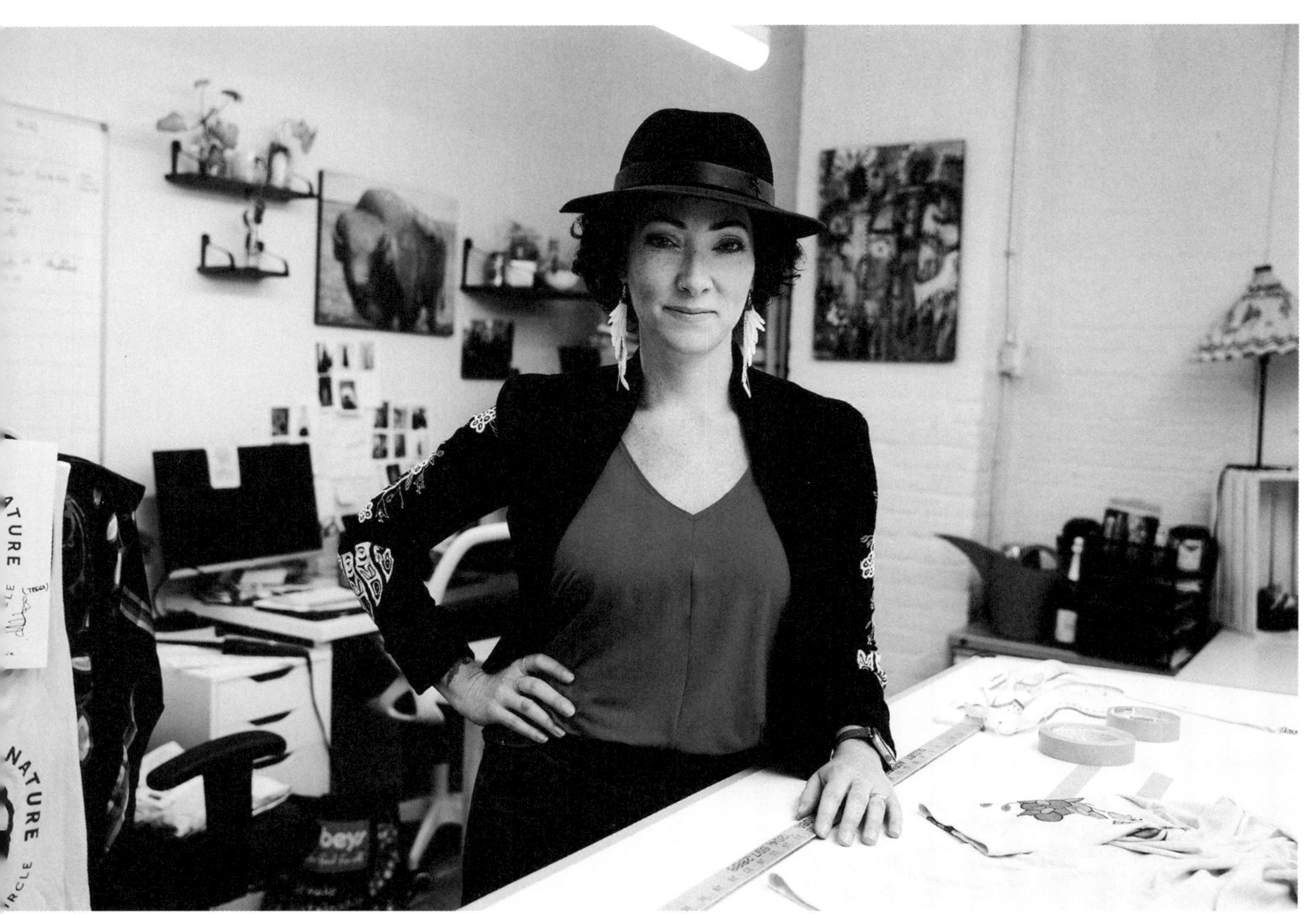
NATURE

Andréanne Mulaire Dandeneau

Founder, CEO, and Fashion Designer, Anne Mulaire

"I started this company with the goal of creating positive change in the fashion industry and the environment."

Can you recall your first favourite piece of clothing? Why was it special?
When I was twelve, my mom took me to a stunning store filled with floral fabric dresses and jackets. I spotted a red dress from Laura Ashley that caught my eye. Though it seemed impossible to purchase due to its high price, I fell in love with the classic style and luxurious fabric. This experience taught me the value of investing in quality pieces.

At what age and stage of life did you realize that fashion would be the focus of your future?
I've always been passionate about both finding better fabrics and creating designs, but I'm not entirely certain which one came first. At the age of sixteen, I began making costumes for my dance concerts due to a lack of affordability and poor fabric quality. My teammates soon began requesting costumes as well, leading to the expansion of my clothing repertoire. While my grandma had taught me the basics of sewing, I wanted to delve deeper into pattern making, fabric knowledge, and advanced sewing techniques.

After graduating, I enrolled in the Human Ecology Textile Science course at the University of Manitoba, which provided me with a comprehensive understanding of textile manufacturing. However, I craved even more knowledge, particularly about the garment-making process. That's when I decided to enrol in the Fashion Design Program at LaSalle College in Montréal, where I gained invaluable knowledge about the other side of the fashion industry.

You grew up and continue to live in the vibrant prairie city of Winnipeg. How does this place shape you as a designer?
Winnipeg has a challenging work season due to the cold climate. People tend to work hard during this time, which keeps them resilient and alert. For me, spending time with family and nature is what shapes my design style.

Your label is committed to a strong set of core values. Was this always your intention when building the brand?
Growing up, I was taught to be mindful of my impact on the environment and to live sustainably. This value has become a part of my identity and guides my actions. I vividly recall my fourth year of studying fashion design when we were tasked with creating a couture dress for our final exam. While my classmates went to the fabric store, I set out to find sustainable materials for my dress. After searching far and wide, I eventually found natural hemp silk, hemp jacquard, and hemp knit to create

my masterpiece. Initially, my teachers were skeptical that a naturally sourced dress would make an impact on the runway, but I was determined to prove them wrong. After completing the dress, I received overwhelming praise from my instructors, who were amazed that every aspect was made entirely from hemp. This experience solidified my passion for sustainable fashion and desire to make a meaningful impact in the fashion industry.

What have been the benefits and challenges in building the brand?

One of the hurdles I've faced is finding enough resources for fabric supplies to support a sustainable brand. To ensure ethical production, I purchase all fair trade and organic materials, valuing eco-fabric and quality. Despite the higher prices, my customers appreciate the fashionable and comfortable clothing that is locally made with ethical practices. Competing with larger fast fashion brands is a continuous challenge I have faced since the start of my company.

Another challenge has been staying authentic to my heritage and Indigenous roots. It has not always been easy to share my story and gain customer acceptance, but I believe that a brand with an authentic identity can create change.

I am grateful to have built a supportive community and have had my family beside me every step of the way.

Anne Mulaire has an extensive online shop and a brick-and-mortar boutique in Winnipeg. All the clothing is made in Canada. Tell me more about the physical space and the vibe of the boutique.

Initially, the boutique served as a display area for clothing items. However, as more customers started frequenting it, I gradually transformed it into a proper boutique. I absolutely adore this space! Our customers not only come here to shop but also avail of our alteration services to ensure that their clothing fits them perfectly. This approach aligns with the slow fashion movement, where customers invest in good quality clothing that is tailored to their bodies. It's a well-known fact that when we find clothing that fits us well, we wear it longer and feel proud to wear it. The boutique also has an interesting feature—it's connected to our manufacturing unit. We provide our customers with a tour of the manufacturing facility, where they can witness how their clothes are made.

Tell me more about the Heritage Prints.

Back in 2005, when I founded my company, my mom asked me how I wanted to present myself in the fashion industry and what my story would be. Without hesitation, I replied, "Just me." Later, I discussed this with my dad, and together, we created prints that reflected our Indigenous roots. We continued collaborating with fellow Indigenous artists to develop designs for various collections, each design telling our unique story of Indigenous history. I strongly believe that fashion and education go hand in hand. As Métis people, we have always lived in harmony with nature. After much reflection, I came to the realization that I aspire to be a designer who remains grounded in my roots.

As the brand has evolved, so have you as a visionary leader. What does this look like for you in terms of personal growth?

My personal growth as a visionary leader within my sustainable brand has been characterized by an expanded awareness, ongoing education, collaboration, adaptability, and a commitment to cultivating a positive impact on the world. By embracing this growth mindset, I continue to evolve and drive positive change in sustainability while inspiring others to do the same.

Who, where, and what inspires you?

I find inspiration in leaders who champion sustainability, natural landscapes, and historic architecture. Emotions also fuel my creativity, particularly those that stem from memorable experiences. For me, travel is a powerful source of inspiration, as it broadens my perspective and exposes me to new ideas beyond my usual surroundings.

What do you enjoy doing outside of work?

I have a great passion for travelling as it allows me to witness a beautiful blend of colours and experience life in a unique way. Additionally, I am a huge fan of tea and drink it regularly as it has a grounding effect on me.

The future of fashion? What can we change, and how can we strive to be less wasteful?

A helpful suggestion is to wear our clothing more often instead of constantly buying new ones. It would be wise to invest in higher-quality items and consider the company's values before purchasing.

As a society, we must shift towards a circular economy, where we consider the entire lifecycle of a product. The future of fashion relies on finding ways to maintain the longevity of our clothing.

Cheap garments often come at a cost, so it's essential to keep the concept of circularity in mind. As a society, we must shift towards a circular economy, where we consider the entire lifecycle of a product. The future of fashion relies on finding ways to maintain the longevity of our clothing.

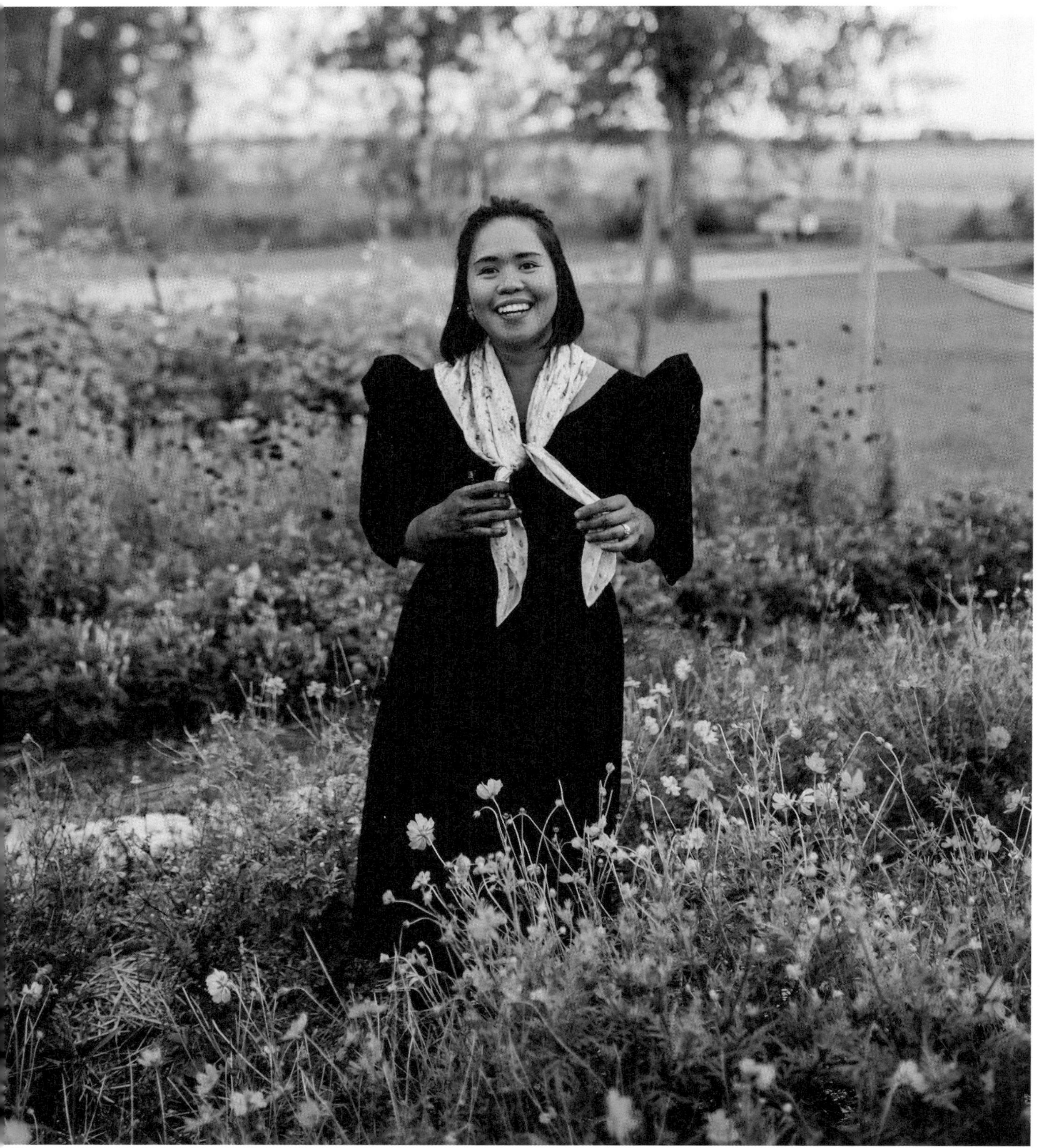

Lourdes Still

Founder, Masagana Flower Farm & Studio

"Looking back, moving to the countryside felt like a new beginning similar to moving to a new country. Tending to the gardens at my new home was symbolic of taking roots, metaphorically and literally speaking."

What is your first memory of flowers?

Sampaguita with ylang-ylang garlands. Sampaguita, or jasmine, is the national flower of the Philippines, and a whiff of this scent takes me back to the time I spent with my Lola Lilia (maternal grandmother) and the end of the school year.

I grew up in a religious Catholic family, and we adorned the saint figurines with fresh flowers every week. It was a weekly ritual followed by lighting the candles and praying the rosary.

Sampaguita necklaces or corsages are also very common floral accessories during end of school year ceremonies and I remember wearing them every year.

The Philippines is a beautiful place and a warm, welcoming culture that I called home for two years. How did the cultural surroundings inspire you?

It made growing flowers seasonally in Canada that much more special!

My cultural upbringing informs how I host friends, family, and my guests at Masagana Flower Farm. There's always food when I invite people over and, in a way, it's how I keep my culture alive. I don't observe Catholicism anymore, but I carry with me spiritual practices that still make sense for me. My spiritual foundations help me recognize that I have a role in environmental stewardship.

What brought you to Canada? First impression of your new country?

I immigrated to Canada in May 2009 through the Manitoba Provincial Nominee Program. I landed in Vancouver first, and I called my parents to tell them about my first impressions. The scent in the air reminded me of the balikbayan boxes we received from relatives in the US. The smell of everything, especially the clothes in that box when we opened it, is the same as what I experienced in Vancouver: fresh, new, and sweet. It also felt like I was in the refrigerator. It was cold!

What is unique about your immigration story? Is there one experience that left a lasting impression?

My main motivation to immigrate to Canada was the same as most immigrants: to help my family out financially. I can't pinpoint anything unique about it, but the whole process of my application felt like a chance at a new beginning, and like anything was possible. Owning a business was definitely not in the plans, but it's also not a completely foreign concept to me. My papa owned and operated a machine shop as a home-based business, and I have my relatives who still run convenience stores. I think that experience left an indelible impression, and it's one of those things that keeps me going.

How did the idea come about for starting Masagana Flower Farm & Studio?

It was a series of events that led to the start of Masagana Flower Farm, but meeting someone who eventually became my husband was a significant factor. Moving to the countryside sparked the idea of starting a flower farm business. My husband already had the property before we met and leaving the city was an easy choice for me. I warmed up to the idea of a slower pace of life.

Masagana Flower Farm & Studio started as a seasonal venture, and my wedding floral designs were a mix of imported and Manitoba-grown flowers in the summer. My conviction to only use low carbon footprint florals grew, and I eventually stopped taking in off-season wedding clients. My first business model was not feasible in the short growing season of the prairies, but an eco-printing workshop in the winter of 2019 at a nearby fibre farm was a lightbulb moment. Diversifying my offering to include natural dyeing activities using farm-grown dye flowers was promising. The rest, as they say, is history.

Looking back, moving to the countryside felt like a new beginning, similar to moving to a new country. Tending to the gardens at my new home was symbolic of taking roots, metaphorically and literally speaking. I finally feel at home at my second home.

Masagana is a beautiful Tagalog word that holds a lot of meaning.

The word *masagana* holds so much promise that there is abundance around me if I look for it. It was in the winter of 2018 that I decided was going to use that word in registering a business name. It is a reminder to myself that everything I need is within my reach. I didn't have a clear vision for the business yet then, but it felt good to aspire to put nature first. It took a lot of trusting that business/clientele who share the same values will follow, eventually.

Working and tending a farm is a year-round commitment. Something you learned about yourself in the process of bringing this vision to life?

It became apparent that I had a lot to learn on how to live by the seasons when I started farming. The plants are teaching me that there's a time for growth and slowing down, and both are equally important. Farming requires your whole being, and you use all your senses. You give a lot of yourself to the land and others during the growing season. To sustain this new way of living, I need to take my cue from nature itself. Otherwise, I'll burn out.

This creative endeavour is a result of that desire to work with nature rather than against it.

"Nature has taught me about patience and letting go of control." Tell me more about this and how it applies to your work at Masagana.

My biggest hope in doing my work at Masagana Flower Farm is to inspire others to reimagine their own greenspaces. I want to believe that by visiting, my guests see the joy I get from what I do. I can only make their time at the farm as memorable as I can, and I let go of any expectations of how their experience will affect their lives.

> Making art is worth pursuing. It is essential for our survival. I hope the next generation in my family will not only want to have their basic needs met but, more than that, have the opportunity to live a life inspired by art.

You also mentioned how pursuing your passion has brought you great joy. How so?

I used to be the type of person who fills up her calendar with social activities. I had to have weekend plans all the time. I took on a lot of different hobbies and volunteered my free time every so often. All of the things I filled my time with made me happy, but not necessarily joyful. One of the things that drew me to Kevin was his easy-going demeanour. He found contentment in quiet weekends reading a book. I mean, I did too, but it was more like a reward after a busy work week that I had to earn the right to slow down.

Joy, I learned, is not found in outside influences. Joy is independent of circumstances; it's an internal feeling.

"My hope is that my life's work will influence my family's next generation."

Making art is worth pursuing. It is essential for our survival. I hope the next generation in my family will not only want to have their basic needs met but, more than that, have the opportunity to live a life inspired by art.

What does success look like for you?

For me, short-term success looks like finishing the construction of my studio and opening to the public in Spring of 2023. Long-term success for me is becoming the type of business owner who puts nature first and who is able to adapt to the changing climate. Also, being able to keep inspiring others to find that joy in their lives. If it's through flowers, great.

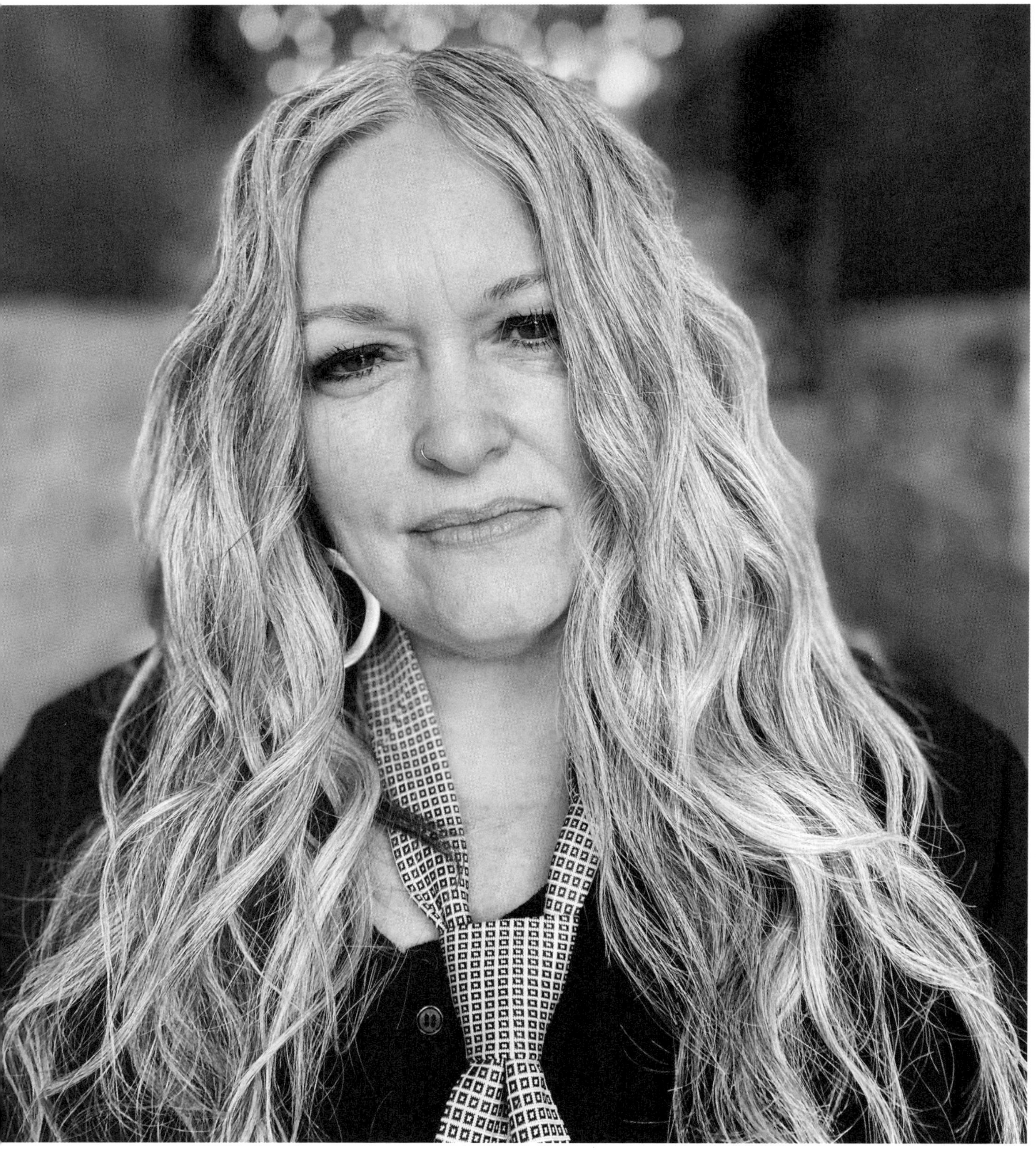

Signy Thorsteinson

Photographer

"People are fascinating. I've always been a people watcher, so capturing people in normal day-to-day life is an extension of this."

What is an early memory of a photo that moved you?

My dad had a subscription to *National Geographic*. While growing up, I was always fascinated by the photographs in this magazine. I was seventeen years old in 1985 when the photo "Afghan Girl" was featured on the front cover. It was such a striking and memorable image. I also have early memories of going through boxes and albums of old black and white photographs my grandparents had—some so small and tattered. Others were so crisp and clear.

You call Winnipeg home. A small but strong city in terms of creative and entrepreneurial spirit. Would you agree?

I was born and raised in Winnipeg with strong ties to the Interlake. I absolutely agree with Winnipeg being strong in creative, entrepreneurial, and cultural spirit. We're such a diverse multicultural city and exposed to so many different experiences. I definitely support local more than I ever have before. I'll champion Winnipeg always.

How does the physicality of Winnipeg shape and inspire you?

I love the different seasons. The constant change of the landscapes makes for a good variety of photography. The weather can make for natural effects, so I try to take advantage of that. The -30-degree temperatures make for a thinner production of street shots, but make me very appreciative of better weather. I'm a hearty Winnipegger. The art and festival scene here can be overwhelming at times. We have First Fridays in the Exchange District; there's so much happening that you have to pick and choose.

Fringe Fest, Folklorama, Jazz Fest, Community Festivals, Folk Fest, Nuit Balance—the list goes on and on. Events like these are the best for street photography. I was once told the best shots are after a parade—and it's so true!

When did the idea come about to document your city?

Photography is not my full-time gig. I work in the insurance industry, which doesn't have a lot of room for creativity. Photography is my outlet.

A colleague told me about Instagram. I was late to that game, but it opened a whole new world for me. Instagram connected me with local and worldwide photographers. It made me want to learn, take better photographs, and find my niche.

Have you done any formal photography training? Do you feel it's essential?

I have no formal training. I shoot and edit with my iPhone and iPhone settings only. I could probably benefit from some training. I don't use a camera with different lenses. What I capture is how it is. I don't think it's essential to always put out my *best* work. In all forms of art, right? My photography is about being in the moment and instant gratification. I enjoy studying the works of other photographers. A benefit, or perhaps not a benefit, is that I don't know what I'm technically doing wrong. There are also some wonderful groups of online women photographers: femLENS, Women Street Photographers, and @mystreet.photo, all of which I draw inspiration from.

How would you describe the photos you take?

I've always been a people watcher, so capturing people in normal day-to-day life is an extension of this. There is usually something that captures my eye—the posture, hair, clothing, or what they might be carrying, pushing or pulling.

There are a few neighborhoods I tend to take photos in more. Osborne Village, where I live, is an easy one. As well, the Exchange District, Downtown, and West Broadway/Wolseley. I like the candid moments of everyday life—this is where we see unrefined beauty.

What have you learned about yourself, photography, and people?

I can do something, learn, *and* improve. I've gained confidence. I've also learned there are people interested in the same images I am and enjoy my work. The community of people I have met has opened doors for me to show my work.

I discovered my passion later in life, which doesn't bother me. I'm grateful to have found something that fills me up.

I've never had someone ask me not to take or post a photo—I always ask first. I've learned that people are mostly good—and always interesting.

"Photography has added to my life." Please explain.

Photography has changed the way I experience life—I'm always looking for an interesting capture. It's more than just a creative outlet for me. It allows me to make a connection with people.

I'm always looking for an interesting capture. It's more than just a creative outlet for me. It allows me to make a connection with people.

You're currently involved in a wonderful philanthropic project, the Front Steps Project, documenting people and places on your iPhone. You're also collecting supplies and funds for Resource Assistance for Youth (RaY), a non-profit street-level agency working with street-entrenched and homeless youth up to 29. What has this experience been like?

At the beginning of the pandemic, when we were all isolating in 2020, I read about the Front Steps Project that had been initiated by a group of women in Boston. They were photographing families on their front steps from a safe distance to document the crazy times we're living in, in exchange for food or monetary donations to their local food bank. I immediately thought of my block and dropped flyers in mailboxes. The response was wonderful; neighbours posted their photos on social media, and I became very busy. I photographed sixty families from all over the city and collected generous donations for Manitoba Harvest. In 2021, I collected personal hygiene products for RaY; I felt lucky to be able to document these families. Some families had brand new babies or were pregnant. Many people dressed up and accessorized their pets with cocktails in hand.

It was so much fun. The connection was, I believe, what we were all craving, not knowing what the future held.

You shoot only in black and white. What is unique about presenting people and places in this way?

I only shoot black and white because that's what I like best. To me, black and white makes the subject the focus of the image, while colour can be a distraction. I like the mood of a black-and-white photograph. Black and white is nostalgic and timeless. I like that the time and place might not be obvious.

A photo experience that left a lasting impression?

The one that stays with me is when Chantal Kreviazuk and I met through Instagram during COVID-19. I'm a big fan of her music and humanitarian work. I was posting about her Park Theatre show I had attended. She asked if I was related to someone she knew. We started an ongoing conversation. She would share my photos on Instagram, which thrilled me; we arranged to spend a day together when she was in Winnipeg performing at Manitoba's 150th Anniversary. I took photographs, and she posted them. Chantal, sharing my photos on Instagram is how you found me.

Do you foresee pursuing this passion full-time?

Even though it's not how I make my living, I still feel I pursue my passion full-time because there's an opportunity to take photographs everywhere, any time of day or night.

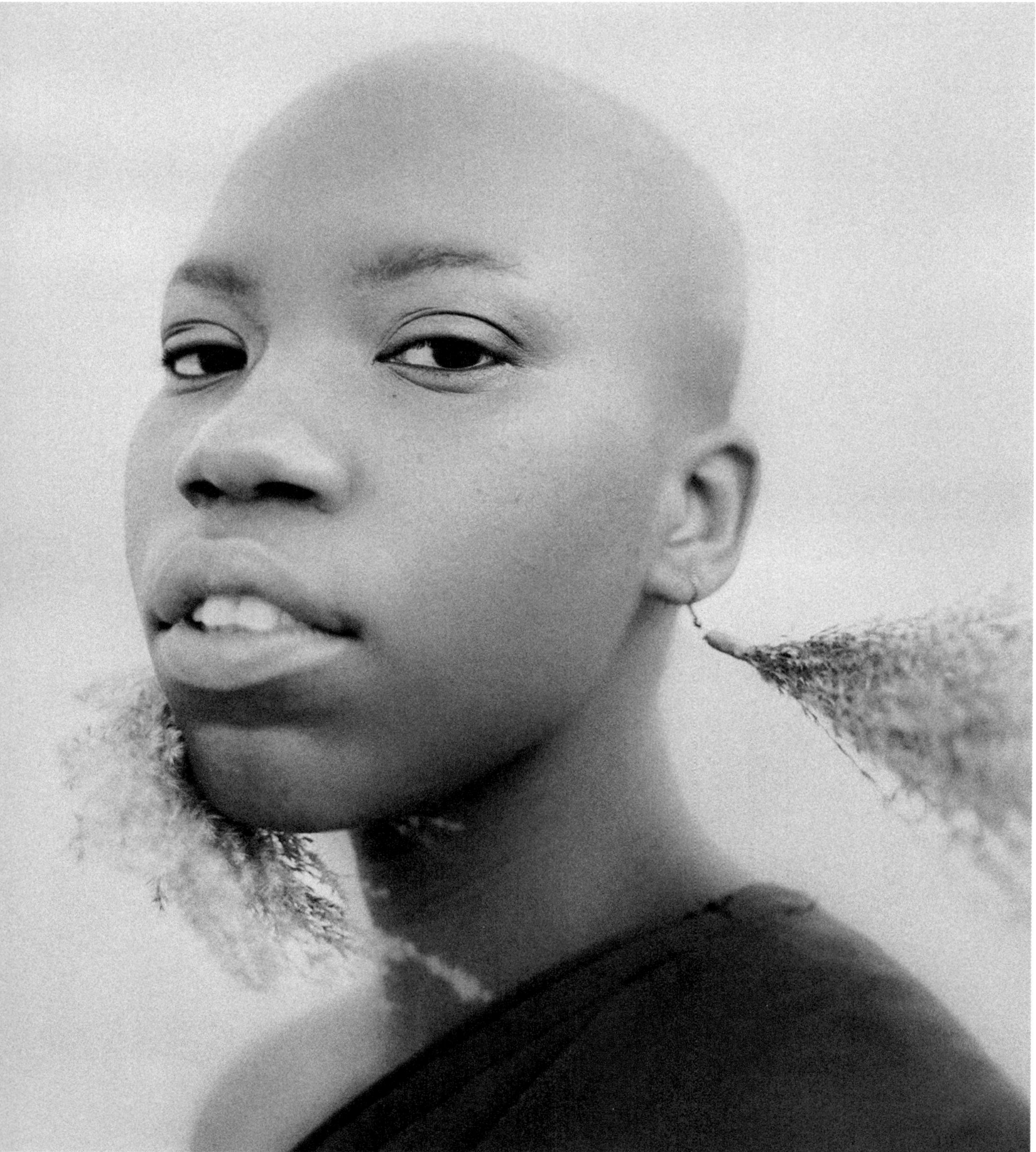

Peace Akintade

African-Canadian Interdisciplinary Poet, Public Speaker, Actor, and Model

"I am blessed to come from a culture that embraces oral traditions such as storytelling, poetry, and hymns. I am blessed to have a family that allows me to yell, and dance, and truly be in the moment around artistry."

What is your first memory of words?

It began with a shout. I was sitting cross-legged on the streets of Ogun State. The masquerade ball was in full gear. Storytellers in bright fabrics of purple, red, and blue stood on podiums. They screamed their philosophies to the growing crowd. Men on ten-foot-tall stilts swung their sticks into the air, trying to catch the flustered bystanders. Prayer warriors dressed in white touched the foreheads of children, whispering blessings and prophecies. At four years old, sitting on the streets of Ogun State, I felt sorrow, happiness, and simplicity. The storyteller weaved my imagination like a skilled seamstress. I wanted to be the seamstress' apprentice. In closing, the storyteller motioned to the audience and asked, "Who would like to stand and preach?" I raised my hand confidently! I really wanted to preach, to inspire emotions like the storyteller. My mom tried to stop me, but with a huge voice, I yelled, "PDP POWER!" A roar of laughter flew through the group! My young self didn't realize I yelled the name of our government. It was the only set of words I knew confidently! That moment set a domino effect that turned me into a storyteller and poet. I am blessed to come from a culture that embraces oral traditions such as storytelling, poetry, and hymns. I am blessed to have a family that allows me to yell, dance, and truly be in the moment around artistry.

You arrived in Saskatoon on April 13, 2012.

I unknowingly assumed that Canada was the name of a campsite. I thought we were staying at the campsite for two weeks, then moving to a warmer environment. After eleven years in Saskatoon, I can confidently say that Saskatoon is home.

My first impression of Canada is the lack of communal appreciation. In Nigeria, we truly believe that it takes a village to raise a child. It took until 2016 before I felt a community connection with Saskatoon. There was a form of emptiness that radiated around the Western environments. I can't greet my neighbours; I have to make schedule arrangements to visit my friends. In Nigeria, if I sat on the streets for fifteen minutes, I would be bombarded with relatives, strangers, or friends. Individualism, in a way, removes the need for others.

Canada and Western culture have removed the concept of *third space* in their geography. Your *first space* is your home; your *second space* is your productivity, aka your school or workplace; but your *third space* is your pure existence. In Nigeria, we have streets, farmlands, and we even have the sky. The land is your *third space*. Kids were encouraged to discover the wilderness and cities in Nigeria. In Saskatoon, I had to find my own wilderness.

Your Nigerian heritage plays a pivotal role in your creative path.

Embracing my Nigerian heritage is an act of resistance. I wear my heritage as a shield and as a two-sided sword. It took gruelling years of ridicule, racism, colourism, and misguided microaggressions before I felt unbridled pride in my culture. As a child, I hated showcasing my African clothes or traditions. I spoke in a British accent; I adopted mannerisms from my white counterparts and refused to talk to any Nigerian kids. It was internalized racism brought on by bullying, coercion, and gifted child syndrome.

My life changed after I started getting serious about poetry. For the first time, I was praised for my mannerisms, speech patterns, and words. I cannot continue artistry without saying thanks to my ancestors, without saying thanks to my mother, my siblings, my aunties, my uncles, and my cousins. To deny and forget my heritage is to deny and forget my blood, my soul, and my air.

"When I first came to Canada, there was an unspoken rule that my identity must be scrubbed." Please share more about what this powerful statement means for you.

In "The Journey of a Villager," I wrote a series of poetry depicting my hairstyles while coming to Canada. I talked about my experiences with bullying during middle school. My classmates would pull my braids in the playground, laugh at my short hair, and in one instant, chased me with scissors to see if it was my real hair. Canada was the first place I ever felt like the *other* or the *minority*. I am in the process of unlearning. By essentially conforming to the bullying and racism, I was allowing hatred to be my story. I refuse to be an angry Black woman; I want to be a Black girl first. I want to learn to love my hair and smile in the face of travesty. My art speaks about Black joy specifically because of these stories. My identity makes me who I am, and I am who I say I am.

To deny and forget my heritage is to deny and forget my blood, my soul, and my air.

"As a Black woman and refugee in Saskatoon, I have had my race and age called out in the community. It can be very hard to practice authentically when you feel like you don't belong."

The act of exclusion will always be present as long as systemic racism still prevails. I am a triple threat in spaces. Being Black, a woman, and an artist will always put me at a disadvantage in multiple spaces. As long as I can remember, artistry always came with negotiations. I was always trying to negotiate my place in a space. Instead of embracing myself, I would make myself smaller and invisible. For the space to feel comfortable in my presence, I removed my authenticity and truth. How can you be authentic when you are consistently lowering yourself?

Currently, I move with the authority of someone who is deciding to make my own table. I no longer feel the need to beg for a seat at the table. I am fashioning my own!

The theme of community and "how one creates a community" is pivotal to your work and process.

From a young age, I was deprived from having a stable and safe community. I missed being in a community, and even more in a collective. Instead of wallowing in self-pity, I decided to use my artistry to understand community.

I am currently in the middle of my artist-in-residence program with Remai Modern Gallery. For my residency, I decided to create a collective of artists, poets, storytellers, and other forms of artistry that didn't have immediate access to poetry. My main focus was to curate a space where people felt comfortable and vulnerable enough to become a community. For four months, I would facilitate the fifteen members through the Remai Modern Gallery and have them interact in the space through a series of poetry exercises. They created amazing soundscapes, and art pieces with each other on their own agency. Each person knew that they had a place in this space. They knew that the community wouldn't be the same without them. That realization opened their vulnerability tenfold.

Please tell me more about the work you do at Write Out Loud.

I am currently a co-organizer for Write Out Loud as a program coordinator. It feels like a complete circle to take the mantle after performing at open mics and slams with Write Out Loud since I was fourteen. My first *aha* moment was with Write Out Loud, and now I get to curate the space to let other youth poets have their *aha* moment. Write Out Loud is a spoken word youth poetry collective on Treaty 6 territory in Saskatoon. We have been operating since 2009. We are an organization led by youth for youth. Write Out Loud seeks to expand the influence of spoken word in Saskatoon to make it an even more insightful and receptive city.

"An award for one is an award for all." Why is this important?

My mother always reminded me of two things: One, to remember the daughter of who I am; and two, that I am standing on the shoulders of giants. Both touch on themes of humbleness and gratitude. I wouldn't be who I am without the support around me. Part of my artistry is knowing my responsibility in the world of poetry. I am paving the way for poetry to become less elitist, fewer classists, more multicultural, and more intercultural. Yes, I am standing on the shoulders of giants, but I have to prepare myself to become one of the giants.

Why is sharing our stories—the real, unfiltered, and unpolished version—important?

As an artist, I am constantly aware of being perceived. I am aware that others base their emotions on my words. I have a responsibility to take care of my audience, but also remind them of the humanity behind my words. I cannot be a true artist if my words are not real, unfiltered, and unpolished. A manufactured artist is an unchanging artist.

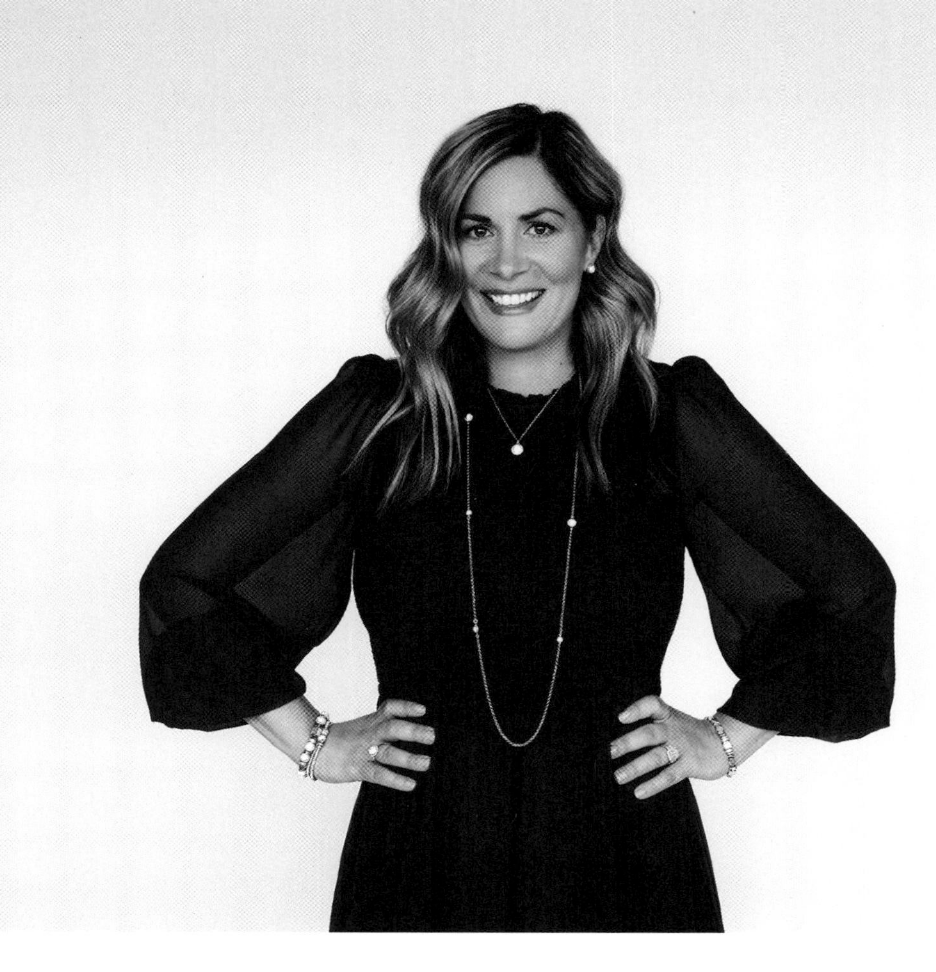

Rachel Mielke

Jewellery Designer, CEO, and Founder, Hillberg & Berk

"I have never really seen myself as a designer but rather as a curator, admirer, and catalyst for a new view on jewellery."

What is your first memory of jewellery?

My first memory of jewellery was admiring the bold and fashionable jewellery collections that my aunties had. They were fashion icons to me when I was little, and their style had a big impact on me. I remember looking through their jewellery drawers and feeling transported by the colours and designs. I loved to see how they styled their beautiful outfits together with jewellery. The looks they put together were always bold, classy, and chic. They were my very first style inspirations.

"I didn't have a lot of special or 'nice' jewellery growing up ... at twenty-three I decided to make special happen for me ..."

I grew up modestly. Jewellery was a luxury that our family couldn't afford, but as I became a teenager my fascination for fashion, accessorizing, and the transformative nature of jewellery began to intrigue and inspire me to begin exploring different mediums of jewellery making and design. When I discovered that I could actually learn to make beautiful pieces of jewellery in my early twenties, I was drawn into the world of jewellery design, and I have never looked back. I remain as inspired and in love with the world of jewellery design today as I was when I was a child.

When did you realize that designing jewellery would be your professional path?

I have never really seen myself as a designer but rather as a curator, admirer, and catalyst for a new view on jewellery. When I entered the jewellery industry, I knew absolutely nothing about it and had no background or education in it. I carved a path that broke many rules in creating H&B from a design perspective. I think that unique view on the product we created is what our customers really gravitated towards. Our product was unique and interesting, and you couldn't find anything like it on the market. I never set out to be a jewellery designer. I happened to fall in love with the product and process and just followed that passion.

You were a contestant on Dragons' Den. It was a "pitch-turned-deal" experience. What did you take away from this experience?

I had been growing my business over the years leading up to my Dragons' Den pitch in the spring of 2008. I had decided in 2007 that I was going to leave my job to focus on growing my business full time, and I did that in January of 2008. I had also rebranded my company to Hillberg & Berk in 2007, so there had been a year of concerted growth leading up to Dragons' Den, but the business was still very much in the start-up phase at that point. What I thought I would take away from the experience was learning about pitching for venture capital and exposure for my brand, and what I really gained—besides getting an investment—was a business partner who has been one of my biggest champions. He has reinforced a value that success in life is measured by the quality of relationships with those that matter most, and not my business accomplishments.

What were some of the challenges of building a your business?

Building a business from the ground up poses continual challenges that must be overcome to continue to grow and thrive. Some of the biggest challenges of the start-up phase are navigating product market fit and being flexible enough to get to a place where you have a commercially viable product. That takes a lot of trial and error and patience. This phase was pretty stressful as cash flow was inconsistent, our team was very small, and I was required to wear many hats, but in many ways, this was also one of the most exciting times in the company journey.

Who, where, and what inspires you and your designs?

I am inspired by travel, art, people in my life, colour, and nature, and I love finding ways to bring the things that inspire me into the design and brand experience work we do at H&B. However, I'm most driven by the inspiration our customers and staff offer. There is a never-ending idea pool within these two groups, and I love listening and being able to uncover amazing new ideas from the people who matter most to our brand. Some of our biggest successes in product innovation and design have come from ideas customers have given to us.

"In everything we do, the reason is women." Why is this important?

My dream is that our customers, interaction with our brand will enhance their lives. This matters to me personally because I want to live in a world where brands care about their people, customers, and the impact they leave and their messages, actions, and products align to that. We are seeing a huge shift towards more transparency and accountability then when I started almost two decades ago, but there is still a long way to go.

> I want to live in a world where brands care about their people, customer, and the impact they leave and through their messages, actions and products aligning to that.

The Hillberg & Berk *Know Her* blog is similar to what we're doing here with the *BLOOM* books. What inspired this?

I believe it's important to honour the reason we exist and showcase stories that inform and inspire. Our blog is an opportunity for us to feature the amazing stories of women in our community, women who we use as models, and incredible women who have inspired us. Bringing the *Know Her* blog to life was the fulfilment of a dream to use our brand as a catalyst for helping connect women to their power.

We share a history with cervical cancer. What was your health journey and how did it impact you?

I began noticing that I was not feeling well in 2019, so I went to see my doctor for a variety of tests. I didn't know I had not had a pap in over three years as I thought it was routine to get one after you give birth, but we discovered that I had not had one after the birth of my son. When my doctor performed a pap, it came back abnormal. This led to meeting with a specialist, a colposcopy, and eventually a cervical cancer diagnosis. This was a shocking diagnosis, as I thought I had been following protocol on getting regular pap tests, had never had an abnormal test, and had the HPV vaccination in my twenties. I found the diagnosis earth shattering, and as a result, I took a step back from my role at H&B during my treatment to focus on my mental well-being and recovery. Although I wish my family and I didn't have to endure the pain and trauma of that experience, going through that set us on a path to a different life post-cancer that I am deeply grateful for. Facing cancer quickly made the priorities in my life abundantly clear and was a catalyst for many changes in my life. I am clearer about my values and how I want to spend my time. Professionally, I believe the experience has made me a more focused leader with softer edges.

What have you learned about business, jewellery, and yourself?

I have learned that there is no playbook to running a business, and you can never let yourself get comfortable because the rules are constantly changing, and only those willing to challenge themselves to keep up with the rapid pace of change in business will prevail.

Every day, I learn more about myself through this journey, but perhaps the biggest lesson has been learning to surround myself with brilliant people, really lean on and let them lead, and continue to work towards making myself less needed every day.

You share that the purpose of H&B is "a deepening passion for the do-good side of the business." What does this look like?

Over our sixteen-year history, we've dedicated over 20 percent of our annual profits to supporting women, generating over 10 million dollars in financial and product support. In 2022, we were able to contribute $250,000 for our national partners: Dress for Success Canada Foundation, the Native Women's Association of Canada, and the Canadian Centre for Gender and Sexual Diversity among others.

Nationally, we work to ensure the organizations that are changing the landscape of women's rights have the funding to continue their vital work. We've seen first-hand how the Employment Suiting Program at Dress for Success empowers women, which is why we give a gift of jewellery to everyone who completes it.

Jewellery marks memorable life experiences. How do you, as a designer, ensure that each piece you create instills a sense of connection and timelessness in the wearer?

I think jewellery is symbolic to us in many ways, as it often represents the most important times in our lives or how we want to express ourselves. It is really important to me that our product is produced in a high-quality manner with expert craftsmanship and precious materials to ensure longevity and beauty. I also believe our focus on listening to our customers and providing back to them the products they are asking for has helped establish designs that resonate with our customers. The most important voice of inspiration to me is her, our customer, and I feel deeply honoured every day to have the opportunity to create beautiful jewellery that so many customers continue to choose over and over.

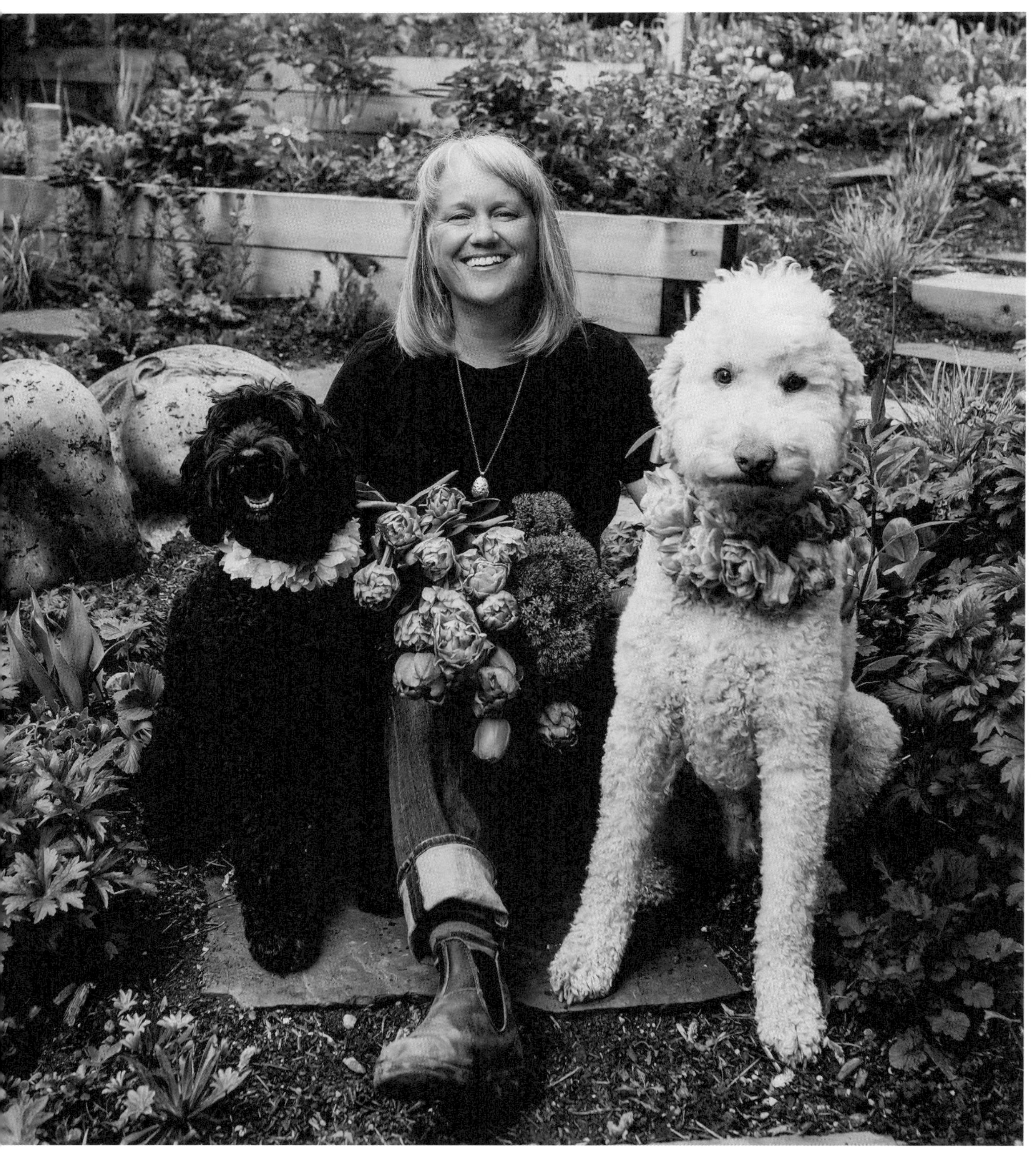

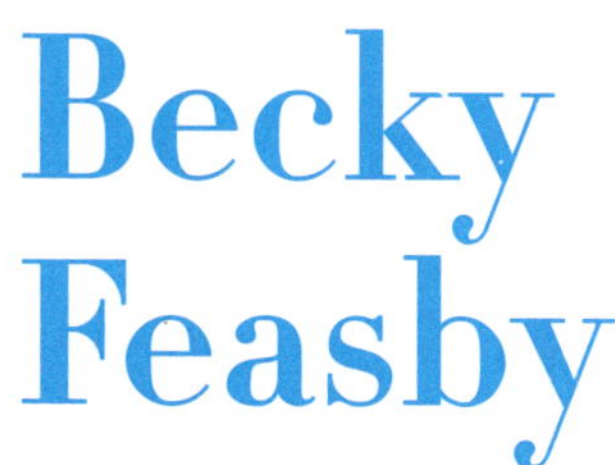

Becky Feasby

Gardener, Florist, and Founder, Prairie Girl Flowers

"My main reason for starting PGF was to develop a business model that stood in stark contrast with the conventional way of doing flowers."

What is your first memory of flowers?

Cutting hyacinths and tulips with my mom for my kindergarten teacher. We cut a nice little bouquet, wrapped the stems in a wet paper towel, and then covered them with plastic wrap and an elastic. All of it was perfect, except for the plastic wrap. But back then, we didn't give it a second thought!

How did the idea for Prairie Girl Flowers come about? Was it a planned endeavour or more of a spontaneous coming-to-be?

Prairie Girl Flowers was both spontaneous and years in the making. My main reason for starting PGF was to develop a business model that stood in stark contrast with the conventional way of doing flowers. Relying solely on locally grown, seasonally relevant flowers, never purchasing or using plastics in my work, and advocating for socially and environmentally responsible practices were the cornerstones of PGF. They continue to be the guiding principles that inform all my work and advocacy work.

You worked at the Alberta Children's Hospital as a Horticultural Therapist prior to starting the business. What was this like?

Working in a hierarchical organization taught me the importance of creating adaptive networks in my work and instilled in me the significance of listening deeply. Being part of a care team looking after the psychosocial needs of patients, families, and staff taught me the importance that "nature" can play in facilitating healing. More than that, though, my work across a variety of patient populations at the hospital helped me understand how important it is to limit our exposure to unnecessary chemicals. When I first started working at the hospital, a local florist approached me about donating several cases of floral foam to the program. The MSDS for floral foam was clear: it contained toxic formaldehyde and carbon black. At the time, that was enough for me to know I couldn't have that product anywhere near sick kids!

What were some of the surprising challenges and benefits of starting PGF?

We are fortunate enough to own one-third acre in inner-city Calgary, where we live. I am so lucky to have a nice piece of land to grow flowers! I use all of these in my wedding and event work. Growing flowers for profit has taught me many things. Most of all, it has taught me the real value of flowers and how the flowers we see today sold at big box stores and grocery chains have lost all sense of worth. If a rose only costs $2 per stem, that means that someone has not been paid along the way, or has been paid so little that they are living in poverty.

"Sustainability is the focus of our work." Tell me more about this and why it's pivotal to your process?

Sustainability is the focus of every decision I make. Whether it's considering the environmental implications or the negative social consequences of a product I use, the sustainability of what I do matters. The floral industry has notoriously flown under the radar of environmentalists for decades. I often think that flowers can somehow hide behind the *pretty,* and consumers can dismiss any negative environmental and social consequences out of hand. Yet the global floral industry faces many of the same issues common in other agricultural products: extensive use of pesticides and herbicides, unjust working conditions, monopolistic governance, and huge amounts of plastic waste.

Sustainability is the focus of every decision I make. Whether it's considering the environmental implications or the negative social consequences of a product I use, the sustainability of what I do matters.

You're the Canadian ambassador for the new Sustainable Floristry Network. What does this role entail?

The Sustainable Floristry Network is a global educational platform aimed at aligning floristry with the UN's Sustainable Development Goals and creating a more environmentally and socially sustainable industry. My work as an ambassador involves communicating with the SFN's founder, Rita Feldman, as well as advocating for better practices here on the ground in Canada.

You're currently working towards a master's degree in Sustainability at Harvard University. What motivated you to pursue this?

As my work as an advocate increased, I realized that I had significant gaps in my education. I needed to learn more about life cycle analyses, the economic principles of sustainability, and the science behind metrics such as carbon output, greenhouse gas emissions, and regenerative agriculture. The program at Harvard ticked all the boxes: academic integrity, an extensive list of great courses, and a short residency requirement. It also gave me the option of completing a thesis, which I was keen to do again—having completed my first master's thesis in Physical Anthropology back in 1997. My hope was to be able to educate myself in order to educate others and increase my effectiveness as an advocate.

Tell me more about the Slow Flowers Movement. Where do you envision yourself and the movement five years from now?

Much like the Slow Food movement, Slow Flowers is focused on creating balance in the world of flowers. Slow Flowers recognizes that there is a disconnect between humans and the growing of flowers—largely as a result of globalization and increased commodification of flowers as an agricultural product.

"We are dedicated to the seasonal flower movement and love collaborating with farmers, growers, and creatives in our community." Why is this important?

The year-round global distribution of greenhouse-grown flowers has obscured our understanding of seasonality. Tulips at Christmas in the Northern

Hemisphere? No problem. And a couple getting married in January can easily have peonies at their wedding—they need to bring them in from New Zealand. Consumers have lost all sense of the seasons and what should be possible. The environmental and social costs associated with our demands matter, though. How workers growing these flowers in the Global South are treated matters. The amount of fossil fuels burned to heat and cool the greenhouses matters. Collaborating with local farmers and growers creates not only community connections, but also ensures that our flowers are seasonally relevant and connected to place.

What is something we may not know about the traditional flower industry? Are we seeing progress in moving towards a more sustainable mindset?

The traditional cut flower industry is an artificial construction of what society has told us we want: roses, gerbera daisies, alstroemeria, lilies, hypericum, and carnations. Most of these are resource-intensive crops that have a long vase life. Longevity, predictability of colour, ability to hold up well in floral foam, and stem length have been the guiding factors determining floral production globally.

The movement toward a more sustainable mindset in the floral industry has been slow. But we are gradually starting to see progress. Academics and researchers are beginning to take an interest in floriculture and uncovering patterns related to the ongoing unsustainability of the industry. Movements such as Slow Flowers have drawn significant attention to some issues. More than that, though, Slow Flowers has given legitimacy to domestic flower growers in North America and has created a new demand for specialty cut flower species, many of which are climate resilient.

I like to think that the world and people generally pay attention to what makes us smile, like the beauty of flowers. Have you seen a rise in sales since the pandemic?

Flowers make us feel connected to the natural world. They feel special because they are special. They are an outward expression of nature's genius and generosity.

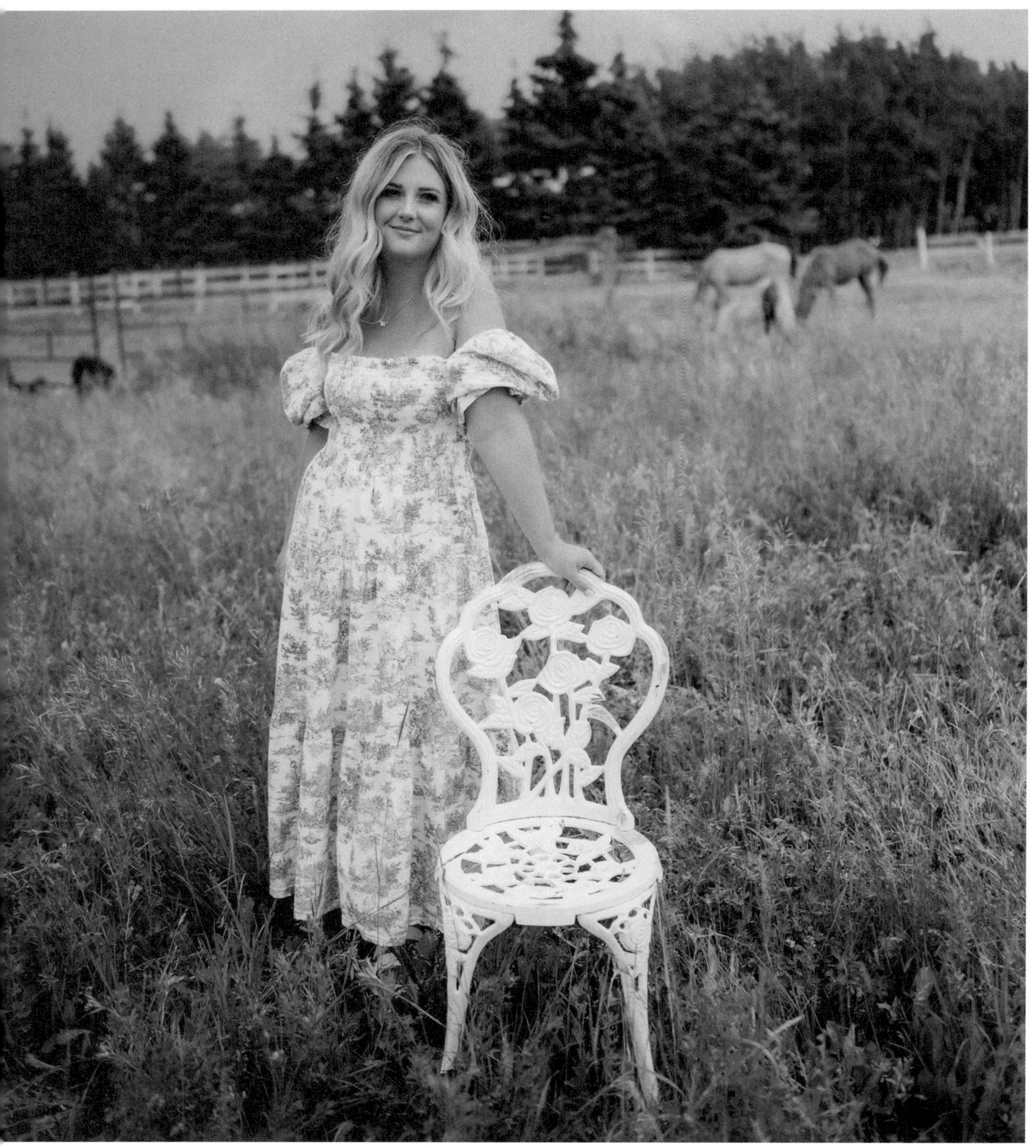

Lindsay Kelloway

Founder and Designer,
Haiku Lane Jewelry

"Jewellery is meant to keep your stories close and the people you love even closer."

What is your first memory of jewellery?

My earliest memory is of my grandmother and her jewellery. Her pieces were timeless and elegant. My grandmother was always dressed as if she was about to go out for fine dining at the country club, even when we were just out shopping for the day. I'd watch her put on her diamond rings, jewelled brooches, and elegant earrings that she stored away in some secret spot, and I was in awe. As she put each piece on, she would tell me their stories, the special people who had gifted her the pieces, and the unique places she had travelled to where the jewellery was purchased. No piece was any less special than the last, regardless of their worth. The piece that always stood out the most was an opal ring gifted to her by a friend travelling in Australia. I thought, "Oh how I would love to have that one day." I knew from here on that jewellery was meant to keep your stories close and the people you love even closer.

Before Haiku Lane, you were a childhood educator.

I didn't dream of being a teacher. This career almost felt chosen for me. I was finishing high school and needed to choose a path. I had never seen this for myself, but I thought I could envision myself in education. I started to volunteer in schools, Girl Guides, and children's festivals. I loved these experiences and started to believe that this was the perfect career for me, as well.

Once I finished university, getting a permanent position was a challenge. There were so many graduates that year, but not enough jobs in the field. Or maybe I was just being too picky. All in all, I wasn't overly disappointed when I didn't find a permanent job. A voice in my head kept saying, "You can teach for a few years, then do something you actually want to do. Maybe you can open a store."

I eventually found a childcare position working in schools. I came to love this new role and eventually became a supervisor.

I spent a few years working in childcare while working on Haiku Lane on weekends. Haiku Lane was starting to become a part-time gig, and I loved every minute of it! It wasn't until I had my first child that I saw how Haiku Lane could become a full-time business. It was not only something I enjoyed doing but could help take care of my family. While on maternity leave, I decided that I did not want to go back to my job and instead see where Haiku Lane could take me. The only way to know for sure was to try.

I love owning my own business. That isn't to say that being your own boss doesn't come with its unique set of challenges. For me, financial planning and setting boundaries are areas I need to work on. Not knowing 100 percent what your income will be in any given month requires smart planning. Designing jewelry and being in charge of this company is something that I enjoy so much that sometimes I don't know how to separate my personal life and work life. It's important to set those boundaries for myself and something I constantly need to be mindful about.

It was on this trip to Maui, completely immersed in new surroundings, scents, culture and people, that I took in the air and felt that this is where my soul is meant to be. Maui is that place for me.

What is the story behind the brand name?

My original *why* started as a creative outlet after a trip to Maui in 2011. My grandparents have a place there, and it always felt like my home-away-from-home. It was on this trip to Maui, completely immersed in new surroundings, scents, culture, and people, that I took in the air and felt that this was where my soul was meant to be. Maui is that place for me.

Haiku Lane was inspired by this magical island. The name Haiku comes from my love of Haiku Mill, an old sugar mill in Maui that dates back to 1860. I loved that they melded modern elements, nature, and vintage aspects into something unique and beautiful.

This venue truly spoke to me. It was romantic. It was a fairy tale. An escape. I was inspired by the artisans that live there and use natural pieces like seashells and gemstones to create unique and beautiful things.

Every year, we have gone to this island. Every year is a new adventure, holds new memories, and new discoveries.

I started visiting as a child. This has evolved to me now visiting with my own family. My grandma has since passed away, so this special place only holds a deeper meaning.

Do you have any formal training in metalsmithing or design?

I have taken metalsmithing classes but have not taken any courses in design. I do think that some formal training and knowledge is important so that I understand the technicalities of jewellery. Once I understand the technical processes, key elements, and steps, then passion, inherent talent, and hands-on experience are vital. Having a story is key. The most beautiful designs are inspired by something important.

Please walk us through your creative process.

When I first envision an idea, sometimes I will create a mood board to gather ideas for a whole collection, and other times I will quickly sketch my idea on a pad of paper. I am very traditional with my design approach and use a sketchpad and pencil. If the sketch excites me and all the inspiration comes flooding back, then I know it is meant to be part of my collection.

Who, where, and what inspires you and your designs?

Now that I have two daughters, I am always thinking about heirloom pieces that I would love to pass along to them. I have designed several pieces with them in mind, including lockets and botanical pieces symbolizing each girl.

Since Haiku Lane came to be on visits to Maui, I will forever have pieces with nods to this island.

Each piece brings me back to my favourite places and reminds me of the special moments with my family.

I have several flower designs that remind me of afternoons picking flowers as a girl, learning to garden with my grandma, and flowers I have received on special occasions.

Where can people find Haiku Lane?

Haiku Lane is primarily online. We have stockists in Canada, the USA, and even in Switzerland! You can find us online, at local boutique markets, and gift shops.

Which jewelry designers do you admire?

Maui Mari in Maui and Olivia Burton.

Why is it important for you to model pursuing a path that fuels and fulfills you?

I want my daughters to be passionate about their careers. If it isn't something they would be doing if they had won the lottery, it might not be the best career path for them. I want them to live a life guided by love and fulfilment. I love that they are surrounded by women doing things that they are passionate about. My mom, mother-in-law, sister, and sister-in-law, as well as the many female entrepreneurs I have befriended, have become role models. Their paths have shown my two daughters that it is possible for them to be anything they desire.

How do you wish for people to feel when wearing Haiku Lane?

I want them to feel deeply connected to their stories, the people they love most, the environment that brings them joy, and the moments they cherish.

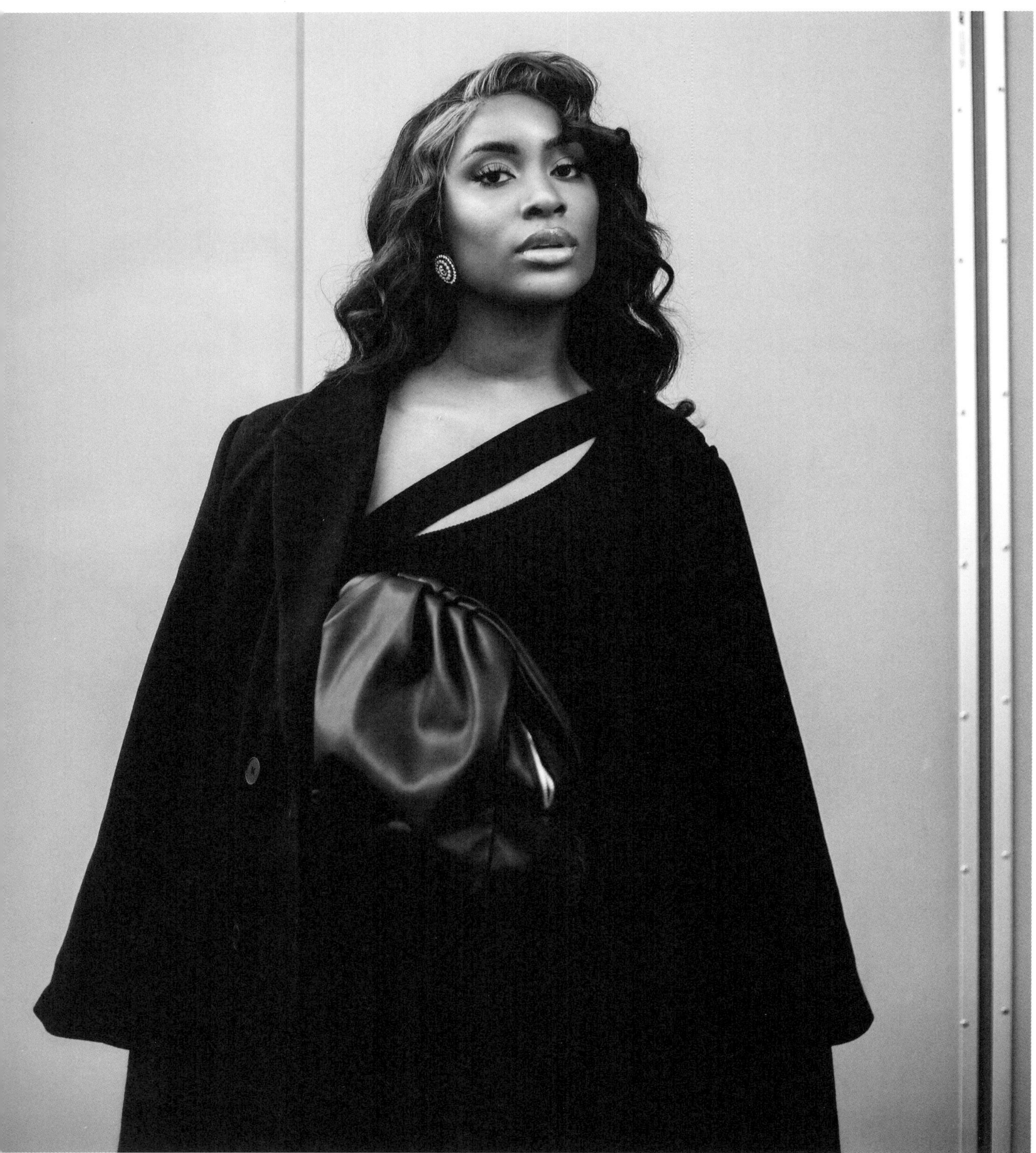

Chinenye Mary Otakpor

Style Blogger and Vocational Rehabilitation Specialist

"I have experienced depressive episodes and the one thing that helped set a positive tone when actively trying to practise self-care was how I chose to physically present myself. A good outfit doesn't solve all bad days, but it's a start. Sometimes, getting dressed is the key to regaining that sense of regularity and purpose for the day."

What is your first memory of fashion?

It's of my older sisters and watching their style evolve when we moved to Canada. I would *borrow* their clothes when they weren't aware and re-style them in my own way. I have three sisters with amazing style, but my sister Nonye was the one I most aligned with style-wise.

How long have you been working as a vocational rehabilitation specialist?

I've been working as a rehabilitation specialist for three years now, but have worked within the mental health sector for seven-plus years. The hardest part of my job is the secondary trauma and compassion fatigue I experience.

Secondary trauma and compassion fatigue are constants within my field of work; however, attending therapy has made a significant difference in how I handle both. I've found a balance and developed several coping mechanisms that allow me to do my job and also take care of myself mentally and physically.

The benefit of this job is how it has helped me grow specific social skills, empathy, and understanding of others, which has greatly improved my platonic and romantic relationships. I am always trying to understand people without judgment, which I see as a great gift.

You shared with me that you started your style blog, *Queen's Playground*, as a healthy creative outlet.

When I first started working in the field of mental health, I felt a lot of sadness and experienced burnout. I knew I didn't hate my job, but I couldn't pinpoint why I constantly felt drained. Before beginning therapy, I knew that I needed an outlet to cope. That was when I discovered Instagram, specifically fashion, on that platform. I loved how people posted outfits *for fun*. Seeing as I had an interest in fashion at the time, I figured why not try myself, and the rest is history.

How do you go about deciding which outfit to wear and post?

The outfits I choose usually depend on my mood and the weather, but mostly on my mood. Some days, I feel a little edgy and other days, I go for simple and classy. Over the years, my style has become a bit edgier and out of my comfort zone, which I love.

Sometimes, I am a little hard on myself and don't post all the outfits I shoot, simply because I become overly critical of myself. If an outfit doesn't fit the aesthetic of my usual style, I will still sometimes post, and surprisingly, some of these looks receive the best feedback.

Who, where, and what inspires your looks?

It's funny because living in Calgary, every time I am out, I have a lot of people asking me if I am from Toronto because of how I dress, which makes me wonder how people in Toronto dress.

I am heavily inspired by Rihanna, Tracee Ellis Ross, and Zendaya. For non-celebrities, I find inspiration in style influencers like Juliette Foxx and Melissa Holdbrook-Akposoe.

One thing all these people have in common is their bold and chic style, which resonates with me. The one person from the list that truly inspires my personal style is Rihanna. We are not in the same tax bracket, but I gravitate towards recreating her style.

What has been the response to your looks and platform?

I am happily surprised that the response has always been good. You can never predict how the online world will react to what you present, so I am grateful that the response has been positive because it has helped push me out of my comfort zone and motivated me to continue creating.

I have experienced depressive episodes, and the one thing that helped set a positive tone when actively trying to practise self-care was how I chose to physically present myself. A good outfit doesn't solve all bad days, but it's a start. Sometimes, getting dressed is the key to regaining that sense of regularity and purpose for the day.

The hair. What inspires a tress transformation?

I love that the hair is noticeable as well. Like with my outfits, I also have different hair for different moods. My real hair is black and short, so experimenting with wigs allows me to try out new styles and colours without damaging my hair. I believe hair can bring together an entire look. Some looks I've shot were perfect, but the hairstyle ruined the entire outfit. I have learned to ensure that the hairstyle I present with each outfit adds to the look instead of taking away from it. I am also very into colour. I love experimenting with colour, and that also translates into my hair. Nothing too crazy, but always bold enough to make a statement.

What are some challenges and benefits since you started posting on *Queen's Playground*? Who takes the photos?

The most surprising benefit is the boost to my self-esteem. I have always been a confident person, but I have found the appreciation that others have for my work has helped boost my self-esteem and encouraged me to step outside my comfort zone.

The main challenge is being my own worst critic. I criticize myself and constantly compare my work to others, but I have to center myself and remind myself of how much I have achieved so far.

> If the goal is to grow your passion and build a platform, consistency and quality will allow your audience and future partners to feel a connection with you and your platform.

I do not take my pictures. I wish I did; it would have saved me a lot of money. It's about quality over quantity. I prefer working with local photographers in the city to get the quality I want.

Dream brand collaboration?

Fenty or NA-KD. I have always wanted to design my own line or collaborate with a company and release a curated collection selected and designed by me. I am putting that into the universe so it can actually come true.

You do a lot of wonderful promotions for travel within your home province.

I never get tired of going to Banff or Canmore. We are truly blessed to have such a beautiful place so easily accessible. Whenever I am feeling burnt out and need a break but can't fully afford a vacation, a quick getaway to Banff or Canmore really does the trick. There are so many activities to explore, from a romantic getaway, hiking, or going to the hot springs to skiing and snowboarding. There's always something to do.

Creative outlets are important. What advice can you offer someone looking for a similar sense of connection to something different from their nine-to-five?

Consistency is key. I had to learn the hard way, and to be honest, balancing a nine-to-five and my platform can be exhausting, but once you find that balance and plan out whatever creative content you have ahead of time, you stay consistent. If the goal is to grow your passion and build a platform, consistency and quality will allow your audience and future partners to feel a connection with you and your platform. I still struggle to find that balance. Don't be hard on yourself if you can't achieve it all right away. It takes time.

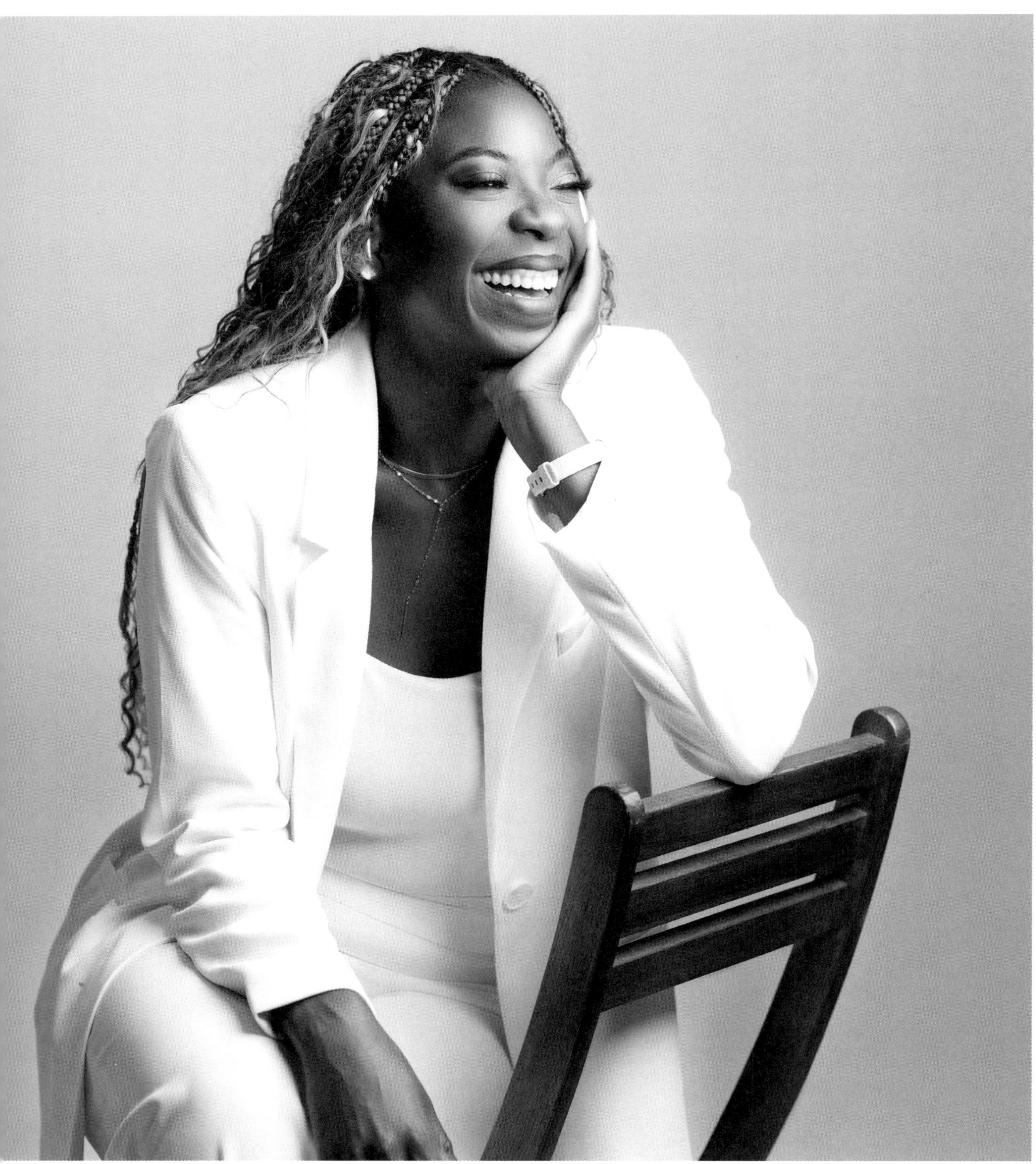

Priscille Bukasa

Writer, Poet, Spoken Word Artist, and Teaching Artist

"The beauty in all this is I never imagined I would ever call myself an artist or be an artist. It wasn't my first choice; I wouldn't even call myself creative, but here I am doing it every day and I wouldn't trade it in for anything."

What is your first memory of poetry?

I was in eighth grade. My English teacher assigned us to write a haiku for class the following day. I went home and attempted to write a haiku, to no avail. The restrictions for haiku stifled my creativity, and I couldn't write. So, I decided to write my own short poem with no constraints. I told my teacher I couldn't write the haiku but that I composed a short poem instead that I would like to read out to the class. It was titled "Identity." After reading it, the class cheered. Everyone loved it. This was the first poem I ever wrote. It was a very positive experience.

How do you feel your early years influenced you as a person?

I was born in Congo in 1991, and shortly after, my family moved to Johannesburg, South Africa, where we lived from 1991 to 1999. This was at the height of apartheid. I remember as a child always being scared in Johannesburg. Something was always happening; our apartment got broken into three times while we were sleeping. As a kid, I could feel the tension of the country and the people feeling restless from the political climate of the nation. I remember staring up at the sky and wanting to move elsewhere because of the fear I experienced with things I had seen or heard. Now, as an adult, I look back at our time in South Africa and think about the sacrifice my parents made to leave their home country and move to a new one with five children, where we didn't have a lot of family, all to provide us with a better life.

You arrived in Canada in April 1999, specifically in Calgary. What were your first impressions of your new country? How do you and your family celebrate your culture and heritage?

Canada was cold. I saw snow for the first time in Winnipeg as we stepped off the greyhound bus that was Calgary-bound. We made snowballs like in the movies we'd seen on TV; we were excited to be here. After twenty-four years of living in Canada, I have still not acclimated to Alberta winters.

Adjusting to the cultural change was something I was not prepared for. Growing up in South Africa, everyone looked like me, and my skin colour was not something I ever thought about. Being the only Black person in class was a strange reality; having to explain cultural things, a new normal. I experienced racism for the first time, which was difficult because I didn't understand why someone could hate you because of your skin colour.

As a family, we celebrate our culture by observing Congo Independence Day. My siblings and I have made the effort to learn our native languages, listen to Congolese music, and stay connected to what's happening at home. We eat traditional Congolese dishes and have learned how to make these recipes from our mother.

Were you creative as a child?

I didn't feel I was very creative because I mostly played sports; I couldn't sing, and I struggled to colour in the lines. Three of my older siblings were musicians, which was my exposure to the arts. As a child, my idea of artists or art was that one needed to sing or play an instrument, as those were the only art forms I knew. I did excel in drama class, and I loved theatre.

Prior to becoming a full-time artist, you worked in marketing. What motivated you to expand your professional path?

The goal wasn't to leave marketing; I love marketing and I still want to work in sports marketing specifically. However, I felt that I was neglecting my craft and not taking my art seriously because of the mindset I had regarding artists.

In 2020, my intention was to give art my full attention; if not, I would never know where it would take me. My mind was everywhere those first few months of the COVID-19 pandemic; the last thing on my mind was writing poetry.

Fast-forward to 2021, when I connected and started collaborating with artists from different disciplines. This opened doors and led to a grant-funded project, which allowed me to get paid as an artist while continuing to work part-time in marketing.

I now have more time to focus on my writing as I work on my own schedule. I'm happy with my present path.

You wear many creative hats. Is the work and the creative process similar for each or do they differ?

The creative process is similar for all the creative hats I wear. They all require me to get into a creative space and allow myself to create without any limitations or fear of making mistakes. Working as a social media coordinator or writing a new poem is all about thinking outside the box and being authentic without any restrictions. Once I have something on paper, I can start fine-tuning it and adjusting to ensure that the poem or the content fits the audience or brand. I often research what I'll be writing about and allow myself to make mistakes and start again. I like to listen to music or other spoken word artists, which inspires me.

The creative process is similar for all the creative hats I wear. They all require me to get into a creative space and allow myself to create without any limitations or fear of making mistakes.

Can you remember your first spoken word performance?

I was nineteen years old, fresh out of high school and in university. A friend I went to church with also ran the African and Caribbean Student Association at the University of Calgary. For Black History Month, he asked me to be part of the artist performing showcase, and I said, *of course*! The performance was in the food court hall; it was busy with a ton of students there to watch or pass through. I don't remember what piece I performed, but I remember it went well! People came up to me and told me how much they enjoyed the performance and my presence. That was the first time I really thought, "Wow, this could be something."

Who, what, and where inspires you?

When an experience inspires me, I feel it. I will then often express the emotions it stirred in me through writing. An example is when, in 2016, Laquan McDonald, a sixteen-year-old boy in Chicago, was shot sixteen times by law enforcement. I remember crying and being strongly affected by this story. I sat with this pain, and whatever emotions I was feeling for those two months became a piece titled "16 Shots."

Creativity can be inspired by both the good and challenging layers in our life. You mentioned a traumatic loss in 2015. How did this experience shape you?

I remember, in my late teens and early twenties, thinking to myself how hard it was to write about love because I had not yet been in a serious relationship. In 2015, I experienced my first heartbreak.

I laughed at my young self for wanting to go through some form of traumatic love experience, which I believed would give me the rite of passage to write about love. The heartbreak was hard, and it shut me down and kept me away from getting close to people. I turned to writing as my outlet during this painful time. I was writing and performing more around the city and at various events. I made a name for myself as a spoken word artist. I believe this challenging time to be the catalyst that pushed me to share my experience through words.

A poet who consistently wows you with their work?

Consistently at the top of my list is Titilope Sonuga, a globally renowned poet from Edmonton, Alberta. She was the first poet I ever saw live. We share a similar journey of immigrating to Canada and being of African descent. She writes about womanhood and her faith. Her storytelling is a journey I can relate to. Her ability to articulate her thoughts eloquently is what draws me to her.

We talked about the rollercoaster ride of being an artist. What advice can you offer others looking to pursue a creative path?

My advice to people looking to pursue a creative path is to just do it, because it's in your heart, and something is pulling you towards this path; give it your best and see it through. Although you will encounter challenges and may feel uncomfortable at times, you will feel joy, and that is the most important thing because you are living a life that brings you fulfilment.

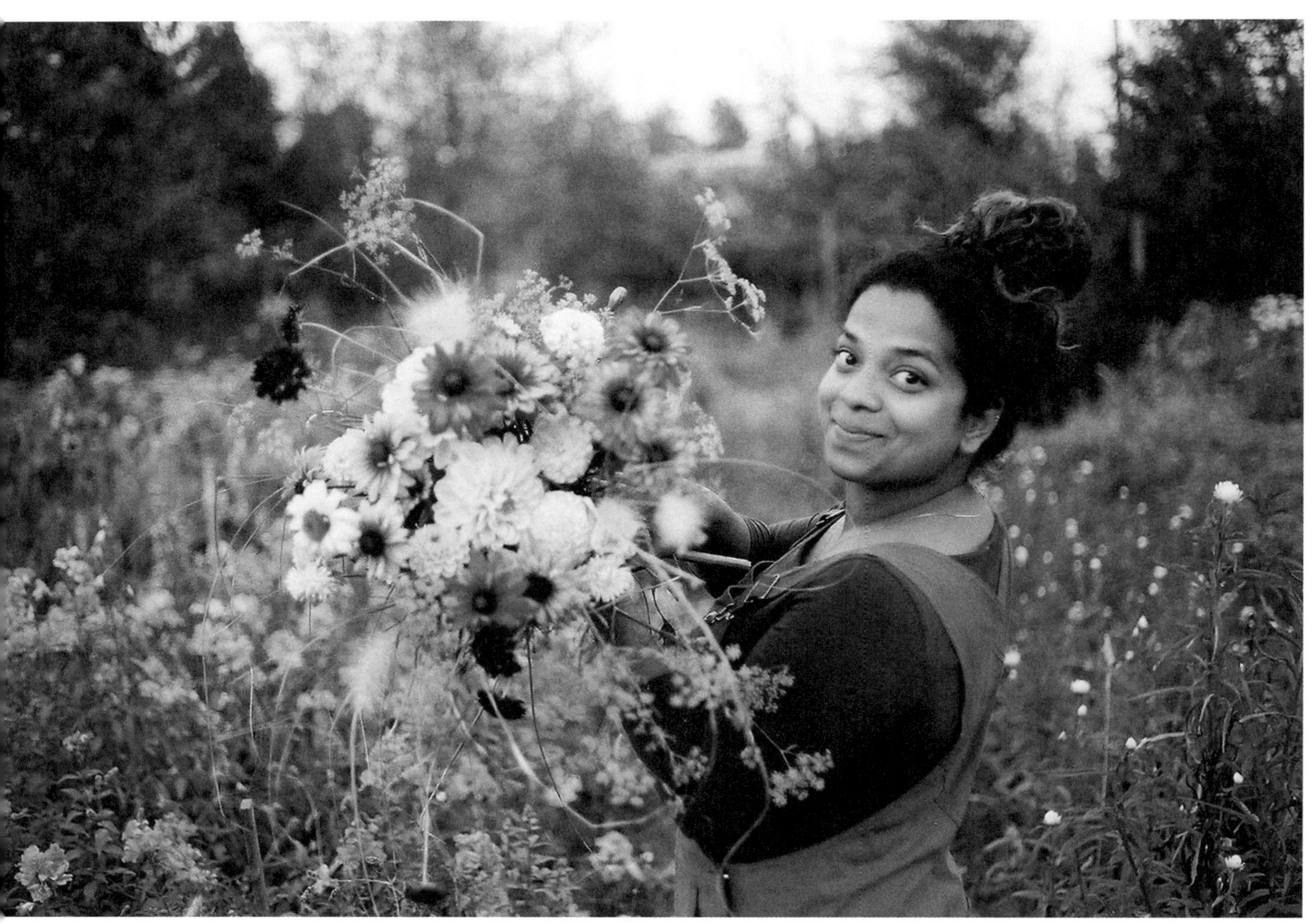

Thanushi Eagalle

Founder, Wild Bee Florals

"It was a time of total reset for many, and it's been the most amazing adventure and learning experience so far."

What is your first memory of flowers?

Jasmine and plumeria (araliya) flowers have a special spot in my heart because they were often used in cultural events growing up. Many Sri Lankans had these plants growing in their gardens, and their smell was intoxicating. I often remember picking up fallen flowers on pathways, one after the other, and smelling them and carrying them home.

Where did you grow up? Was nature a pivotal part of your childhood?

I grew up in Sri Lanka near Colombo and moved to Toronto, Canada when I was nine. Nature was always a very important part of growing up because of my dad, grandparents, and aunties. Whether exploring nature with my family, playing tag in my aunt's gardens, or staring up at parrots on cashew trees at the end of the driveway waiting for a school van, I always felt surrounded by nature.

When did the idea for Wild Bee Florals come about? What were you doing prior to pursuing this passion?

The idea of pursuing flower farming full-time came about when I lost my full-time job during the pandemic. I was already growing flowers for sale part-time at Farmers on 57th, which is an urban growing space in Vancouver, but the idea of living the entrepreneurial life came out of just thinking, *why not?* I have always dreamt of this idea, so if this is not a good time to start, then when is? It was a time of total reset for many, and it's been the most amazing adventure and learning experience so far on this path.

At the end of 2020, you left Vancouver and moved to the Comox Valley on Vancouver Island to pursue flower farming full-time and embrace the rural lifestyle. What have been the benefits and challenges of this transition?

We knew we couldn't afford to live in Vancouver with the lifestyle we wanted, and the community always felt transient. My partner Aaron and I were searching for a place on the West Coast that resonated with us and was full of folks we connected with. When visiting a friend in Courtenay and checking out the farmer's market, I felt so welcomed by everyone I talked to. That visit really inspired me to move out to the Comox Valley. In terms of wanting to operate a farm filled with beauty and creativity, that was a dream I've had since my early twenties after completing graduate school. It has been one of the most challenging projects I have taken on, but it's also so rewarding. I have come to learn not to hold on to failures and to keep moving forward through farming. There really haven't been too many challenges with this transition, aside from how expensive farmland is! The Young Agrarians organization has been a really good resource for folks who want to start farming by leasing land.

"I see the world through many different lenses, one being the intersection of evolutionary biology and informal education." Tell me more about this and how it applies to your work with Wild Bee Florals.

With this project, I wanted to ensure that whatever I did was done with a sustainability focus. Starting with soil enhancement and how plants are nourished, processed, and gifted, every step had to be completed in a way that supported local biodiversity. If any practice didn't serve that fundamental pillar, then it was not something we wanted to bring into our operation. I also know first-hand the healing effects of being surrounded by natural beauty and creating art, so I have been offering lots of workshops based off the farm to the Comox Valley community in collaboration with other creatives.

What is regenerative farming, and why is it important?

Regenerative farming focuses on soil enhancement because good soil health leads to better crops, and, very importantly, the sequestration of carbon. There are so many farming practices that fall under the regenerative agriculture umbrella. At our farm, our priority is to make sure soil is never bare, to compost whenever we can, being mindful of our irrigation practices, and ensuring that there are food sources for pollinators and birds. Small-scale regenerative farms are powerful tools to combat some of the environmental issues we are facing.

Are we seeing a shift within both the floral industry and the consumer's mindset?

I think so. More businesses are communicating about their sustainability targets, which helps raise awareness that businesses and consumers can make important decisions towards a better future for our local ecosystems. For example, using seasonal florals only, or not using floral foam.

"We aim to be an ethical brand that doesn't compromise on style and focuses solely on flowers grown in BC."

What I'm trying to communicate is that so many beautiful varieties of flowers and colours can be grown here on Vancouver Island and in the province of British Columbia. We are used to the media, especially social media, telling us what's cool and trendy, and that can lead to people wanting a specific colour or a flower variety, which is quite toxic

> Often, society can make people feel like they are not good enough or they are not where they should be in life. A lot of folks feel lonely and are seeking genuine heart connections. Thus, ensuring everyone has access to connecting with our flower farm, through programming, farm visits, volunteering, etc., is important to me.

to come by when not in season or grown around the world. Instead, if folks open up to using seasonal flowers sourced from their local community, they can be blown away by the amount of beauty that can be created without detrimental effects on the planet.

You recently spent some time in Sri Lanka. Did this inspire some ideas for the farm?

Sri Lanka is amazing because there are so many micro-climates. What I found fascinating during one of my recent visits was how productive small front yards and backyards were for growing flowers. Nuwara Eliya, where there are lots of tea plantations, has great growing conditions for cool flowers. I really appreciated how neighbours were collaborative in floral distribution. They were in a place where locals grew the flowers, and then a flower harvester would visit multiple gardens to pick those flowers and transport them to city hubs like Colombo.

Inclusivity is a pivotal part of the work you do.

Often, society can make people feel like they are not good enough or they are not where they should be in life. A lot of folks feel lonely and are seeking genuine heart connections. Thus, ensuring everyone has access to connecting with our flower farm, through programming, farm visits, volunteering, etc., is important to me. I feel so good when folks I have never met visit and feel inspired. Hosting more farm events is part of our future planning.

What does life look like for you away from the farm?

To be honest, the farming journey is quite all-encompassing from spring to fall. When I'm not in the field, I appreciate great meals with friends, DIY projects around the house, ocean or river dips, photography, and canoe trips. I have recently started some drop-in sewing classes and have been loving them!

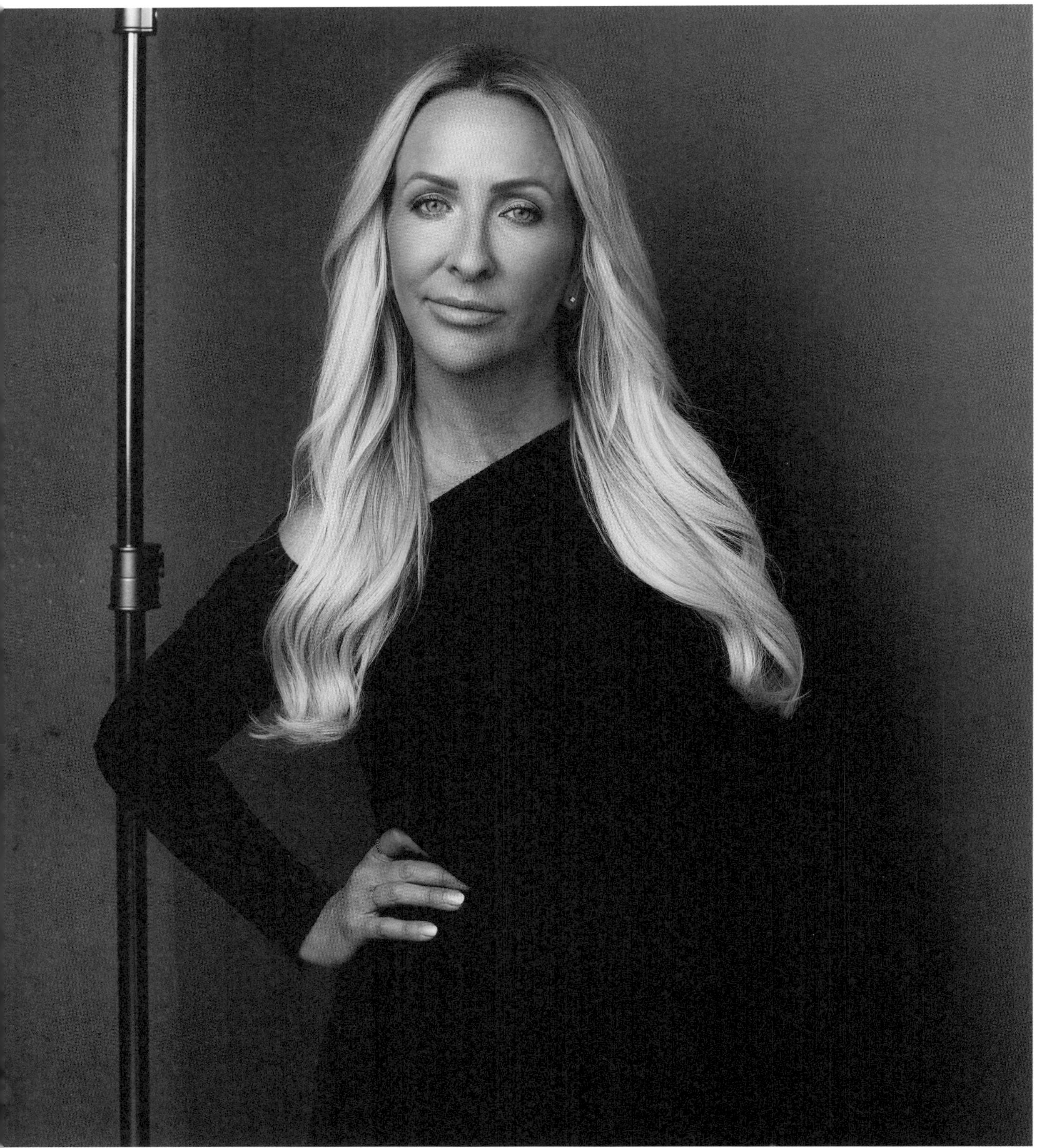

Karen Hoekstra

Founder and CEO, k'pure Naturals

"As a self-proclaimed 'overachiever' who was addicted to hustle, my journey has helped me get centered and make mental health a priority, balanced with building a business."

What is your first memory of the ritual and experience of skincare?

I remember being in elementary school and using and St. Ives blue mud masque and Noxzema cream to wash my face. I can smell both of their distinct scents when I think about them. I've always enjoyed the process of the skincare ritual, especially when winding down in the evenings. Although, I now do my evening ritual at dinnertime, as often I'm too tired to do it right before bed.

Inspired by your youngest son, k'pure began as an interest in chemical-free products. Tell me more about this.

Discovering that toxins were being absorbed through my skin and into my bloodstream and breastmilk, mainly through antiperspirants and body lotions, was pivotal in my clean product journey. I had originally started with a bowl of coconut oil mixed with baking soda and arrowroot powder that I kept under the bathroom counter, to replace aluminum-filled antiperspirants. This evolved into our best-selling deodorant, Get Closer, and our body scrubs and butters.

"I'll always be the girl that started selling natural deodorant on the internet, wondering what might happen if I just kept going." What year did k'pure officially open for business? Has it felt like an organic evolution?

I officially launched the website in February 2016 after selling the products at my fitness studio and on Instagram for two months. The growth was absolutely organic, as it took many months for me to believe that people would keep buying it! Every month, I was sure it would be the last, and I would continue on with my fitness studio, but people kept requesting the products, and I kept formulating new ones, until I finally had to choose between my gym and k'pure. I believe imposter syndrome is a very real experience for women, so working through that has given me confidence not just in business but also my personal life.

Prior to starting k'pure you were a personal trainer and bootcamp instructor. How did your previous work prepare you for your current role as CEO?

Health and wellness have been a priority for me for a long time, so fitness and clean products were naturally a good fit. In fact, the women at my boot camp were the original test subjects for the deodorant! We had a beautifully connected community of women at the studio, and having those women allowed me to translate that feeling of community support into what we now see as the *k'pure community*.

You're a single mom to four children. Wow. How do you build the business while also having this other important role?

At the beginning of k'pure, when I would start work at the studio at 5 AM most days and work on k'pure at night when the kids were sleeping, there was zero balance and almost zero sleep! The kids were small then. My daughter was only sixteen months old when I launched the website. I've never really loved the word "balance" as it puts too much pressure on mothers. We either feel like we're working too much or not working enough. I have learned how to manage my time better now and always take weekends off. It's always evolving as the kids get older and their needs change.

I imagine self-care factors in somewhere. What does this look like for you?

Daily exercise and meditation are key for me and my self-care. I love things like spa days, but self-care is taking care of myself daily with little acts of care like reading and going for runs.

What have been some of the highlights and challenges of building the brand?

We are now in over 300 stores across Canada, and our team has grown to six people, which is beyond my wildest dreams. Seeing my products on store shelves and in peoples' homes is always a *pinch-me* moment! I still find managing people to be a challenge, as I am a creative at heart.

How do you go about developing and deciding upon a new product?

In the beginning, I was making products that I needed in my own home. It would always start with finding recipes and then tweaking in ways I thought would be better. Then, customers would request certain products, and I would research and develop those. All of our earliest products were tested and developed in my kitchen. I had no desire at the beginning to delve into skincare and stuck to body care products, but it was an organic progression, and now skincare items are my favourite products to develop.

You're very active on social media. How has this helped you connect with customers?

I originally feared that moving to an online-only platform, instead of seeing my community in person, would mean I would lose that connection, but I was able to translate that into an amazing community of people with a much farther reach. I really love hearing people's k'pure stories and how our products and my story have impacted them and their families' lives. I like to tell my story and the stories behind the products, which gives customers a feeling of belonging to the community.

Giving back is important for you. What does this look like for you personally and professionally?

Giving back is of huge value for me. Personally, I like to give back quietly to my community, and professionally, I like to work with charities and causes that can really benefit from our voice. I have a role in Acts for Water here in Canada, which I'm very passionate about. I love to give back to causes that are really impacted by financial donations rather than being lost to corporate costs.

I really love hearing people's k'pure stories and how our products and my story have impacted them, and their families' lives.

You're very open about your personal journey—finding self-love, therapy, and spirituality. What has this looked like for you?

I have been in weekly personal therapy for over three years, which has transformed my mental health, which then trickles down to every aspect of my life, both personally and professionally. While going through my divorce, I learned that trying to numb the pain was only causing me to numb all of my feelings. By feeling all the emotions, I was able to find peace and joy along with the sadness. My spiritual journey has been life-changing in the last year as I began daily meditations, and journaling. I have learned to be present for my children, loved ones, and my k'pure team and community.

Who, where, and what inspires you?

My children and watching them grow and evolve. My mother and grandmothers and their stories of strength and perseverance. All of the amazing women in my life who have supported me and lifted me up on my journey. I love reading stories and hearing podcasts about people who have overcome adversity, addictions, and hard knocks to be their best selves.

My biggest love is the west coast of Vancouver Island, Tofino and Ucluelet. It is where I go with the kids to recharge and reconnect with the ocean and nature.

I am a long-distance runner, and some of my best ideas and most spiritual moments have come while on a long run.

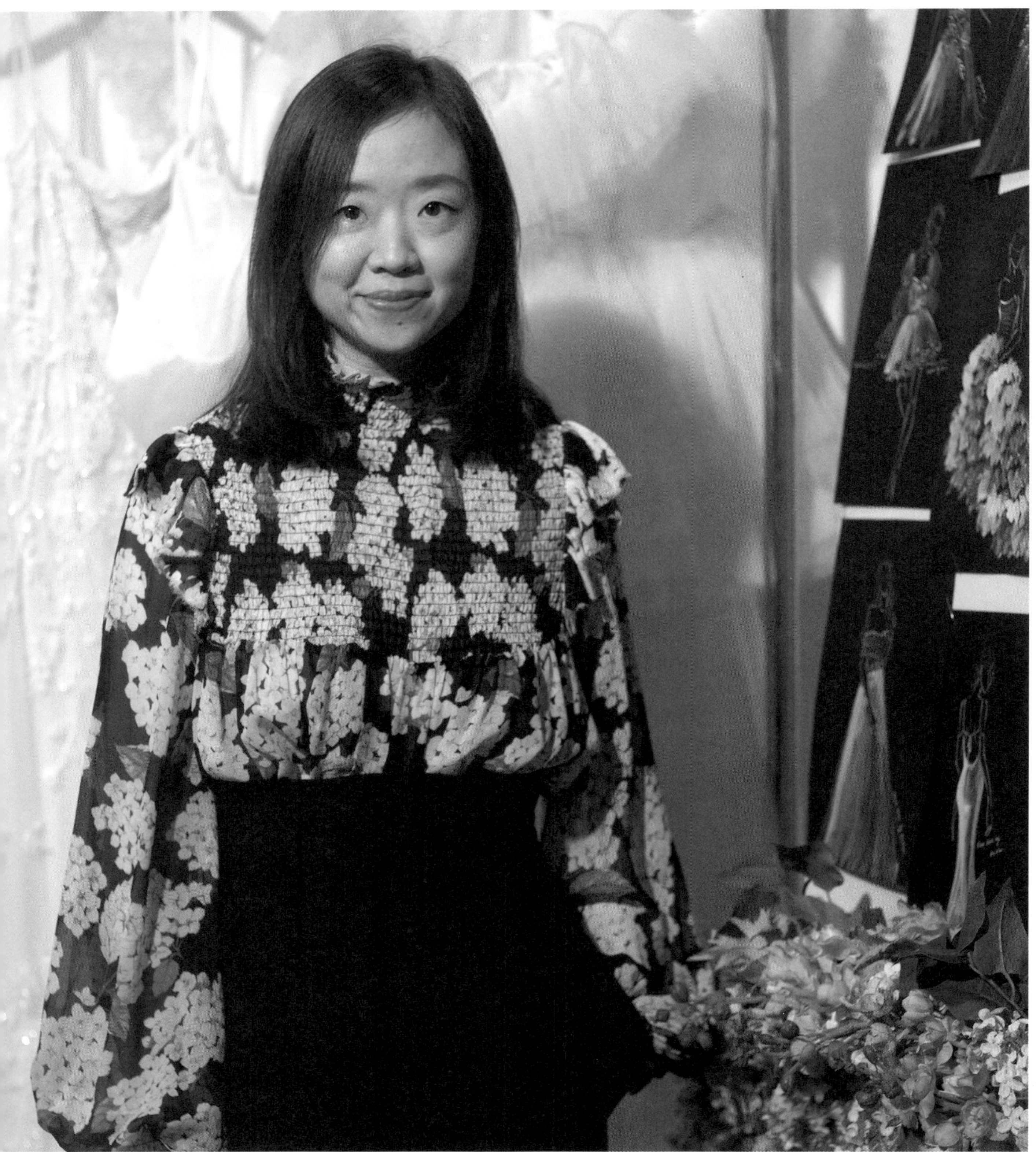

Ou Ma

Owner, Designer, and Creative Director, OUMA

"Fashion design is not just art, but is also strongly connected to the current economy and human consumption behaviour, as well as a reflection of culture."

Your first favourite item of clothing?

It was a black velvet dress with puff sleeves and a ruffled bottom my parents bought me when I was about five years old.

You were born and raised in Beijing. How did the geography and culture shape you?

I love Chinese culture, especially art and philosophy. I grew up playing in ancient royal parks in Beijing and watching my grandfather doing traditional Chinese painting. What influences me is the idea of *harmony*. Chinese culture values proper and balanced coordination between things. That is me. I am never too bold, both as a person and as a designer. Being modest, understated, and in control is what I value, which is expressed through my work. There are no protruding elements or a standout colour on my dresses. Instead, everything seems to blend well and play harmoniously with each other.

You completed a bachelor's in sociology upon your parents' request prior to pursuing fashion.

Being a fashion designer was a secret I'd been hiding from my family. When at high school in China during the early millennium, it was considered a not-so-serious job that would lead to an unstable lifestyle. The college entrance examination in China was extremely intense, so I was grateful to study sociology at the Communication University of China. The four-year bachelor's program provided me with a solid understanding of what I wanted to pursue as a career. Fashion design is not just art, but is also strongly connected to the current economy and human consumption behaviour, as well as a reflection of culture.

In my sophomore year, I started to show my mom my fashion talent, and she became the biggest supporter. She agreed I could attend a fashion program if I finished my sociology bachelor's degree. She said, "Fashion is hard; so is any major. Prove to me you can finish at least one degree seriously." Back then, I didn't understand what she meant, but now I appreciate her push. Otherwise, I would have dropped out of school and possibly been left unprepared for my current path and profession.

What were your first impressions of New York City?
I visited New York when I was ten years old while my parents were working in Washington, DC. My first impression of the city was similar to that of so many other visitors: crowded, noisy, and dirty. Living in New York completely changed my view; the subway is dirty still, but it is so efficient; the streets were always crowded, but people were energetic; the noise was endless, but so were some amazing street artists' music and subway performances. It was like a dream come true and I was absorbing everything I could while living there.

After FIT, you worked for Ralph Lauren's women's collection and Calvin Klein's made-to-measure atelier, both highly respected names in the fashion world. What were some key things you learned during this time?
The experience of working at high-end fashion houses, especially as a design assistant at Ralph Lauren's women's collection, broadened my vision of fashion. It was my first job right after college and I was able to attend meetings with Ralph himself. It was quite eye-opening to see how he interpreted inspirations and designed three women's collections throughout the year. He was such a legend, but still very hands-on with details when designing the collection.

When working at Calvin Klein's made-to-measure atelier, I assisted in selecting fabrics for red-carpet looks for celebrities such as Anne Hathaway and Christy Turlington. It felt unreal to see my favourite celebrities wearing gowns on the red carpet with my contribution.

In 2014, you were selected to present a five-piece capsule evening wear collection made of cotton fabrics at New York Fashion Week. Congratulations!
My specialization at FIT was knitwear because I was intrigued by making textiles myself. I dyed and felted my own yarn for my knitwear senior collection, and then I transformed the knits into printed patterns on cotton fabrics for the Supima Design Competition. The pressure was intense! I remember the morning of the competition: I was walking down to Lincoln Center. It was a bright, sunny morning. I remember it clearly because I saw this as a sign—I would have a bright future. I presented one short dress and four long evening dresses as the first collection coming down the runway. My parents, best friends, and FIT mentor were watching and cheering me on. I didn't win, unfortunately, but what the experience gifted me was much more than a title.

"Hardest decision for me was when I left New York. It was my second home where I spent my 20s, discovered who I am, and built my connections. I chose to move to a city (Vancouver) that I had only visited 3 times, to be with a guy I had only dated for 6 months (although I'd known him for 17 years) and embark upon a new life." Tell me more about this move in 2016.
It was a rather irrational decision because I relocated for love, but I would probably make the same choice today. My life in New York was intense and all work. If I stayed, I may never have evolved into my own brand. I wanted a change and a better work-life balance. The move in 2016 was the challenge I needed. I handled the transition well, made new friends, started my business, got married, and adapted to a new city. My motto was, *if I can make it in New York, I can make it anywhere*. I am thankful for that impulsive decision because it pushed me to do what I really wanted to do and realize my own potential.

What inspired you to focus on bridal and a zero waste policy?
When I first moved to Vancouver, I had to decide whether to work for a fashion house or start my own business. Making custom bridal dresses was my side gig in New York, and I loved making one-of-a-kind dresses for brides.

Sustainability is very important to me. Fashion itself is a high-waste and polluting industry, especially the wedding industry. The idea of saving up the money for just a one-day event made me think about other ways to save for the planet without compromising on the wedding itself.

"My first collection failed in the Vancouver market. But the failure turned into a success during the pandemic."

The pandemic was a pivotal time for my business as I offered short dresses, pantsuits, and bridal separates, which, at the time, were in high demand. I was able to cater to brides who had a short turnaround time due to restrictions. My revenue tripled the total from the year before.

You have a young son, Hudson. How has motherhood changed your approach to your profession?

He knows I'm a bridal designer, and he's very proud of his mom. This is motivation for me to do better. Growing up, I measured one's success by grades achieved at school and accomplishments at work. But being a mom taught me life has so many dimensions and is so much more than a measurable career path. When he was sick, especially when he had a stomach ulcer this past winter, I had to sacrifice work to take care of him. Work can happen at any time, but my child's health and our quality time together is easily lost. I am clear now about what my priorities are and can better pace my company's growth in a more balanced way.

My hope for the future is that there will no longer be any restrictions on what brides can and cannot do on their wedding day.

What is your vision for the brand?

I am glad the hard work paid off. I foresee OUMA being a global bridal brand that empowers women to be true to themselves when it comes to choosing a wedding dress. My hope for the future is that there will no longer be any restrictions on what brides can and cannot do on their wedding day.

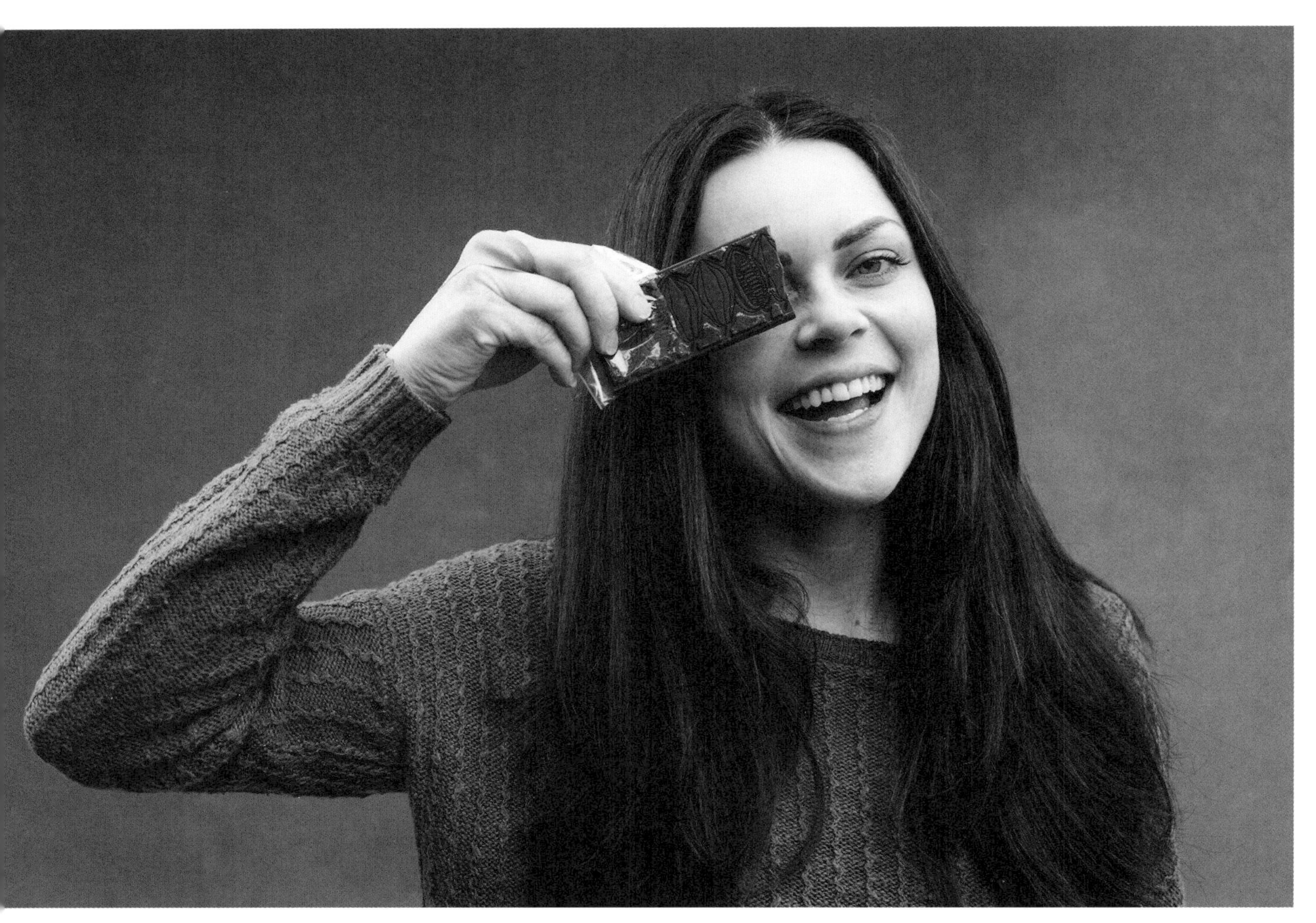

Mara Mennicken

Chocolatier,
The Good Chocolatier

"Good chocolate is also very much about how it's sourced, who benefits from consuming it, and what impact it has on the environment."

What is your first memory of chocolate?

I want to say it was in elementary school when we went to the Cologne Chocolate Museum. I remember lining up at their massive chocolate fountain to dip a cracker into this liquid gold. What a dream! Another thing I just recently learned is that my mom successfully stopped breastfeeding me after letting me have a hot cacao at night. That was the only thing that worked.

Where did you grow up? How did the culture shape you?

I grew up in Rösrath, a small city near Cologne in Germany, and have been coming to Vancouver since I was sixteen. I always knew I wanted to live somewhere else and experience something different from Germany. When I was seven, I told my mother, "When I'm old enough, I want to live really, really far away, where nobody can visit me." At sixteen, I guess I was old enough, and Canada was far.

"I've always been concerned with the story behind a product."

I think caring about the background of a product originated from how I was raised.

When I was twenty, I travelled to Thailand, where I visited local markets with makers who produce the products they sell right at their stand. I saw poverty, happiness, and contentment, which formed a different lens about consumerism. I'm not 100 percent sure which part of the trip shaped the direction of my career path most, but I returned with clarity on how and where I wanted to use my energy. It started with studying sustainable design in Cologne and getting numbers on the many industries and world issues related to climate change and globalization. I then developed an interest in social sustainability, which led me back to Canada.

The Good Chocolatier came about from your strong sense of doing good...

I started The Good Chocolatier at twenty-five while still studying, so there wasn't too much of a career path beforehand. The Good Chocolatier was a side hustle; it was very much aligned with what I was studying. I studied Community Leadership and Social Change at Capilano University in North Vancouver because I was curious about the social aspects of sustainability. When I finished my studies, I had already taken over The Good Chocolatier but also started working full-time at Dudoc, a Dutch company for sustainable urban development. Since March 2020, I have been focusing 100 percent on The Good Chocolatier. I have a heart for people and sustainability, and I want to have a positive impact on the lives of people that too often are overlooked. Although being a chocolatier or entrepreneur wasn't my initial goal, it's worked out. When I learned about social enterprises, however, it was like a light bulb moment, covering so many of the values I hold—The Good Chocolatier is putting the theory into practice.

"I think that good chocolate changes people's lives—in terms of happiness and so much more."
For me, good chocolate means not only that it's delicate, rich, smooth, shiny, and has layers of irresistible flavours. Good chocolate is also very much about how it's sourced, who benefits from consuming it, and what impact it has on the environment. The brilliant thing about good chocolate is that the more you eat it, everything around you and inside you just gets better.

Did you do any formal training to prepare for this new path, or was it more of a hands-on, learn-as-you-go approach?
Totally hands-on. I was first introduced to the world of craft chocolate in 2015 by Pierre Gruget, the former owner of Chocolat Natural/The Good Chocolatier. I was fascinated by the health benefits and boost in concentration it gave me while studying, so I asked if I could volunteer with him. After a year, I went with him to the kitchen, saw a chocolate grinder for the first time, and learned about tempering. In 2017, everything went quickly; he told me that he was moving back to France with his family and planned to sell his business. Being curious, having learned about social enterprises, and already being persuaded by his slightly addictive craft chocolate, I considered this opportunity. When I made my decision in May 2017, I had one month to learn how to make chocolate and run a chocolate business before he left for Europe. In reality, I learned in one month how not to break and burn everything, while the real learning happened afterwards.

Is everything produced in Vancouver?
I'm not a bean-to-bar producer, but I make my recipes from a combination of raw ingredients and different sweeteners. The winnowing and roasting are not done in Vancouver. The benefit is that I need less space for additional machinery. I like to be central, and real estate is pricey. This also means that the sorting of the beans, quality control, winnowing, and roasting are done at the farm level, which leads to more employment. Although there is more flexibility when sourcing the beans directly, and many chocolatiers pride themselves on their roasting technique, I don't think it's necessary for us. It took us a very long time to find the right quality cacao with the perfect, minimal roasting, but we *absolutely love* the cacao we source now; it's unique, bold, light-roasted, and has flavour notes that are incredibly nuanced and sophisticated.

"Social enterprise should be the future of business." How do you incorporate this ethos into the brand?
When I was learning about social enterprises, the concept was completely new to me. I thought every company's goal was purely financial, and if a company turned philanthropic, it was often after a huge financial success. It's not uncommon to see a social mission be a pivotal part of a business platform nowadays. Consumer mindsets are changing; they're making more conscious decisions about what they buy, and so are producers. The number of certified B Corporations has grown consistently over the past ten years, from only 707 in 2012 to over 4,400 in 2022.

The Good Chocolatier employs adults who are autistic. Why is this important?
My biggest concern has always been the job market and who does or doesn't have access to it. I investigated marginalization in Vancouver and found that

most people have slid into that category because of an inability to find a job rather than an inability to perform work. That was especially true for adults with autism. Work gives them purpose and a sense of belonging. The Good Chocolatier is an employment-based social enterprise and hires neurodiverse adults because I saw a need and found the right organization to make it a reality. It all started with a chocolate-making workshop at the PALS high school, and I'm lucky to have found such a great, supportive, and sustainable partnership with their adult program.

Who are some chocolatiers and brands that you admire?

Mānoa Chocolate in Hawaii. They grow their own cacao and make everything from bean to bar. They also just recently added a wine bar to their cacao bar. I've watched almost every episode of CraftChocolateTV, hosted by Dylan on YouTube. They invite people from the industry to talk about the different aspects of chocolate making—from sourcing and storing cacao to fermentation, the right machinery, and pairing chocolate, as well as what can go wrong in every aspect of this sweet business.

Is there one particular flavour combination that received a thumbs down at the taste-testing stage of development?

Before deciding on my seasonal flavours during COVID-19, I did an extensive taste testing with whoever wanted to participate from my newsletter list. Participants first voted on seven out of fourteen flavours. I then produced the top ten voted flavours, sent them out, and received another round of feedback. The final sample party was a virtual Zoom chat where it all came together. While keeping the comments I received in mind, I improved the recipes and launched our Seasonal Bonbon Bag with five of those flavours. The Divine Thyme with Basil and Lime flavour proved to be a challenge. I, along with many others, thought it's to die for, but for some, the response was more like: "I'd rather keep my basil on pizza!" or "Too much Italian seasoning."

Maybe I'm still CEO, maybe I'm not, but The Good Chocolatier will still be around to enjoy, providing people with awesome, real chocolate that has a positive impact.

Where do you hope to see yourself and The Good Chocolatier in ten years' time?

I want The Good Chocolatier to be one of Canada's most well-known and loved brands. A perfect souvenir to take home for visitors. I hope to employ at least twenty more neurodiverse adults and find innovative ways to integrate them as the business grows. Maybe I'm still CEO, maybe I'm not, but The Good Chocolatier will still be around to enjoy, providing people with awesome, real chocolate that has a positive impact.

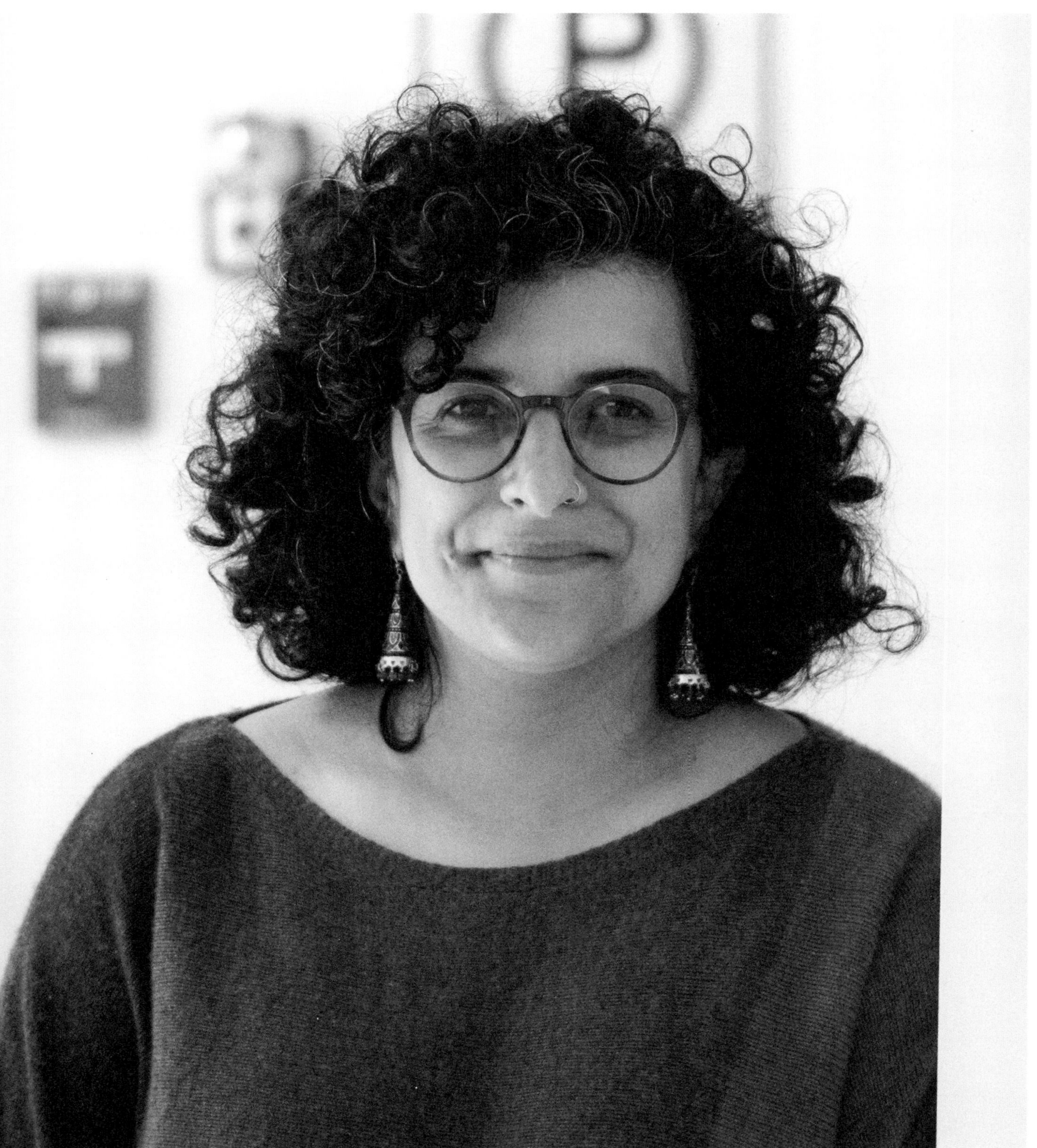

Jag Nagra

Illustrator, Graphic Designer, and Visual Artist

"Once I realized that my art could help me voice my stance on certain topics or meditate and reflect on things happening around me, it became second nature."

What is your first memory of art?

I grew up in a multigenerational home and had two of my uncles living with us, one of whom was a poet and an artist. I remember being enthralled with the ease with which he drew, and often tried to replicate his drawings. I looked up to him a lot and though he's not with us any longer, I often think about him whenever I create a new piece.

You're a self-taught artist. Have you taken any formal training? What do you feel makes a great artist?

I graduated from the Art Institute of Vancouver in 2006 with an advanced diploma in Graphic Design, so I have carried many of the design rules I learned into my art practice. In 2012, I decided I wanted to quit my in-house graphic design job, but with my work experience, I was worried I would only land more jobs exactly like the one I wanted to leave. So, I decided to take on a 365-day project to teach myself how to illustrate. Ever since then, my style has evolved drastically, but the curiosity is still there. These days, I start all my art by drawing with pen on paper.

"A Subway Sandwich Artist™ turned Artist Artist." I'm intrigued.

Just before I started art school, I worked at Subway for about eight months, making sandwiches with the official job title of *Subway Sandwich Artist™*. I thought it was a hilarious evolution of my art practice.

How would you describe your art?

My art connected me to my South Asian roots for the first time about three years ago. It's been an interesting journey of self-discovery. I draw from themes of the intersections of my own identity, being a queer Punjabi woman. I use themes of empowered women; I draw brown skin, and I draw Indian motifs and patterns. My art is hand-drawn and very saturated in colour.

Is there anyone that resonates deeply with your aesthetic and mission as a painter?

Honestly, more than one person; it's this incredible network of South Asian creatives in Vancouver who inspire me. I think because I felt alone in these kinds of community settings for most of my life, I really value being part of the art scene here. I'm constantly amazed by what people are accomplishing; it's inspiring and uplifting.

Can you please walk us through your creative process?

All of the work that I do starts with pen on glossy printer paper. I find that the glossiness allows the pen to glide more smoothly and creates more solid lines when I digitize my work. Once I'm happy with my drawing, I bring it into Adobe Photoshop on my computer to clean it up, and from there, I bring it into Adobe Illustrator to colour it in. That's how most of my workflow goes.

You've shared that art and social activism are closely tied to you. How does it inform how you create?

Once I realized that my art could help me voice my stance on certain topics or meditate and reflect on things happening around me, it became second nature. One often ties in with the other. In the last couple of years, whether it was the fight for LGBTQ+ acceptance, the Black Lives Matter movement, or the farmers' protest in India, I've found that I create art around those topics, which helped me process what was happening.

Why is making art accessible in the public realm pivotal to your process and passion?

I never grew up going to art galleries or museums regularly and I think subconsciously, I felt like I didn't belong in those spaces. Whether it was a lack of representation of the intersections of my identity, or just having a financial barrier to going, it just never felt like my voice could be heard in institutions like those. I think that really helped shape the kind of work that I do. Art in the public realm is available for anyone to take in and interact with for free. I also know that in large part, South Asians as a whole don't frequent art museums in large numbers, generally speaking. I want people, like my parents or grandparents, to experience art in places where they're comfortable. That's what inspires me the most. I like being able to take my kids to public spaces where my art lives and let them experience it in their own way in a more casual setting. I should also say I'm not in any way opposed to having my work in galleries—in fact that's a goal of mine—but I want to be able to create a good balance between two worlds as far as where my work exists.

You spoke of connecting more strongly to your South Asian identity in your thirties through community advocacy and your art.

I started volunteering with the Punjabi Market Collective, which was a group of volunteers working to revitalize Vancouver's historic Punjabi Market. This neighbourhood was vital to creating community and a sense of belonging for my parents' generation, and over the last fifteen to twenty years, there hadn't been much investment in the neighbourhood, and the market as we knew it was looking bleak and neglected. When I started volunteering as the creative director, it was the first time in my life where I had made South Asian friends who were all connected through our culture. I grew up in a very white town and outside of my extended family, so I didn't know many South Asians. Ever since 2019, I've been on this ongoing path to reclaiming my roots and feeling proud to be Indian for the first time in my life in a meaningful way. It's had a direct impact on the kind of art I create now. If you had seen my portfolio pre-2019, you would never know an Indian woman had created the art. Now, all my characters have brown skin and South Asian features. I take pride in it, and I feel like I've come home for the first time in my life.

"Finding my queer identity." What did this look like for you?

For me, my queer identity and my South Asian identity took a long time to intersect. I never quite felt like I fit in with my South Asian peers—and in queer spaces, it didn't feel very South Asian. It was through an organization called Sher Vancouver that I found people who looked like me. In all the work I do, I think in some way, the intersections of my identity come through, not even by force, but because my perspective and my story are the only ones, I can draw inspiration from.

You became a mom during the pandemic. Congratulations! How has becoming a parent changed and inspired you?

Yes! My wife and I have two incredible children, and honestly, all my perspectives changed when we had them. I want to give them a sense of confidence and value in themselves that I didn't start finding for myself until a few years ago. We have a four-year-old and a two-year-old. In hindsight, I suppose having a pandemic baby allowed us to very much *chill out* and experience life with them at a much slower pace.

Is there one piece of yours with which you feel a special connection?

I don't think I could pick out one particular piece. I don't take any of this for granted, and because I told myself for so long that I couldn't draw, when I do now, and when I can, I take a lot of pride in my work. I'm kind of protective of it. I save almost every single black-and-white pen drawing in a file folder. They're all a part of me and a part of my journey. In a fire, that file folder would be one of the possessions I would try to save if I could.

> Art in the public realm is available for anyone to take in and interact with for free. I want people, like my parents or grandparents, to experience art in places where they're comfortable.

Why is art important?

Art is a wonderful way to educate people. It's a great way to connect people. Often, people don't even realize that art is all around us. Whether it's textiles, jewellery design, or more *traditional* mediums, art is everywhere. For me, art is an important way I see the world. It helps me process, it helps me meditate and slow down, and above all, it's helped me find my voice and find myself.

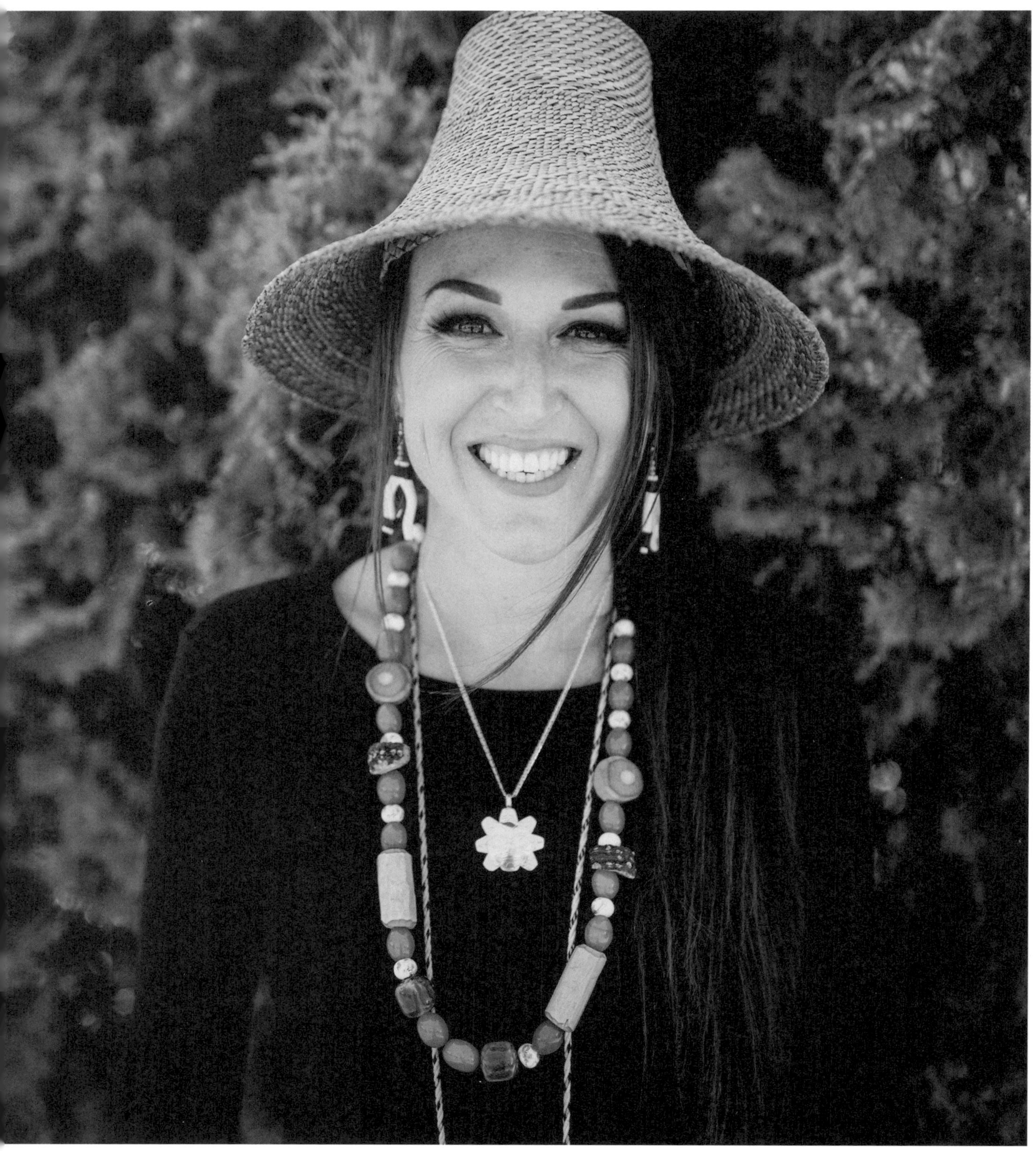

Avis O'Brien (Nalaga)

Artist and Consultant

BRITISH COLUMBIA

"My life path is rooted in making sure that what I went through can now be used to create systemic change in the lives of other Indigenous folks who are living with the impacts of trauma."

You grew up in Alert Bay, a village on Cormorant Island off the northern coast of Vancouver Island. How did the physicality of the place and the culture shape you?

My ancestry is Haida, Kʷakʷakəw̓akʷ, Irish, and Scottish. I belong to the Kawaas Sdaast.aas Eagle Clan from the village of K'yuusda in Haida Gwaii and the Gigəlǧəm n̓əm̓ina of the Ligʷiłdax̌ʷ people of Cape Mudge, which is one of the seventeen Tribes of the Kʷakʷakəw̓akʷ. The lineage I was born into is quite the dichotomy. I inherited a great deal of privilege from my Irish and Scottish lineage, being born into a body with white skin. I also grew up with economic privilege, in the sense that I did not grow up in poverty. My dad worked incredibly hard to ensure my sisters and I had a good upbringing. I also inherited oppression, trauma, marginalization, and abuse from my Indigenous ancestry and loss of positive connection to my Indigenous identity. I grew up very ashamed of my Indigenous ancestry. Because I am white-passing, I got to pretend I was someone I was not.

Thankfully, I had access to my culture growing up. I remember learning traditional dancing in preschool. The culture is strong in Alert Bay because, during the fifty years that potlatch was made illegal, the 'Namgis people continued to potlatch underground. I carry the deepest gratitude for the n̓əm̓ina's (families/clans) that kept our sacred ceremonies and way of life alive. They risked their lives so our culture could survive. And it did.

What inspired a professional path to help others?

In 2013, I was studying Indigenous studies at Langara College and worked for Vancouver Coastal Health in the mental health and addictions field. I was doing street outreach and was burnt out. The symptoms of PTSD were very present, and I took medical leave from my job to rest.

My time at Langara was transformative. I was learning about my peoples' history for the first time. All of this knowledge helped me make sense of my own life and lived experiences. This awakening was integral in my decision to drop out of Langara and quit my job at Vancouver Coastal Health authority to focus on my work with cedar.

Your work focuses on healing through culture.

Healing through culture, through the land, and ceremony, is something I did for thirteen years. I received so much relief emotionally, mentally, spiritually, and physically and wanted to share this with others.

The workshops offer safe spaces for healing in community. Together, we learn about the science behind how and why engaging in our culture is healing. We explore how the land can assist in the safe release of traumatic memories that get stored in our bodies. Together, we learn and experience the healing powers of culture and connection to land while simultaneously reclaiming all the parts of ourselves that were systematically taken during colonization.

Do you feel your personal trauma gifted you with this sense of purpose to help others heal?

Yes. My life path is rooted in making sure that what I went through can now be used to create systemic change in the lives of other Indigenous folks who are living with the impacts of trauma. It is called a survivor's mission; to use one's lived experience to facilitate change in the lives of others who are also struggling.

Having experienced homelessness, IV heroin addiction, and survival sex work has gifted me with the ability to empathize with others' experiences. I know what it's like to pull oneself out of the trenches. I also acknowledge the privilege that I had to have a family that was there for me through this period of my life. I'm not sure I would have made it out if I didn't have my family there for me when I reached out for help.

"Finding my cultural identity."

My journey with reclaiming my cultural identity began when my sister Meghann taught me how to weave in 2009. I watched her from a distance, confused by and uncomfortable with what she was doing. I was still carrying a lot of shame about my identity and didn't understand weaving. When I thought about Indigenous people, I thought about the negative stereotypes that exist in society.

When attending Langara College, I started to meet Indigenous women, who, in all their power and beauty, are doing incredible things in the world. This, along with watching my sister start to reclaim her identity, changed the narrative for me. I began to see that it was not a bad thing to be Indigenous. There was this power waiting for me to connect to.

> I carry the deepest gratitude for the n'əm'ina's (families/clans) that kept our sacred ceremonies and way of life alive. They risked their lives so our culture could survive. And it did.

How does being a parent inspire the work you do?

When I found out I was pregnant, I started thinking about what I wanted for my daughter. I want so much more for our future generations. It is the sole reason why I do the work I do, so that with each generation, we get stronger, rooted in our identity, and thrive.

How do you ensure that you're incorporating self-care?

One of the ways trauma still shows up for me is staying busy. When we keep ourselves busy, we avoid having to feel. Slowing down to stop, turning inwards to what is happening internally, paying attention to what I feel inside my body, slowing down enough to feel the emotions, process them, and allow them to flow through.

I love linking my breath with movement through yoga practices, weaving, drumming, dancing, and singing. Therapy is another tool I utilize. I have been in therapy for fifteen years and will continue to receive that support for my wellness until I no longer need it.

Please share more about the Suicide Prevention Initiative and land-based healing program.

łokʷimas—You are Strong, is a Kʷakʷakəw̓akʷ Youth Suicide Prevention initiative that was inspired by the passing of Tamika Mountain, a 'Namgis Youth. I didn't know Tamika personally, but her passing propelled me to not want to live in isolation with my own experience of living with the spirit of suicide. I put the thought out into the universe and within a couple of months, I had pulled together a Kʷakʷakəw̓akʷ suicide prevention team and started to develop the curriculum. Things fell together seamlessly and quickly. When work is supposed to happen, the path is very clear.

In this initiative we move away from programming that looks at suicidality as an individual problem and aim to address Indigenous trauma as a societally collective problem.

We support youth to stay alive, because staying alive is an act of resistance. Our program offers education on the impacts that trauma leaves on our autonomic nervous system, because suicidality does not show up when our nervous system is regulated. We assist youth to develop skills to regulate their nervous system through singing, drumming, dancing, and cold-water cleansing. Youth are also offered space to explore learning Kwak̓wala, as there is much research that proves language is a protective factor against suicide. Communities that have higher numbers of Indigenous language speakers have lower suicide rates.

Land-based healing programs support folks to release traumatic memories that are stored in our bodies to the land.

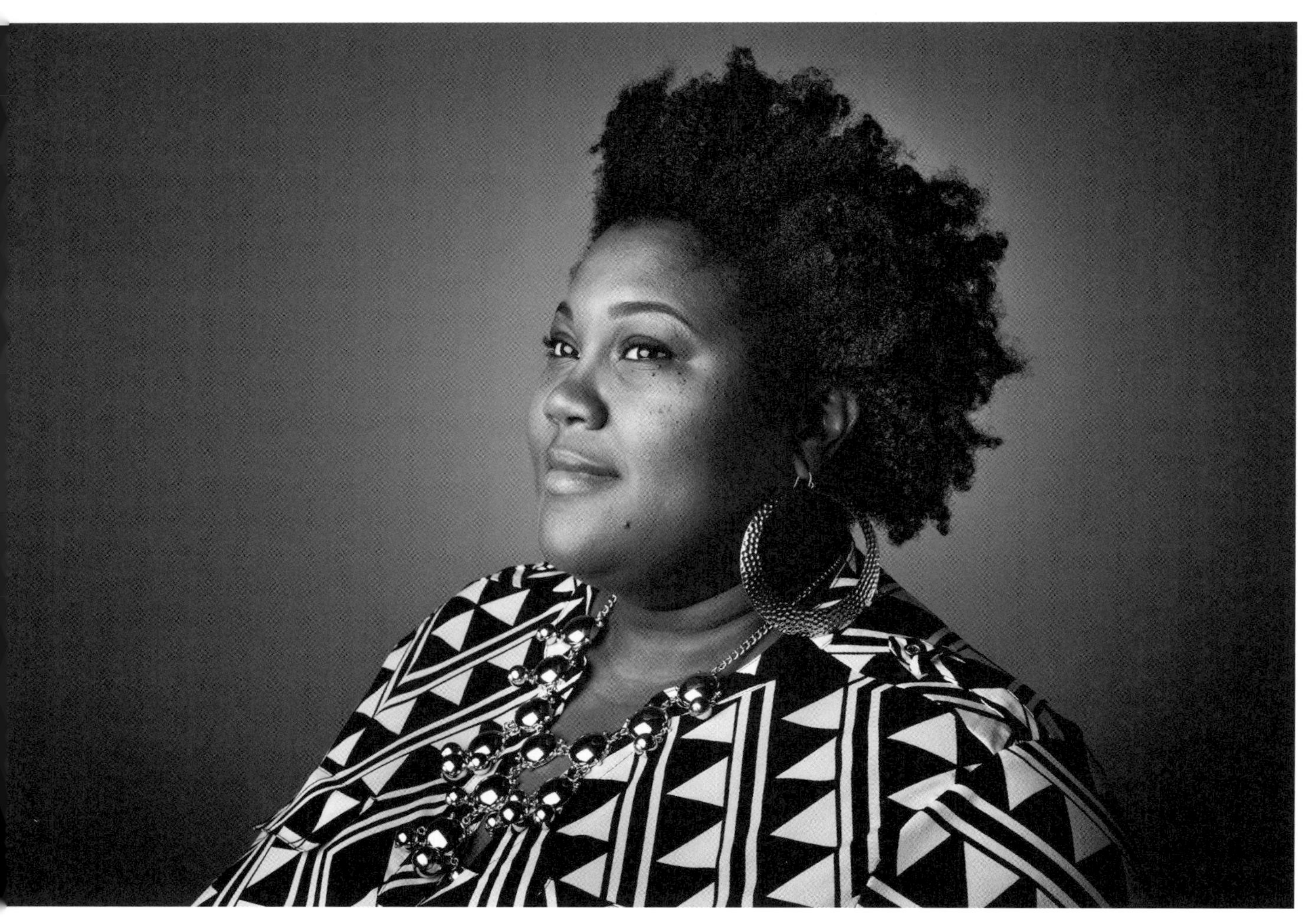

Dawn Pemberton

Vocalist, Teacher, Facilitator, Choir Director, and Radio Host

"Soul music is a way to express the spirit, what's on someone's mind and in their heart."

What is your first memory of music?

My first vivid memory of music was when I was about four years old, and I was lying underneath an ironing board playing. My older sister, who is fifteen years older than me, took me to her voice lesson because she was looking after me that day. I was in the other room while the lesson was happening, but I remember mimicking the sounds that my sister and the teacher were making. At one point, they looked at me and smiled in a *how cute* sort of way.

Do you come from a musical family? Was your love of and interest in music encouraged?

Yes, my family is very musical. All of my siblings play multiple instruments, and I grew up watching them and hearing them play. I wanted to be just like them and do what they did. My brothers played the drums, guitar, bass, alto sax, and percussion, and my sister sang and played piano. It just seemed natural. We had steel drums around, and my parents always played music to relax or inspire them while cleaning or working. My love of music was encouraged and nurtured, and I was exposed to a lot of different styles of music because of my parents and siblings: punk, heavy metal, rap, soul, funk, house, jazz, gospel, calypso, soca, reggae, and jazz.

You were born and raised in Vancouver, a vibrant city known for its diverse musical scene. How did growing up in Vancouver motivate and inspire you as a musician?

I think the music scene in Vancouver is more diverse *now.* However, growing up, it was really mostly a rock, punk, and jazz town. Sure, there were folks playing other styles of music, but you had to really work hard to find them, and you definitely wouldn't hear different styles on the radio. I really had to look elsewhere for inspiration. Things now are a lot more diverse and there is a more connected musical community that is supportive of different styles and interests. It's nice.

At what stage of life did you realize that music was your path?

I think I was about sixteen when I realized that music was what I was obsessed with and all that I liked to do. Even if it was hard work, it was fun. I have my degree in jazz studies, and I'm currently applying to start my Master of Music. Formal education is great, but I have learned so much from being curious, creating strong relationships with mentors, listening to albums, and connecting with others. I think formal and more organic ways of seeking wisdom are equal and valid.

What about soul music resonates with you?
Soul music is medicine. It was created by people coping with having their dignity and humanity denied for hundreds of years. Its roots are deep and connected to field hollers, gospel testimonies, and shouts. Soul music is a way to express the spirit, what's on someone's mind and in their heart. You don't need words to get the meaning of a soul song. It's a feeling, a visceral experience that we can all relate to because we are all human, and that's why everyone loves it.

You were the winner of the 2015 Western Canadian Music Award for Urban Recording of the Year. Congratulations! How did this feel? Did it at all change the way you approach your craft?
It felt really nice to be recognized by the musical community, my peers, and fan, to have something that I worked on and dreamed about be appreciated by others. Winning didn't change the way I approach my craft. It could, but I work hard to write and create for the sake of creating and not to win awards or be *popular*. I also think that it made me proud to know that soul music was being recognized in BC and in Canada where it's not as prevalent in the music scene as it is in the US or Europe. I think after winning, people started paying more attention to what I was up to and to who I am, which is kinda cool. I definitely had more opportunities arise, which has been a blessing.

What was your first time performing live in front of an audience like? Was there an aha moment that resonated with you saying, "This is what I'm meant to do?"
I love connecting with people on stage, bandmates, and audiences. I feel like a midwife to stories, songs, magic, and emotions. I often feel like a part of me goes away and someone else, spirit, or God takes over. I like myself the most when I'm on stage, especially when I feel there is freedom to be playful and explore. It's an amazing thing.

Which three musicians inspire you?
I'm inspired by so many people. It's hard to choose just three. However, I *can* say that I'm inspired by all creative and artistic people in general, musicians, visual artists, fibre artists, potters, dancers, and floral arrangers. I think the three things they all have in common is creating something from nothing. I love watching the evolution. All creative people selflessly offer up something beautiful for the world to engage with, and a by-product of that is that they are leaving a part of themselves in the work.

A song that moves you. Every. Single. Time.
It has to be "Ain't No Way" by Aretha Franklin. It cracks my heart right open every time.

Dream collaboration?
I would love to collaborate with Herbie Hancock or Charlie Haden! I love their artistry, their hearts, and their musicality, of course!

> Music is for everyone. You don't have to be an expert or a professional to feel and experience its power.

Music brings people together. During the pandemic and tough times in history, we've seen music bring magic, meaning, and lightness to our lives.
Music is magical. It can bring us outward, take us places, and unlock many emotions. It can also invite us to look inward, slow down, and reflect. Music can be done in large communities, and we can experience it by ourselves. Music is for everyone. You don't have to be an expert or a professional to feel and experience its power.

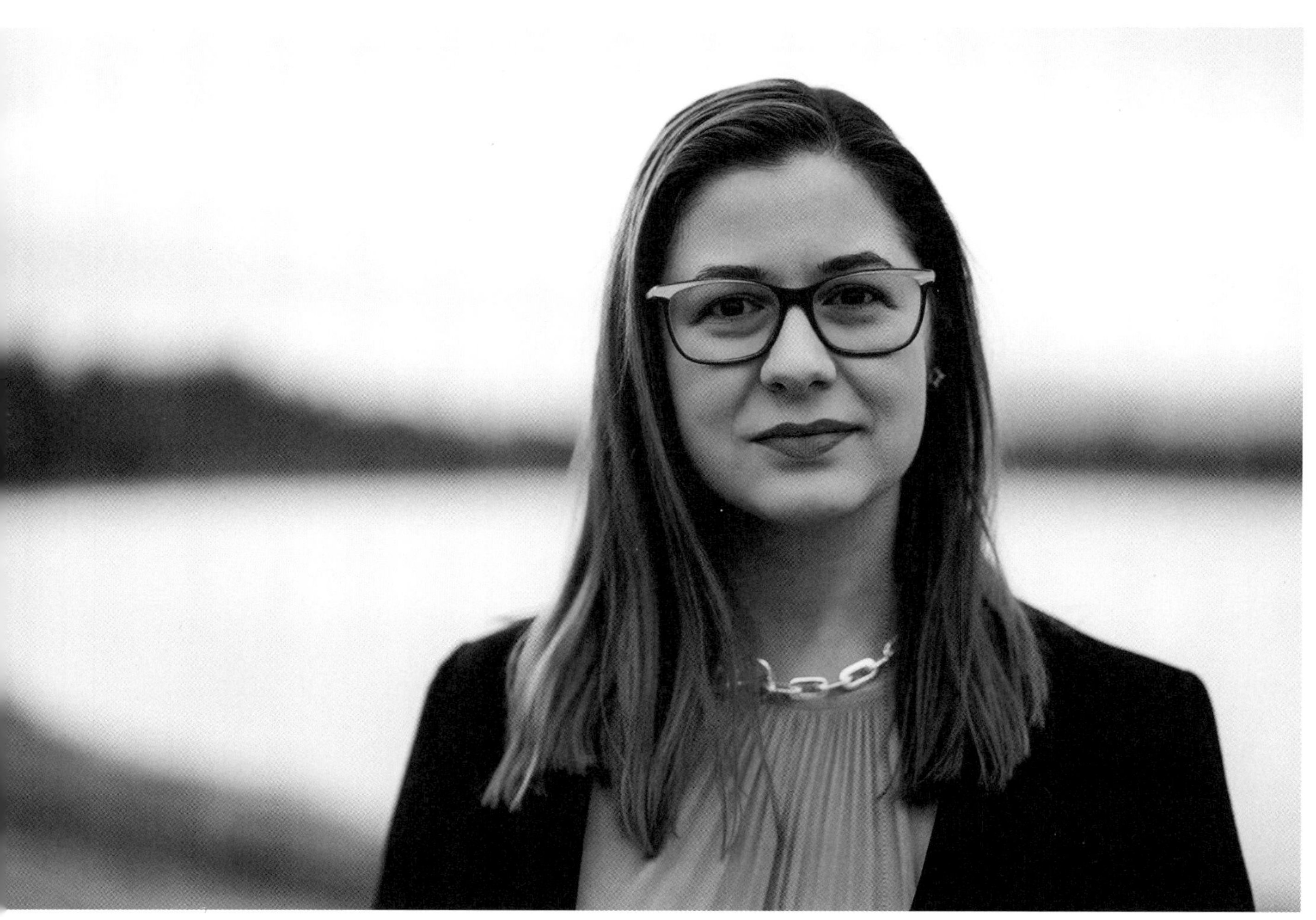

Amy Robichaud

CEO, Mothers Matter Canada, and Former Director, Dress for Success Vancouver

"In order to manage my depression, I've learned that rest, leisure, and play aren't things that I should feel guilty about engaging in. Rest is part of work, and play is part of productivity."

An early memory of helping someone?

I was the type of six-year-old who would scold total strangers for littering. As a child, my energy was very directed toward the environment and recycling. I have it on good authority that I was a terror about proper waste disposal.

At what age did you realize that your professional path and passion would involve giving back?

My family would tell you that it was pretty obvious from the get-go. At the same time, I was convinced that I was going to be an astronaut, a marine biologist, a lawyer, or a jeweller. As I entered my teenage years, I realized that helping others was really what lit my fire, and to be honest, that awareness hit fast and has lasted.

Prior to landing the executive director role at Dress for Success Vancouver, what was your previous work experience, and how did it prepare you for your current position?

When it comes to being "in charge," absolutely everything in my previous experience helped prepare me for a formal leadership role—and at the same time, nothing could have prepared me.

I have spent my whole career in social impact and philanthropy. I've been the charity office intern, office manager, program coordinator, and fundraiser. I've worked in-house at charities, as a fundraising and governance consultant, and on the giving side.

I came into Dress for Success Vancouver with a broad knowledge of the *how* and *what* of the philanthropic sector. This set me up really well for the strategy. What I couldn't have been prepared for, and what I think you can't be prepared for until you actually sit in the CEO or executive director role of a small shop, is the sheer scope of the role. Each day, I'm the spokesperson, the controller, the key revenue generator, the IT specialist, the HR advisor, the inventory manager, and the janitorial staff. This job is a constant test of prioritization, focus, and boundaries. I love every minute of it, but it is very much a position that you have to do on purpose.

I also dearly love leading people, caring for their wellbeing and championing their excellence, and I learned a lot about how to do that from people who led and managed me. Some of that was learning what not to do, but most of it was learning that the trick to leading and managing a team is that you need genuine affection for and belief in them.

My goal, ultimately, isn't to help individuals, although that is necessary. My goal is to change our society so that this work isn't necessary. I can't completely succeed in my job until I've eliminated the need for my job. How's that for a retirement plan?

What are the challenges and benefits of working with Dress for Success?

I believe I have the best job in the world. Each day I have the privilege of leading a team of amazing humans, both staff and volunteers, who are dedicated to empowering women into good jobs, financial independence, and personal success.

I believe that the perennial challenge in any leadership role is to remember that an organization is made up of two things: people and processes.

Dress for Success can't meet our mandate if we are not properly investing in the women who work for us by providing good pay, benefits, and a culture of growth and care. It took three years to ensure we pay all our staff a living wage and to lay the foundation for a culture that values and invests in employees. The charitable sector struggles with toxic workplace cultures that demand more for less from staff because it is *for a good cause,* and that leads to burnout and high turnover.

At Dress for Success and Mothers Matter Canada, the goal is to create and lead teams that actively engage in a healthy counterculture each day, and it takes work and constant attention.

Why is it important to give back and help build communities?

Since opening our doors in 1999, Dress for Success Vancouver has empowered over 41,000 women into the workforce. The full economic inclusion of women in the workforce means a more robust and resilient local economy, which we all benefit from and need.

Mothers Matter Canada has transformed over 60,000 lives since 2001, and research tells us that when mothers thrive, children flourish—doing better in school and earning more throughout their eventual careers. When each of us is stronger and living a sustainable and connected livelihood, our communities and neighbourhoods prosper.

What is unique about working in your sector?

When women are facing social and economic isolation, they are usually experiencing a complex web of barriers that prevent them from thriving and reaching their full potential.

In working to help women overcome the most unequal and difficult circumstances, we can and do count each woman, mother, child, and family that we serve as a success. Yet, until the systems and circumstances that cause this work to be necessary are eliminated, we'll never truly, fully succeed.

My goal, ultimately, isn't to help individuals, although that is necessary. My goal is to change our society so that this work isn't necessary. I can't completely succeed in my job until I've eliminated the need for my job. How's that for a retirement plan?

"I do this work while living with Major Depressive Disorder."

When you live with a chronic illness of any kind, you get really good at identifying what it is that works and doesn't work for you—and then you get really good at adapting so that you can spend more time with what works and mitigate what doesn't.

In order to manage my depression, I've learned that rest, leisure, and play aren't things that I should feel guilty about engaging in. Rest is part of work, and play is part of productivity. We are all at our best when we deeply engage in both; I just have less margin and more pronounced consequences for getting that balance wrong.

"My work to advance women's equality and to create a more inclusive world IS my identity."

My work isn't just my job; it is my job and my calling, and how I intend to leave my mark on the world. What gets me up in the morning is the same, no matter if I'm going to work or if I'm going grocery shopping. I'm always asking, *how do I leave this day, this week, this place, this world more inclusive than I found it?*

Who inspires you?

My mom is always at the top of my list. There are a lot of folks, in their thirties, who wake up one day, look in the mirror, and say with horror, "Oh my god, I look like my parents!" I love that I've grown up to be like her, in appearance and spirit. She's got more gumption and leadership in her little toe than most people.

A small yet significant step someone can take to get involved in giving back...

Just start. If you only do one thing to give back, become a monthly donor to an organization that is doing work you deeply support. You don't have to give a lot each month, but give something and make the commitment of a subscription.

Most specifically, become a monthly donor with Mothers Matter Canada or Dress for Success Vancouver. See? I'm always working.

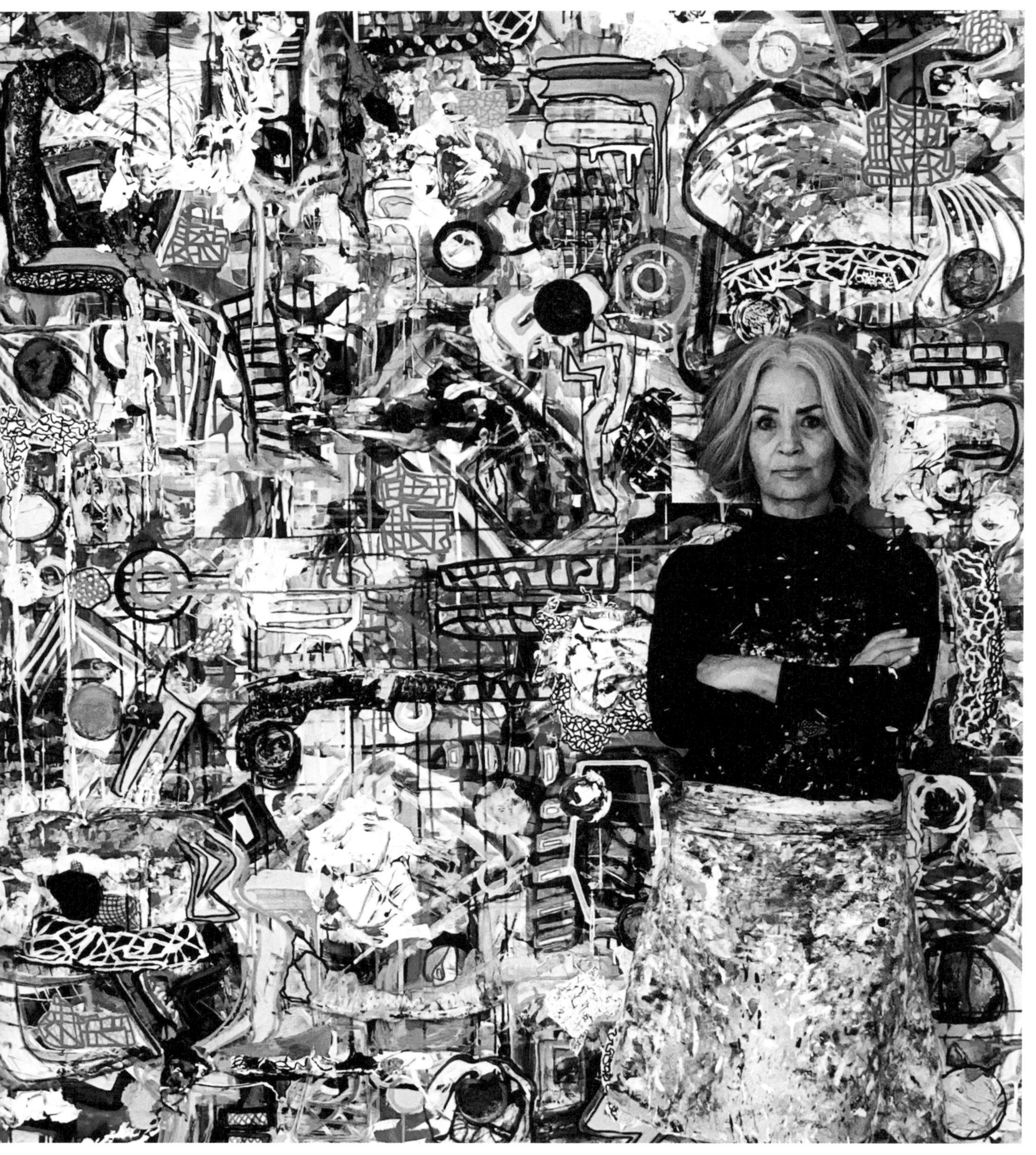

Carla Tak

Painter, Parker Street Studios

"Art brings a joyous dimension to life."

What are your first memories of art?

My first memory of art is at age twelve when I was doing a book report on Picasso and saw his studio and incredibly large, beautiful paintings. The experience moved me so much that I declared that I was going to be him. Creating art came at age fourteen when I attended art school and felt like a failure. Experiencing art came when I was twenty-seven, just getting divorced, and bought my first watercolour painting from a local LA artist.

How did your surroundings shape you? Personally and professionally?

I was born in Holland accidentally. My parents had gone back after the war to finally meet each other's prospective in-laws and extended their trip by four months. We returned home to West Vancouver, where I lived for fifteen years. I was lucky that I grew up in the 50s and in a beautiful home and neighbourhood where I played and explored outside. My parents were Dutch, right off the boat after the war, and my father had inherited a large sum of money, which made us stand out from the other Canadian families on our street. I did not get spoiled in any way whatsoever. If anything, I had more chores and responsibilities than any of my friends.

My young life instilled in me the following three things: early freedom to play, a hard-work ethic, and not being intimidated by wealth. All three factors shaped me in my personal and professional future.

You mentioned having survived intense early childhood trauma. Are you comfortable sharing what this was?

I would like to preface my response and share that I have made peace with and found forgiveness for everyone who was involved in my trauma. I believe individuals who traumatize others have been deeply hurt themselves or have inherited some trauma generationally.

My trauma began at a year old, with sexual abuse by a babysitter. I also witnessed my father trying to shoot my mother. On another occasion, he tried to throw himself out the window; this happened before age nine. As a teenager, I had no parental guidance, became promiscuous, and did a lot of drugs. I quit school at fourteen, left home at fifteen, and then left Vancouver for LA at fifteen with a thirty-four-year-old American sculptor, my then boyfriend. Nineteen years later, I would return to live in Vancouver.

My therapeutic practice began accidentally when I was attending art school at the age of fourteen. Fritz Perls, of Gestalt and "Primal Scream" fame, was doing a teacher training session. I took part in these sessions and found them interesting, not because I thought I was struggling in myself; at that time I still believed I was living a normal life. I did not start my serious therapeutic journey until I was twenty-four. Before that my work ethic, that was imprinted upon me at such a young age, really came to my rescue. I had to survive and was already supporting myself at age fifteen. Work gave me comfort, took me out of my head and brought me great satisfaction making money.

My therapeutic journey over the last forty years has involved a psychiatrist, reiki master, psychologists, and group therapy. I was very fortunate that I felt compelled to stick with therapy, otherwise my life would have had a very different trajectory.

Now having spent all these years gaining insight and tools, I mostly feel at peace with the past trauma; it is something that happened to me, but I am not it! I even have a feeling of gratitude. I feel these experiences took me to a deeper level within myself which afforded me a greater understanding of the psyche and more compassion and forgiveness towards others.

Most importantly I believe I was given a huge gift and that is the well of inspiration that I have in my art practice, which I find available to me at all times.

"At age twelve, I dreamed of becoming an artist . . . and at fifty, I reclaimed this dream." Tell me more about the process of changing the course of your professional path in midlife.

I moved back to Vancouver from LA at thirty-four with my young daughter. Although I had a great mind and enjoyed business, I was not passionate about my work. I was always trying to find other ways to make money.

When I was forty-eight, my daughter graduated and moved to New York. The dollar exchange was at 40% so I decided to earn some US dollars by bringing great artists from Vancouver to NY. I had everything lined up but couldn't pull the trigger. I was in a session with my reiki master complaining about this, and she pointed her finger at me and said, "You need to paint, and this is your homework." My reply was, "I don't paint or do homework." "Well, don't come back then," she said. That was the beginning. Within six months, I had a studio, and after two years, I was painting full-time.

Who inspires you?

My daughter Hollis' wisdom, strength, and vision inspire me. Myself and all my teachers for the incredible work we've done together. And my husband Chris. He's British, seventy-eight, and still doing personal work.

How would you describe your art?

Intuitive. Strong. Passionate. Original.

What do you require to be creative and productive?

I have the most incredible studio space, thanks to the Beedie family, who have dedicated Parker Street Studios, a 100-year-old building, to artist spaces.

My twelve-year-old vision, of seeing myself in a huge studio, came true!

I'm in my studio six days a week. I only listen to classical music and enjoy the solitude my studio affords me, and I need that to be creative.

Is there anyone that resonates deeply with your aesthetic and mission as a painter?

My favourite era is post-war abstract works by female and male artists. The fact that these artists *lived to work* and painted abstract works resonates with me.

I feel these experiences took me to a deeper level within myself which afforded me a greater understanding of the psyche and more compassion and forgiveness towards others.

"My business acumen has helped me tremendously..." What does this look like for you?

I feel having a good business mind can be very creative. and My over forty-plus years of business experience helped me tremendously as a creative.

When I began collecting art, I was interested in the business of it, never thinking that I would become an artist. Early on, I could see what was not working for artists. Once I began my art career, I knew quickly that I would make my own rules regarding what worked best for me.

Why is art important?

It brings a joyous dimension to life and good health.

What words of advice can you offer someone looking to explore a profession in the arts?

Be you. Work hard. Don't take people's opinions personally.

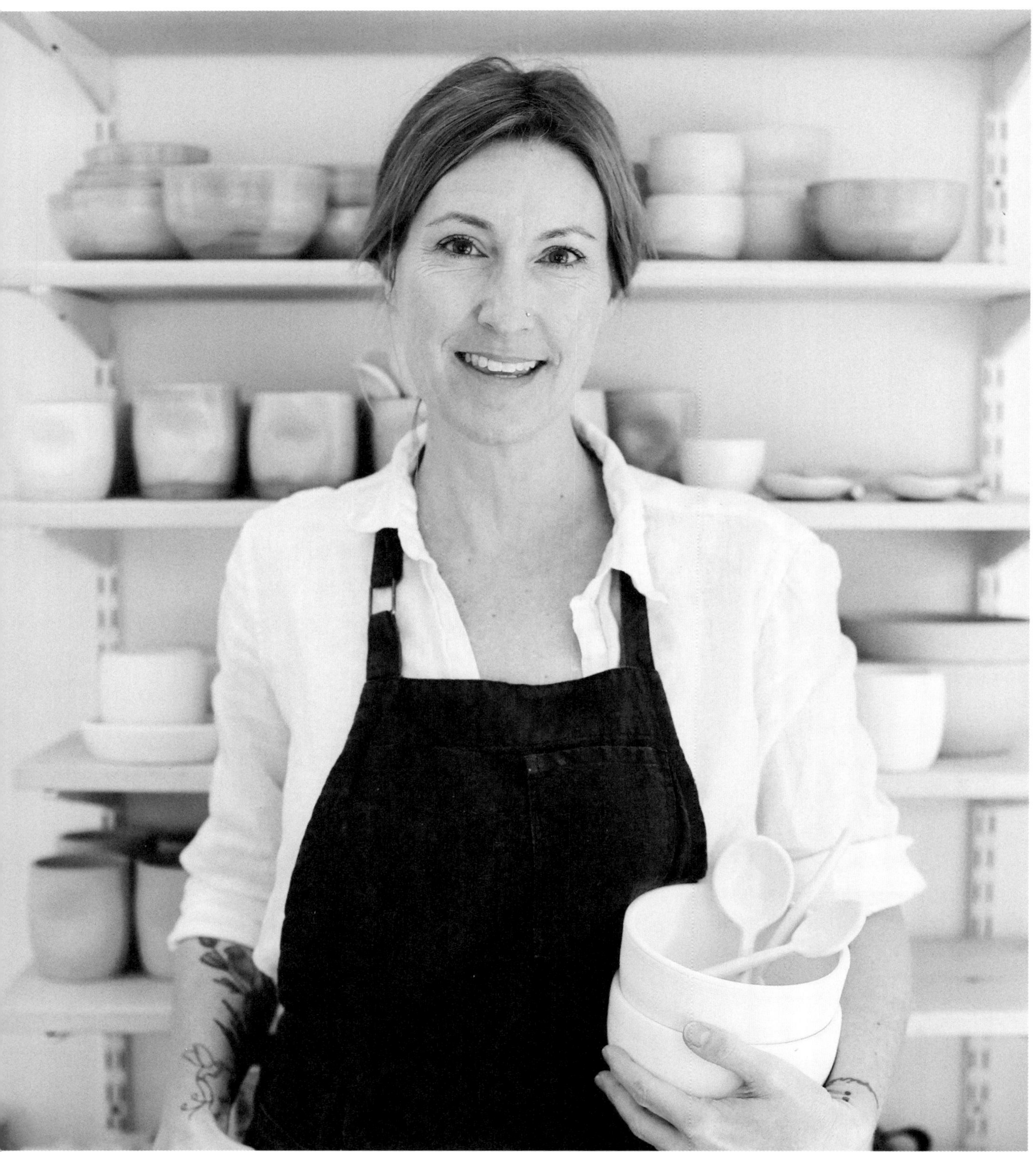

Kim Taylor

Potter and Photographer

"I love telling stories through my work and helping the subject of those images see the beauty that their own story tells."

What is your first memory of taking photos?

I've had a camera for as long as I can remember. I still have old photos and negatives from photos I took in elementary school. My grandfather was a photographer, and I have such sweet memories of time spent looking at old slides on his projector when we were children. I'm pretty sure I carried my little camera everywhere I went.

"I've had a number of chapters in my life, the last one which looked very different to my current one . . ." Was there a specific moment, or was it more of a realization over time that your path needed to be different?

After nearly twenty years with my ex-husband, where I wasn't in the workforce, instead staying home to raise our four boys, I found myself, for the first time, on my own and navigating the path back to a career. I did pottery for a while and loved it, but when my partner and I sold our property where my pottery studio was, I needed to reconsider what I wanted to do. Photography was an easy choice for me, as I have always loved it. During my years as a potter, I was often torn between making pottery and wishing I could be making photos of me making pottery. So, when I was finally able to focus on photography, the first thing I wanted to explore was making photographs of creatives, makers, and craftspeople. It's amazing where your path takes you when you're open to possibilities.

You mentioned the previous chapter being filled with travel and comforts compared with your current one, which is filled with joy and the self-satisfaction of building something yourself and finding success doing it. How do you define success?

At fifty-two, I'm finally in a place where, for me, success is based on happiness. That could be happiness in my work, happiness in life outside of what I do to earn a living, and happiness with my family or my friends. If I've learned anything, it's that I would choose joy over affluence every single time. I'm finding that I need less and less when it comes to material things, and instead, I am finding gratitude in the things I already have or the things I am working towards.

You shared that a pivotal part of this shift occurred when you reconnected with a former love after twenty years apart. Tell me more about the journey.

When I reconnected with the man I had loved twenty years before, it was as if everything suddenly shifted to where it was meant to be. I felt home. I felt safe, seen, and heard. Over the last six years, I have been able to let down so many walls. I've seen myself through his eyes, and my confidence has grown exponentially. I've allowed myself the grace to experiment with my photography, adopt an abundant mindset, and follow my intuition with a sense of peace. It's allowing me to really discover what I want my work to be and to work out what I envision. I'm really grateful for that.

Would you agree that perhaps there may be a direct correlation between pursuing your passion as a photographer and your statement: "The realization that I really need far less than I thought. I'm no longer chasing things to find joy. Joy comes simply by being in this sweet life."

I think that my statement absolutely informs my work. I think that mindset allows me to seek simplicity and beauty in the world. My photographs reflect my appreciation of finding joy in everyday ordinary moments. My greatest feeling of accomplishment these days comes from making photos that allow others to see that same simplicity and beauty. I love telling stories through my work and helping the subject of those images see the beauty that their own story tells.

Who, where, and what inspires you?

I am endlessly inspired. Sunny days inspire me, gorgeous windows with beautiful light coming through, the sea, or any water really. Travel and other cultures inspire me to see the world differently. I am most inspired by other creatives who have found their voice through their gifts and are sharing them with the world. I may see the images of an incredible travel photographer, and it doesn't make me want to be a travel photographer, but it certainly makes me want to build my own body of work. Inspiration does that for me.

You co-founded a non-profit in 2013 in Uganda. Tell me more about this.

Nearly ten years ago, while in Uganda photographing the opening of a children's home, Dr. Isaac Lufafa and I asked, "What would happen if we shared knowledge?" That question was discussed in a children's hospital in Uganda started by The Grow Hope Foundation and Tusubira Village. Over these ten years, we have empowered hundreds, if not thousands, of women in rural Uganda through education, mentorship, modelling, and friendship. We aren't an aid-based organization because the women we work with need skills and tools more than they need aid. Nine years ago, Isaac purchased a five-acre compound that became Tusubira Village. Our goal is to create a self-sustaining program that will eventually become a model that can be replicated throughout Uganda. The beauty is our program isn't dependent on my trips to Uganda. I always look forward to being able to visit and capture the work that's happened when I've been away, but I know that the program is in great hands at all times.

My photographs reflect my appreciation of finding joy in everyday ordinary moments. My greatest feeling of accomplishment these days comes from making photos that allow others to see that same simplicity and beauty.

You're a mom to four boys. You shared that you're "coming to the end of in-person parenting after twenty-eight years of that defining who I was." This is a big moment for both you and your boys. What are you feeling?

I'm actually writing this from Seattle, where I visit once a month to see my boys. If I'm honest, the initial transition was an emotional one. I've raised these incredible, kind, funny, connected boys with whom I have a wonderful relationship. Not having any of them in my home felt strange at first. But I see them happily building their own lives, and it is almost as if I now have permission to begin building my own life in this new chapter. They are all so brave, and they inspire me to be the same. I had twenty-eight years of doing the thing I wanted to do since I was a child—have a family of my own. I had never really envisioned this season, but now that I've acclimated to having so much more time for my own pursuits, I'm finding that I am filled with excitement for what's coming next.

Words of advice to others looking to embark upon creative entrepreneurship?

One of my favourite quotes by Rainer Maria Rilke is, "You are not too old, and it is not too late to dive into your increasing depths where life calmly gives out its own secret."

Where do you envision yourself in ten years' time?

I'd like to be travelling with my photography, telling stories through images. I hope that we will be living on our property on our little island just off the west coast of British Columbia. I dream of a simple life when I'm home, gardening with my love, visits from our five children, and watching for whales on our back deck overlooking the sea.

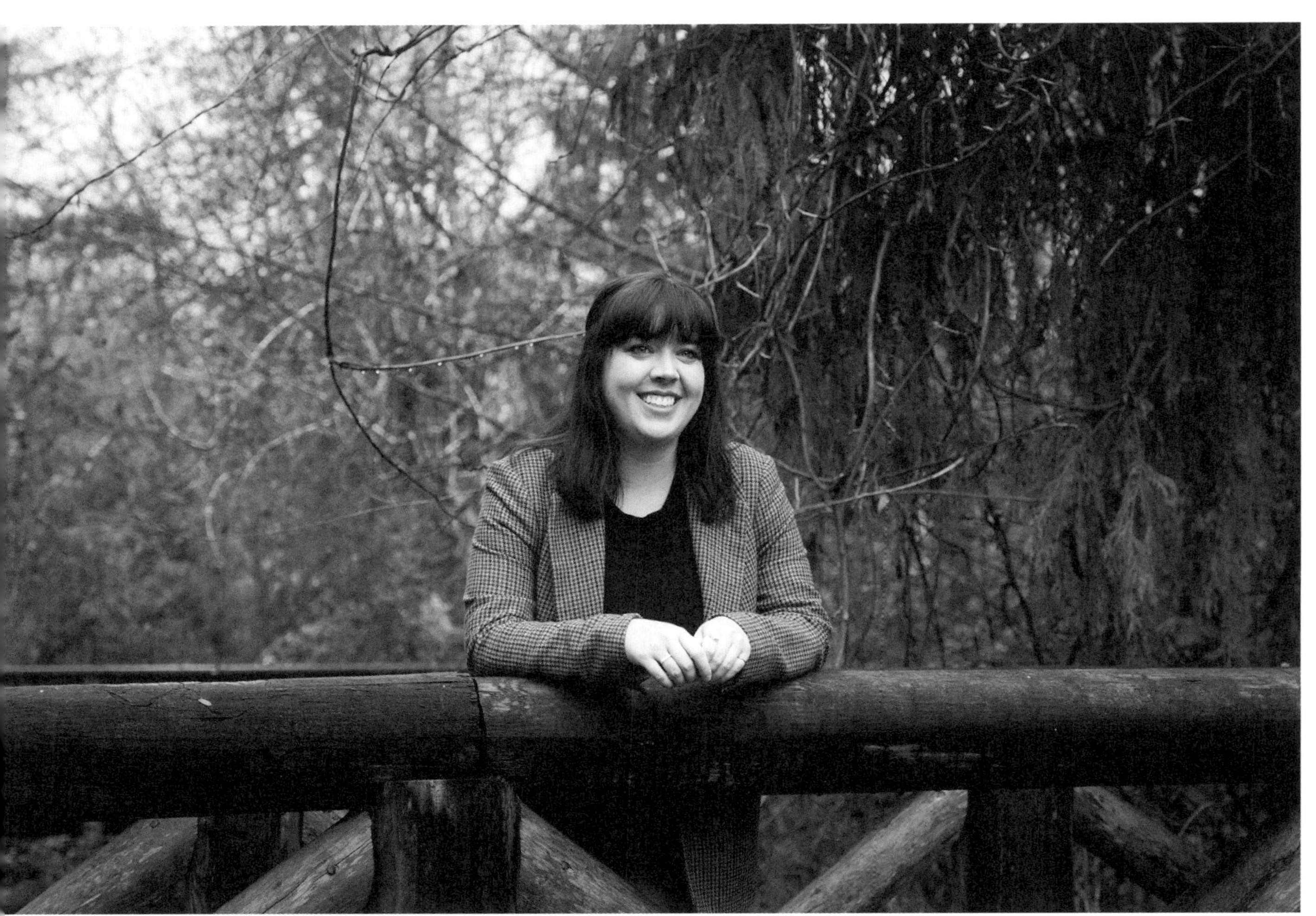

R.S. Twells

YA Author

"The manuscript in my hands represented a new me who had the courage to step out of my comfort zone and loudly proclaim that I wanted to be an author."

What was your favourite book as a child?

In grade six, my teacher read the book *Among the Hidden* by Margaret Peterson Haddix out loud to the class. The story had me on the edge of my seat. It was so thrilling and thought-provoking for my little grade six mind that as soon as he finished reading it, I asked my parents for the rest of the books in the series. They dealt with political issues and loss, something I hadn't thought about. It opened a whole new world of what books could be.

Was writing something you've always done?

It definitely wasn't. To me, writing was something you had to do in school. Writing was work, so why would I want to do it on my own time?

Growing up, some of my friends were creative and capable of writing stories that would make us laugh, but I was never the "creative" friend. I saw myself more as the "average" friend. I was someone that was good enough to pass at a lot of things, but not fantastic at a single thing. The first time I thought I could actually write something was in my grade nine English class when we were given an assignment to write a short story. I did the project in an hour and was pleased that I completed it so quickly because then I could move on and do other things. My teacher ended up submitting it to a short story contest, and I won second place. That grade nine second place short story later gave twenty-year-old me the courage I needed to begin writing *The Field Agent*.

"My struggles dealing with being a young adult led to me to writing my first book, The Field Agent."

Growing up I looked up to my sister. In my eyes, she was perfect. She always knew what she wanted to do with her life: she wanted to be a nurse, and that is what she became. I, on the other hand, never knew what I wanted to be as an adult and that caused me a lot of stress. I didn't want to be an adult. I wanted to be a teenager.

When I graduated high school, that caused me a lot of grief, knowing that I couldn't go backwards. I felt frozen in time, unsure of where to go.

Not knowing what to do, I decided to turn my hobby into a career. I have been around horses since I was twelve and thought I could become a riding instructor. I took a job at a stable, mucking out stalls and feeding horses early in the morning. During these mornings, I had a lot of time to think, and I didn't want to think. Instead, I created stories in my head. In the beginning, I was the main character in these stories as I was working away cleaning the stables. Slowly, I took a backseat in the stories in my head, and these twin brothers showed up. They were teenage boys going through what teenage boys go through, but there was also something special about them. They grew up at a school, studying to become spies. To top it off, one of the boys, Bennet, seemed to have the same challenge as me. He was going through life, not really sure what he was doing and putting his brother on a pedestal. I put down my shovel, picked up a pen, and started writing a story that held a piece of myself in the main character. The manuscript in my hands represented a new me who had the courage to step out of my comfort zone and loudly proclaim that I wanted to be an author.

It was the accountability that started to give me purpose in my life, a reason to feel like I was moving forward instead of always looking backward at what I could no longer have. When I started telling people that I was writing a story, I now had a reason to finish the story.

When the first book was published and people started reading it, I then became accountable to a whole new group of people.

An author who wows you with their work?

Ally Carter was one of those authors in high school, and every time she wrote a book, I would have to run out to get it. Her books were about girls dealing with friends, boys, and, most importantly, doing the impossible. Carter has a different book series about spies, thieves, and teenagers who lived in embassies trying to stop the fall of democracy. I ate it up. Her books are fun while also being inspiring. I have been a slow reader my entire life, which makes me appreciate the short length of her stories. She knows her audience is growing, giving her inspiration to start writing adult novels with the same excitement and adventure.

It was the accountability that started to give me purpose in my life, a reason to feel like I was moving forward instead of always looking backward at what I could no longer have. When I started telling people that I was writing a story, I now had a reason to finish the story.

Who, where, and what inspires you?

Horses will always be my first inspiration. *The Field Agent* came to be while around horses and story ideas continue to come to me while horse riding. My horse, Maple, is incredibly patient with me while I often just sit on her with my Notes app opened, hurriedly writing down an idea before it slips away.

Many people in my life inspire different characters in The Field Agent. The main female protagonist, Darcy, is inspired by my sister, Stephanie, and my friend, Alexis. The two of them are the strongest people I know yet have the biggest hearts. It's fun to write scenes with Darcy in them because I can just ask myself, "Would Stephanie or Alexis do this?" If the answer is yes, I will keep writing.

I grew up volunteering at a summer camp during my teenage years and then went and lived on campus for a year of college in England. These two experiences combined helped me plot out what the school Bennet and his brother attend would look like.

When young writers ask me how to find inspiration for their own stories, I tell them to go out and experience life.

"Writing my first book brought me out of a dark period."

When I had my first panic attack in high school, I remember thinking, "Wow, that was a lot of crying." Then, when I was in my early twenties, and nothing was getting better in my head, people started opening up more about mental health and taking care of yourself. A friend encouraged me to go to a counsellor.

At the same time I was starting counselling, my main character, Bennet, popped into my head. He was going through a lot of emotional stuff at the beginning of his story, and I was going through my deep spell of depression—it was nice to have someone to lean on who understood the feeling of not wanting to live anymore, even if they were a made-up person in my head. Writing the first book, I was able to use my depression to inspire Bennet and what he was dealing with.

The problem with dealing with depression, while my main character was dealing with it as well, is that it kind of gave me permission to stay in that dark period. I had to work very hard to separate myself from Bennet's feelings.

Who have been your biggest supporters?

I kept my writing to myself for a long time before I finally had the courage to tell my best friend, Megan. We were shopping in Sephora, and I began to tell her about these characters and this plot that was dancing around in my head. She was floored that I was capable of juggling this whole world that was constantly expanding as one book expanded into four.

My parents have been beyond supportive. They have blessed me with an office space in their house even though I usually leave my manuscript in piles everywhere but my office.

One of my biggest supporters is sadly not here anymore. My grandpa passed away before my first book came out. He would walk around his seniors' home telling the other grandpas and grandmas that they would soon see my book proudly displayed in bookstores. I dedicated my second book, *The First Traitor*, to him.

You self-published *The Field Agent*. What have been the highs and lows of going this route?

The immediate high was knowing that my book was going to be published. It felt so good when I first signed up to be self-published, knowing that my hard work writing Bennet's story was actually going to be worth it.

A huge low was the lack of support. With self-publishing, if you don't get the word out about your book, no one is going to hear about it. The work doesn't stop just because the story has been written.

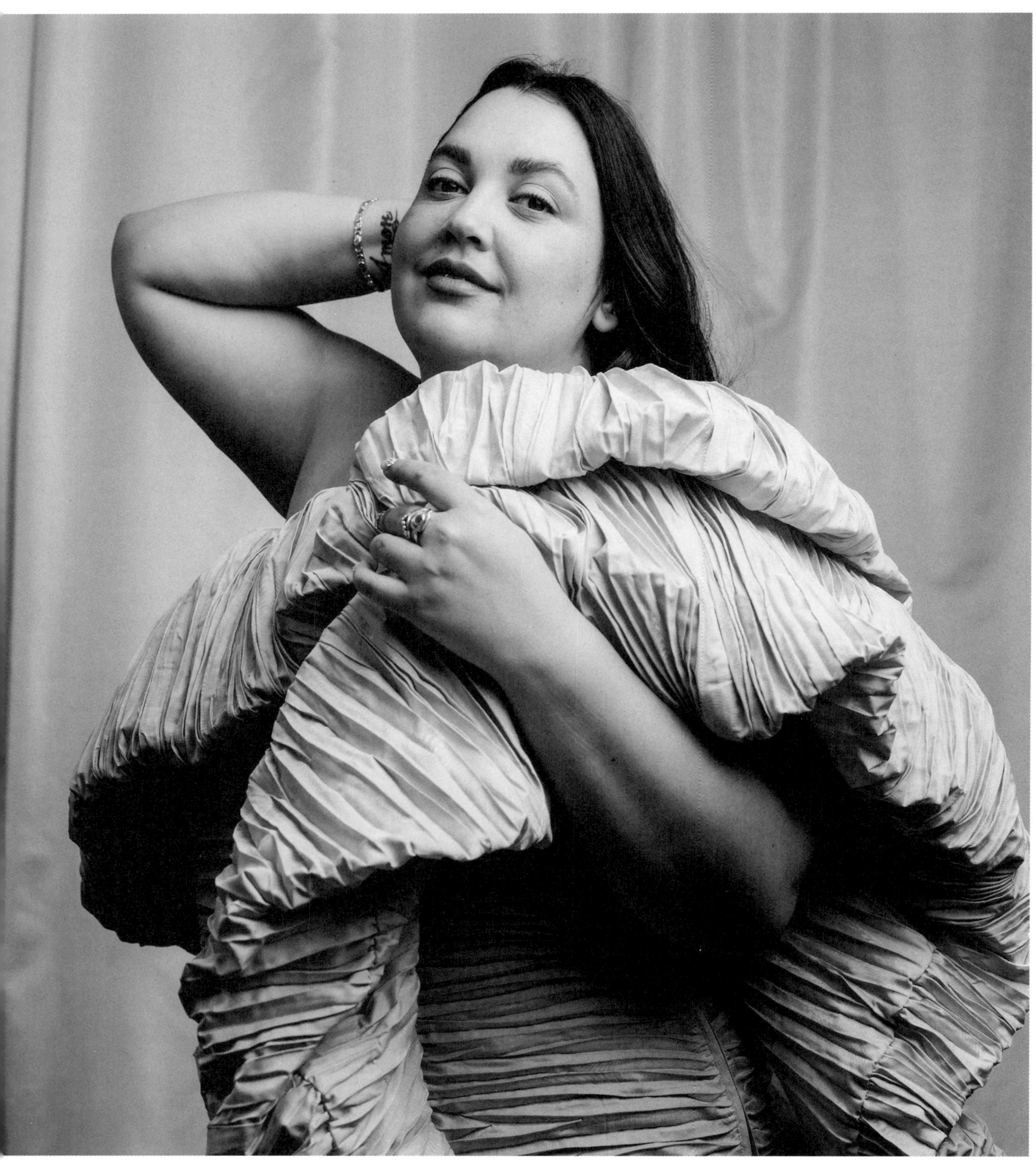

Sylvia Tennant

Curve Model, Founder, and Designer, Zaleska Jewelry

"I believe a good designer tells a story, and there are many ways to do that."

What is your first memory of jewelry?

My mom and aunts were always wearing jewellery. One of my favourite memories of jewellery is a camping memory. My parents would take my brother and I to Kettle River in the summers to camp, swim, and jump off the rocks. The water was freezing cold, so my mom rarely went in. Instead, she would watch us from her camping chair, making pearl necklaces with a variety of beads and stones. She's the kind of person that can make camping feel glamourous.

At what stage of life did you realize that designing jewellery was your passion?

I became fascinated with making jewellery in university. Despite my love of fashion, there were so few places that sold my ring size. Then, I saw a woman carefully weaving a wire-wrapped ring at a local bead store and realized I could do that as well. I was quite pleased with myself for finding a creative solution to my accessorizing problem, but had no idea that this moment would ultimately change the course of my life.

Who, where, and what inspires you and your designs?

People who are confident with their personal styles really inspire me. It could be someone I see in a magazine, on the street, or on my feed. If I get a vibe, my brain goes into design mode. I also visualize new pieces by looking in the mirror and imagining how to adorn the places jewellery lives on my body. Designing in larger batches allows me to tell the full story of a collection, which is often inspired by my life and the things I'm passionate about at that time. Each collection is like a timestamp of who I am and what I'm experiencing.

We share a mutual love for the island of Bali. Tell me more about your connection to this special place and its role in Zaleska and your life.

Bali is one of the world's meccas for silversmithing, but I fell in love with the island before I knew I wanted to expand my business there. It started as my tropical playground, and now it's where I go year after year to bring my sketchbook to life. Bali made it possible for me to jump from doing a few handmade designs to fully realizing my potential as a creative director. I'm incredibly grateful to the talented team we have on the island—they are so important to me.

> I love the element of discovery that comes with travel and the feeling of experiencing a new city for the first time. That energy will forever inspire me.

You and your partner, Rod, love to travel. How does travel fuel and inspire you?

I love the element of discovery that comes with travel and the feeling of experiencing a new city for the first time. That energy will forever inspire me. Give me a great restaurant recommendation, directions to the best vintage shops in town, and a comfy bed, and I'll be a very happy traveller.

Do you feel that a good designer draws on both formal training and inherent talent, along with real-world experience and a passion for creating beautiful pieces?

I have a degree in fine arts with a focus on sculpture and photography, but no formal metalsmith training. I believe a good designer tells a story, and there are many ways to do that. I used to be self-conscious of the fact that I outsourced most of my production, but now I'm so grateful for it. I know my strengths lie in other aspects of the business. I pinch myself all the time because I create alongside some of the most talented silversmiths and carvers in the world, and they allow me to fully express my vision beyond what I'm personally capable of.

Zaleska is a size-inclusive collection of beautiful, handmade pieces. Why is this pivotal to both your passion and purpose as a designer?

I know first-hand what it's like to walk into a store and have nothing fit my body. Creating a size-inclusive jewellery brand means challenging archaic size ranges. It's important for people of all sizes and shapes to feel considered as consumers, and that's one of the big reasons Zaleska continues to exist. I passionately believe that people deserve to wear designs that help them express their personal style, and this informs every decision we make.

"I want to make people feel considered as consumers and to encourage the importance of size inclusion in fashion." In addition to the stunning jewellery line you design, you're also an in-demand curve model, working with several brands. What are some of the highlights and challenges of working in this sector?

I modelled very casually in my twenties. During the pandemic, I began photographing my jewellery on myself out of necessity. Looking at the images with an editorial eye was very healing, and I grew confident in my understanding of how my body moves. I've since signed with an agency, and the journey so far has been incredibly rewarding. The entrepreneur in me loves getting a behind-the-scenes look at the brands I work with, and my only challenge has been navigating the balance between my existing business and newfound career.

What do you feel is your role as a curve model?

Diversity in media is extremely important. I didn't grow up with it, and I'm proud to be a small part of this new era.

Jewellery has marked many of life's memorable experiences. Why do you think we have such strong connections with our pieces?

Jewellery is a very intimate purchase. Like clothing, it has the power to introduce you before you speak. There are myriad reasons why people feel connected to heirloom status, symbolism, and gemstone lore, to name a few. My job is to create jewellery that I love, and if people find it cool enough to put on their bodies, then that is the biggest compliment I could ever get.

How do you hope people feel when wearing your jewellery?

I hope people feel like the highest vision of themselves.

Where do you see yourself and Zaleska in ten years' time?

I'm keeping an open mind about the next decade. If history repeats itself, I'll be living out my wildest dreams and learning every step of the way.

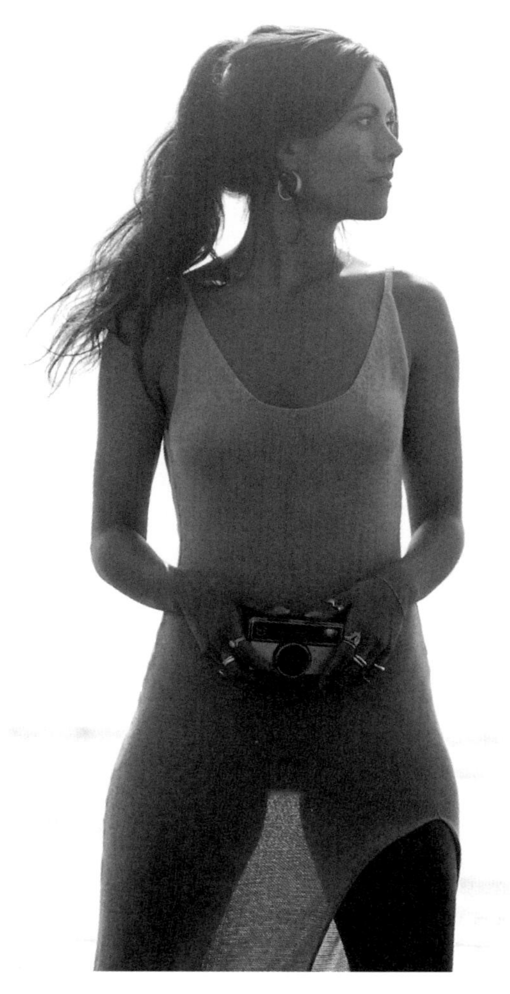

Olivia VanDyke

Photographer

"Photography helps capture an essence that cannot be articulated into words. It is my inspiration and my work to translate this into a photograph."

What's your first memory of a photo that moved you?

I can't point to any one moment in my life that marked its onset, but I can reflect on a photograph I made that held so much: my grandmother, standing in her kitchen, her wrinkled hands holding a recipe. It was a beautiful expression of her love language, the simple act of cooking, and the emotion radiating from her still touches me today.

This photograph spoke to me in ways beyond my understanding and opened the door to a plethora of emotions I could never have expressed on my own. As I look back upon it, I am moved by the beauty of that image, which allowed me to explore photography with feeling and emotion.

At what age did you begin to have an interest in photography? What about photography inspires you?

From my father, I was introduced to the art of photography. His love for film photography and his passion for capturing life's moments is something that I have always admired and have immense gratitude for. As I grew older, I realized the power of photography and its ability to capture and translate these moments. Looking through the lens of nostalgia into his and my own past gave me an insight into the essence of the art.

I didn't understand it at the time, but photography unlocked the door to my soul. It was a way for me to express and connect with my own creative mind. As far back as I can remember, I was photographing my friends. My walls were filled with inspiration from each photograph I developed and printed. I found solace in the art of capturing my life and I felt free to create.

Through photography I find myself practicing gratitude within each frame, as it allows me to pause and appreciate what can sometimes be overlooked. The beauty of how the light illuminates someone's face, the intricate patterns of water rippling on the surface of the ocean, or the look in someone's eyes when they open up and share their truth with me.

Photography helps capture an essence that cannot be articulated into words. It is my inspiration and my work to translate this into a photograph.

Did you do any formal training in photography?

I did! I fell in love with photography in the darkroom. I would spend four hours every Wednesday night in that red-lit room, sometimes spending weeks on a single image. I found the process to be extremely therapeutic. While I learned how to use a camera properly in school, I learned how to create art on my own.

I realized the power of photography and its ability to capture and translate life's moments. Looking through the lens of nostalgia into my father's and my own past gave me an insight into the essence of the art.

I think there is something to be said about being raised in an artistic home; my mom was an artist, and my dad is very connected to nature. I was always exposed to life in an imaginative way. I believe every single human being has a unique and insightful view of the world that could be translated into a photograph if they felt drawn to doing so.

"I see the camera as a tool to heal and connect. Both for me as well as for my subject."

Stepping in front of a camera is a very vulnerable space to enter into. I have to tap into my own body, step into my own vulnerability, and create a safe space for others to do the same. Through this process I have found we can connect with each other in a very unique and powerful way. Striving to cultivate harmony, safety, and closeness so that we may understand each other.

By holding space and witnessing someone experience their vulnerability so closely, I have had to experience my own. The truth finds us in this space. Vulnerability becomes power. It becomes art. It's been an incredible gift to experience.

Your work focuses on nature, humans, and branding. What is special about shooting these subjects?

The expansiveness and vitality of a natural landscape invites you to step into yourself as you are. Guiding a person into the wild and witnessing them experience their vulnerability so closely is an ultimate inspiration and exchange.

It's what is recognized in my creative work that brands want to be a part of. It's also been a way for me to find *my people* more specifically; I am very selective with who I work with. It's important to me that our values are in alignment and that there is a mutual respect for nature.

How does the process differ when photographing different categories?

From my perspective, I'm creating unique work across different subjects, but what's been fascinating is the reflection I've received from my community that they recognize my work, whether it be branded, creative, or an image made of a wild animal.

There is a lot of similarity between shooting humans versus wildlife, as you attempt to capture the raw and pureness, the essence of it all. The overlap between the photography and all its elements creates a unique synergy that makes my heart swell with appreciation for the beauty of it all.

Travel plays a pivotal role in your life.

I'm inspired by the places I travel to, and I find immersion in a different culture or country is a great way to broaden your perspective and align and reframe your world. These days, our reach is further than ever, and our touch is closer than ever. How can I represent humanity in its many unique ways with my art? Through travelling and meeting people in different countries, I can learn about their way of life, views, and what lies beneath in their eyes. Something that transcends language and words alike. It brings me closer to understanding the beauty of the world.

How do your surroundings inspire you and your creativity as a photographer?

I am currently based in Vancouver, BC. However, I've spent no longer than three months of the past fifteen in Vancouver. You could say I'm very much living and breathing a nomadic lifestyle. Being home allows me to appreciate the beauty and culture of my surroundings. It is a place full of love and compassion, a community in which I am grateful to be a part of artists, family, and friends close enough to be family. I am in awe of the wildness and beauty of British Columbia and enriched by the experiences of travel and the wildness of the world. Travel has opened my eyes to how diverse our planet is, yet no place can compare to home. I am grateful to have a space to ground and reflect on the experiences I've had while being abroad. With open arms, I am welcomed back home to reflect on all these wonderful moments that have become part of me.

A memorable shoot that stayed with you?

A specific moment that has stuck with me was coming across three puma cubs on the side of a mountain.

We watched as the last hint of daylight, a sublime warmth, and two rainbows washed away beneath the mountains. The crescent moon pinned to the sky as dusk set the scene. In the midst of such vast and breathtaking beauty, three puma cubs perked their ears towards us in curiosity from the hilltop as we watched with reverence. Giving rise to the notion that what we do to the Earth, we do to ourselves, and that the only tenable choice is compassion, love, and reciprocity.

"Human connection is key in everything I do."

Human connection is the key to my work. It would be impossible for me to produce the art I do without that connection. As I look back at all my work, I can see that connection not only shapes it, but also binds it together in a way that transcends the boundaries of time and space, a reminder that we are one. Connection has been a part of my life and my photography, and it will never cease to be a source of inspiration for me.

Intention.

It's often a word I used to describe my work and a way for me to find meaning in all that I do. Taking a slow, mindful approach to everything helps to bring peace of mind and view life from a new perspective. My intentionality is what shapes my reality and guides me in creating the life I desire.

What do you hope people feel when viewing your images?

Through my work, I strive to create a feeling of unity and understanding, to make people feel seen within its frame. If I can do that, if my art can give someone that feeling, then I know I have done my job.

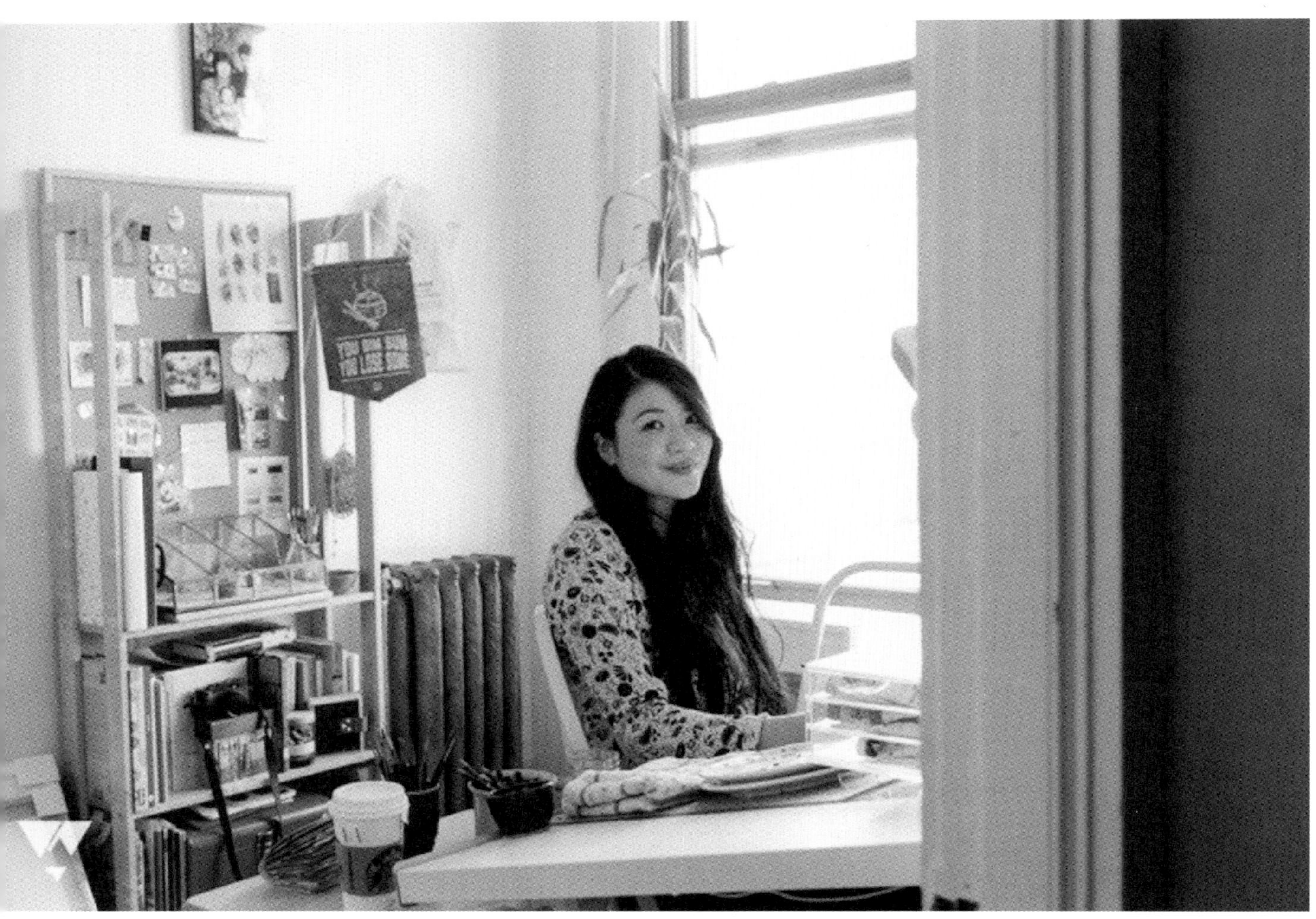
YOU DIM SUM
YOU LOSE SOME

Janice Wu

Artist and Illustrator

"I use drawing as a way to understand the world around me."

What is your first memory of art?

One of my first memories of experiencing art as a child was gravitating toward the arts and crafts volume of my children's encyclopedia set. The book was filled with colourful pages of DIY crafts that repurposed humble, everyday materials to make art. I remember the excitement of embarking on a new creation and using my imagination to create something beautiful out of very little. It was one of the first things that made artmaking feel like magic to me.

Was art and creating a pivotal part of your development through childhood and adolescence?

I would say that throughout my life, I have always felt compelled to create. This compulsion to be creative feels innate, natural, and internal regardless of what it means to identify as an artist. However, the thread that carries through the development of my art practice remains the same. I use drawing to understand the world around me.

You were born and raised in Vancouver, BC. How does the physicality, creative energy, and culture of your hometown inspire you and your work?

To be entirely honest, I'm not sure how my hometown has inspired my work directly. Much of my work addresses family history, a reclaiming of my heritage while confronting what it means to be a child of immigrants in this country. Perhaps, in some ways my work speaks to Vancouver in a perspective that is more intimately rooted in family and my community.

At what stage of life did you realize that pursuing art was to be your professional path?

I started working as a freelance illustrator almost eleven years ago while I was studying for my BFA at Emily Carr University. As grateful as I am for the education, most of my growth as an artist happened outside of school, working on personal projects and in the work I did for various clients throughout the years.

How would you describe your work?

My work is loving, precious, and sentimental. All adjectives that I had been told in both straightforward and in subtle ways as an art student to stay far away from, since this description meant that my work could not be considered as serious. I now dismiss this notion as untrue and quite misogynistic. Over time, I've come to embrace that the accessibility of my work doesn't make it any less poignant or important. I liken my creative process to a botanist taking field notes of flora to study, examine, and ultimately understand the specimen they have chosen to pluck from the natural world. My work is meticulous, and the slowness is deliberate. It is a process of deep and loving consideration for the subject.

"The diasporic experience as an Asian Canadian, cultural belonging, family history and the immigrant experience play a pivotal part in the work I do." What inspired you to focus on art that "appreciates the beauty and hidden narratives in the overlooked, fragments and ephemera, poetic possibilities of the everyday elements in my culture."?
A lot of my work has been and continues to be an expression of what it means to be unapologetically Chinese in this country. As a child of immigrants, a large part of my art practice centres around *Chineseness* and how it is constructed, both in my identity and in its perception. The rise of anti-Asian hate that the pandemic brought on to my community has been heartbreaking, eye-opening, and disillusioning to witness and experience. As a Chinese Canadian artist, my voice matters, and I continue to make art that questions the ideology of Canadian identity and of cultural belonging. The personal is political, and in that spirit, I continue to make work in hopes that my community will feel seen and heard.

My work is meticulous, and the slowness is deliberate. It is a process of deep and loving consideration for the subject.

You've referred to material culture. Please explain what this means to you and how you incorporate it into your art?
Material culture is a recognition that objects hold meaning and that they tell stories. Many of the objects I choose to render are normally considered meaningless or mundane, and my work challenges the viewer to see these fragments and traces of our daily lives as more. What I find energizing about the response to my work is that there are so many ways to interpret material culture: memory and nostalgia, design history, issues of sustainability, and collective excessive consumption. They can all be found in noticing the overlooked.

Do you have a specific space in which you work? What do you require to be creative and productive?
I work from a small home studio that overlooks the Fraser River in New Westminster. It's surrounded by windows and has a lot of natural light, which is crucial!

Who, what, and where inspires you and your work?
My inspirations tend to change and roam, but right now, I'm inspired by unexpected colour combinations, cultural symbolism in packaging design, the rich visual history of Cantonese opera in Vancouver's Chinatown, and colliding materials of various sizes and textures in the same composition.

What words of advice can you offer someone looking to explore a profession in the arts?
Find your voice, stay true to it, and keep making art. Your work will connect with those that it is meant for.

Why is art important?
Art allows us a space to dream. It has the transformative potential to shift cultural mindsets, challenge perceptions, and to reimagine beauty.

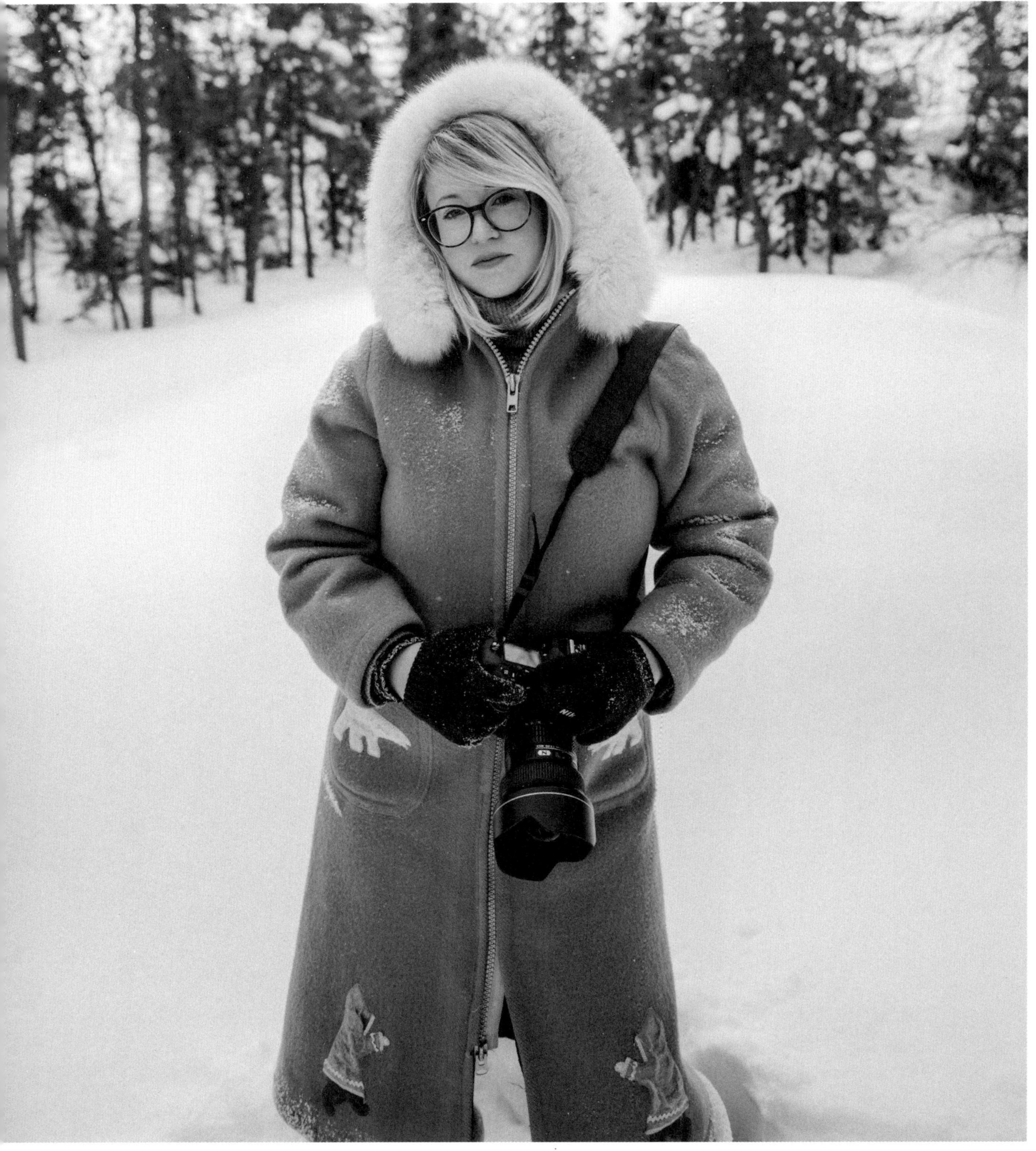

Angela Gzowski

Photographer

"Connecting with your subject or story is so important, and when I started to be more present it drastically changed my work, and also who I am as a person."

At what age did you begin to have an interest in photography?

I've always gravitated towards the arts, as I'm a very visual person. Since I was a little kid, I was running around with a camera. My late father came to Yellowknife in the 70s, where he started Arctic Divers, a commercial diving business. They worked across the Canadian Arctic doing underwater diving and welding, which, because of the conditions and location, mainly meant they were diving underneath the ice. A lot of his work involved videography and photography, and he always had a passion for photography, even outside of the diving world. Since I can remember, we always had cameras around the house, and I guess that I just sort of picked it up by osmosis.

Do you feel that a good photographer possesses an inherent ability to see and capture moments, subjects, and messages in a unique way, combined with formal training?

I attended NSCAD University. I have a Bachelor of Fine Arts with a major in Photography. I believe that technical ability can always come with training practice, and time, but the major player that sets you apart is having a style and creative eye that is your own. Being an artist and not just a photographer at the end of the day.

You were born and raised in Yellowknife and continue to live and work up north. How does this place shape and inspire you?

One day, I could be snowmobiling in -40 and photographing in the middle of nowhere, and the next, I could be shooting corporate studio shots. We live in a unique place, and it has its challenges, but at the end of the day, you are left with a place like no other, which leads to artistic highs that I don't necessarily get shooting elsewhere.

I really enjoy sharing the stories of my fellow northerners through my portraits and photojournalism and promoting our wide range of local businesses through my commercial work.

My photography helps to inform the rest of the country about the issues that we face in the North, showcases the NWT as the amazing tourism destination it is, and brings the people who help shape our home to the world.

My job has led me to meet a lot of different people, experience and learn about so many different things and I would have never had the opportunity too if I didn't photograph here in the North.

How would you describe the focus of your work?
My main focus is portraiture. I could never get bored of photographing people. In portraiture, the images need to reflect the person or give a sense of who they are.

Over the years I've worked tirelessly to hone my craft and style, creating a consistent look and feel to my images that my clients have grown to rely on. Simply put, I don't just take the photos; I help with, and oftentimes lead, the entire creative process.

You're an accomplished professional in commercial, editorial, and portraits. How does your approach to a shoot change depending on the job?
I shoot differently for editorial versus commercial or a portrait series. Sometimes you have no time to plan, and you have to go with the flow. I prefer to obsessively plan for light and scout out locations as much as possible beforehand. I also really like to be pretty close to my subjects when shooting. I find I form more of a connection rather than shooting with a really long lens super far away, and in the end, the images are stronger.

Your work has appeared in several respectable publications and platforms, such as *Canadian Geographic*, *Maclean's*, Netflix, Parks Canada, and the CBC. Congratulations! You've also photographed Prime Minister Justin Trudeau. This is an impressive résumé. To what would you credit your body of work?
Drive is for sure a huge part of being able to have so many opportunities, but overall, just go for it. Asking people who you may be nervous to photograph, or taking the initiative to create opportunities rather than wait for them to come to you is important. I would rather ask and have someone say no than to have never even attempted.

I feel like the biggest struggle is the battle with myself. Pushing myself each day and making sure my work grows and evolves. My work is essentially a representation of myself and, as hard as I try, I can't just put it away. It can take an emotional toll when your work is "you," and I have learned that separating your art and work is an important thing. Although I still struggle with it, I believe it's a major player at not making yourself go crazy.

What do you feel are the benefits of mentorship, especially for someone in your field?
When I was done university, I lived in Halifax for a while, freelancing, and working at a camera store, and as an assistant to two local photographers, Marvin Moore and Dean Casavechia.

They taught me a lot about interacting with clients and setting up on location for commercial shoots. They taught me about the ins and outs of the business. This was a valuable resource and experience to have.

How do you grow as a photographer? I imagine that your ideas, inspirations, and motivations evolve as you do as a person.
I'm at a point now where I have really tightened my style and craft and need to make sure I don't stay stagnant. I do take a lot of time to not shoot. I used to have my camera on me at all times, which sometimes can take away from just enjoying moments in your life.

Another lesson I learned was not to hide behind my camera. I was thinking more about the technical aspects than the story or person I was shooting. I

I could never get bored of photographing people. In portraiture, the images need to reflect the person or give a sense of who they are.

didn't engage enough and ask questions. Connecting with your subject or story is so important, and when I started to be more present, it drastically changed my work and who I am as a person. I'm always learning, and with that, my work evolves and changes with me.

What's been one of your most memorable shoots? I appreciate that it's hard to choose just one.

I have tons of shoots that are memorable, but one recently that was particularly amazing was a nearly two-week NWT Tourism photoshoot in Nahanni National Park. For twelve days, we made our way down the majestic river by canoe and rafts, camping at different locations in the park with the river guide company that had hired me. I had arranged models that came along on the trip, and I was shooting both stills and video each day. I grew up in the Northwest Territories without knowing that this amazing location was just a flight away. While I was in my own territory, at times, I felt like I was in a different country shooting. It was so inspiring and exciting. There was so much to capture, and it was even better knowing I was in my own backyard and going to be sharing it with the world.

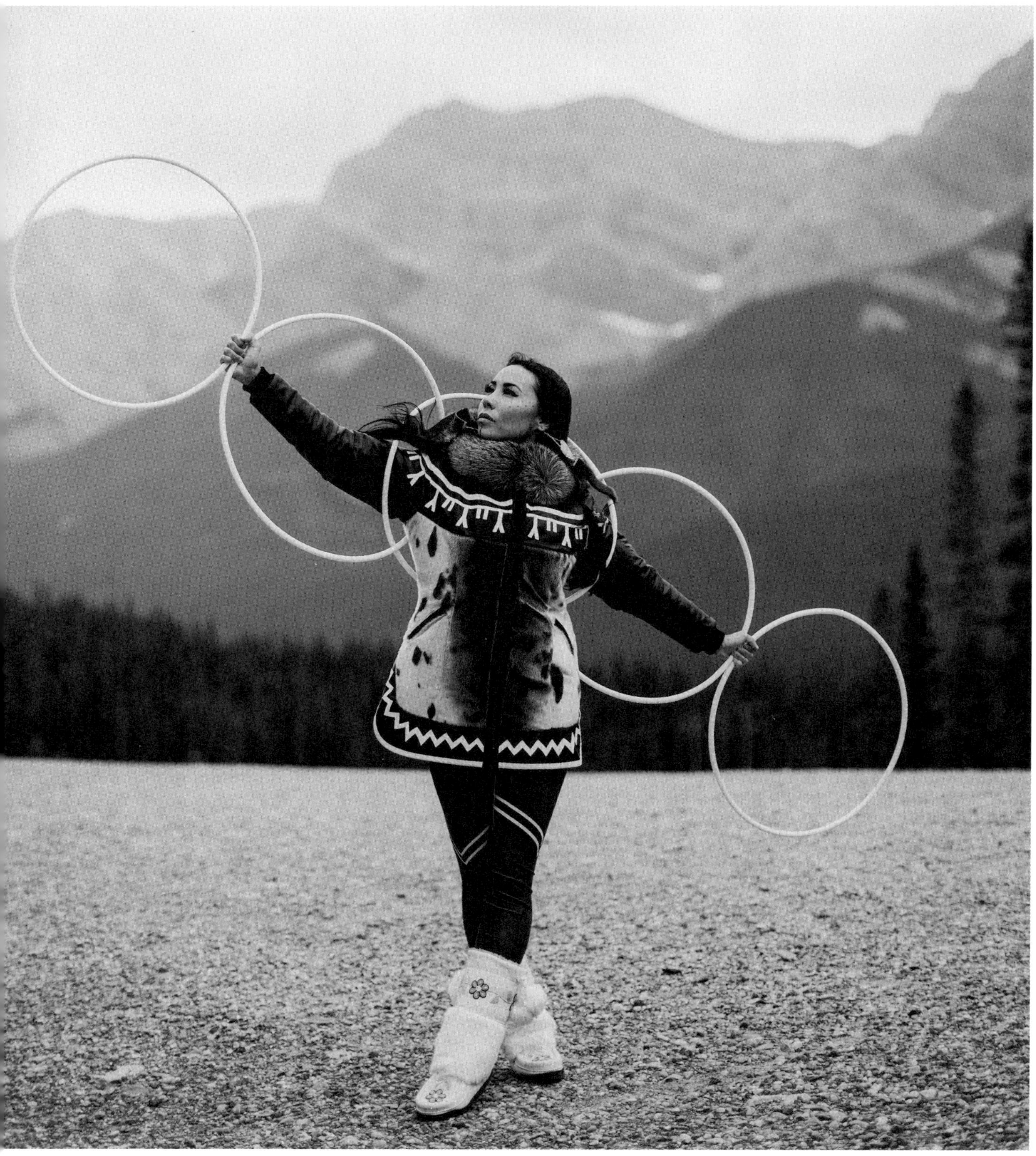

Marika Sila

Inuk Actress, Hoop Dancer, Fire Performer, and Motivational Speaker

"Serving humanity and doing things in a good way is always at the top of my mind in everything I do."

What is an early memory of movement?

I used to grab the hula hoops when I was young and play with them during lunch break by myself. I was so content just being with the hoops all recess, just me and the hoops. I remember getting into a meditative loop with them. I found so much peace with them, even at a young age.

You're from Yellowknife. How did the physicality and culture of this place shape you as a person and a professional?

My culture and inherent connection to my spirituality are at the core of who I am and everything I do. My inspiration and connection to myself are rooted in my culture and heritage.

At what age did you realize that pursuing a creative path in film, television and stunt work was to be your professional journey?

As a child, growing up, we would visit my grandparents in Vancouver. Our neighbours there were in the film industry, and every once in a while, they would bring us on film sets. One day we saw the *Scooby Doo 2* set, and in my mind, it was so magical being on set. It was around that time when I decided I wanted to be a director someday, and as time went on, I became obsessed with the movie *Miss Congeniality*; I probably watched that movie a hundred times before I turned twelve. That was when I started getting curious about acting. The stunts and special skills stuff came later in life. After I quit drinking, I found hoop dancing, which led me into more movement-based hobbies and sparked my interest in martial arts. I started daydreaming of roles I would love to play in the future and realized I should start taking stunts and special skills more seriously to prepare myself for such dream roles.

You wear many hats: actress, hoop dancer, fire performer, and motivational speaker. Do these different roles overlap?

Yes, and no. I feel like everything I do feeds into each other. Ultimately my goal is to continue to build a platform so I can inspire as many people as I can along the way, and everything I do is with this in mind. It is easy enough to stay focused as long as I am following my intuition.

Many of your talents require strength and special skills. What does training look like for you now?

Training for me consists of a lot of weightlifting, hoop dancing, or martial arts. I try my best to do my workouts in the mornings before the day gets too busy, but I often leave it till later in the day if I am working a lot. My brother once told me, "It's not about finding time, it's about making time." This has motivated me for years to make time for what I love, even if it is late at night.

You're the owner of RedPath Talent Inc., an Indigenous talent agency and production company named after the Indigenous phrase, "walking the red road," known as walking a path dedicated to sobriety, health, and wellness. Tell me more about what inspired this approach to both your business and overall outlook.

I have personally been walking the Red Road for nine years now. I gave up drinking and partying in my early twenties, and I owe much of my success to that single life choice. I believe it is important for Indigenous youth to have a role model to look up to that is living a sober, healthy lifestyle. It is a powerful choice for anyone to walk the Red Road. I believe it leads us to our highest selves. Therefore, I decided to name my company after that phrase, *walking the Red Road,* in hopes to inspire others to walk their version of the Red Path.

> I believe it is important for Indigenous youth to have a role model to look up to who is living a sober, healthy lifestyle. It is a powerful choice for anyone to walk the Red Road. I believe it leads us to our highest selves.

"In all the work I do—I do it for my family, my loved ones and my community." Why is this pivotal to pursuing your path?

Family and everyone I love is always at the forefront of my thinking. Doing what is best for everyone around me drives my every career move. Some people are just driven by money. I am driven by the idea of creating the most beautiful life so I can share it with everyone I love. Of course, money is part of that, but it goes further than that. I just want to be able to give more to my family, my community, and the people that I love.

An on-set experience that left a lasting impression?

Every set I step on leaves a lasting impression. There is something so magical about being on set; you will never experience the exact same day with the same people in the same location ever in the film industry. And that makes me fully embrace and live in the moment when I am on each film set. One moment that made me laugh was when I was working on *Ditched*. There was a scene where I made this contraption into a deadly slingshot. That entire scene was really fun and funny to film; everyone on set was having a good laugh. But what is so great about working on set is that you are working with a bunch of theatre kids who are making amazing money doing what they love, so there are always moments of fun and laughter.

In summer 2022, you and your brother Jesse Cockney appeared as a team on *The Amazing Race Canada*. Tell me more about this experience.

Being on *The Amazing Race Canada* taught me a lot about teamwork, perseverance, problem-solving, and living in the moment. The entire month we were away, we didn't have our phones, so it was a refreshing break and reset away from technology. Jesse and I worked really well together and ended up placing second. It was an experience I will always remember and cherish forever. We have always been really close, but after the race, we have a sibling bond like we did when we were young. I don't think a lot of adults can say that they are just as close to their siblings as they were when they were young. I am forever grateful that the race brought us together like it did.

Do you consider yourself to be a role model? What does this mean for you?

As an influencer and actress, I have a long way to go, but I do have a large enough platform that I know many women and youth look up to me. I don't take that lightly, and I always do my best to lead with my right foot forward, walking on this Red Path, because being a positive role model for someone can change their life for the better. I have received messages from people who have told me they are a few years sober because of something I posted about sobriety a couple of years ago. That means a lot to me, and I care deeply about those who look up to me.

How does being a role model fuel your spirit and passion for building a platform that inspires others and brings awareness to Indigenous rights and issues?

Often, when I am tired of posting or self-doubt creeps in, I think of the one person who might need to hear what I have to say, and that is enough for me to keep going. I always try my best to connect with the Creator and ask what it is I should be speaking about that day. I find it is on those days when I am creating from a place of service where my videos do the best. Serving humanity and doing things in a good way is always at the top of my mind in everything I do.

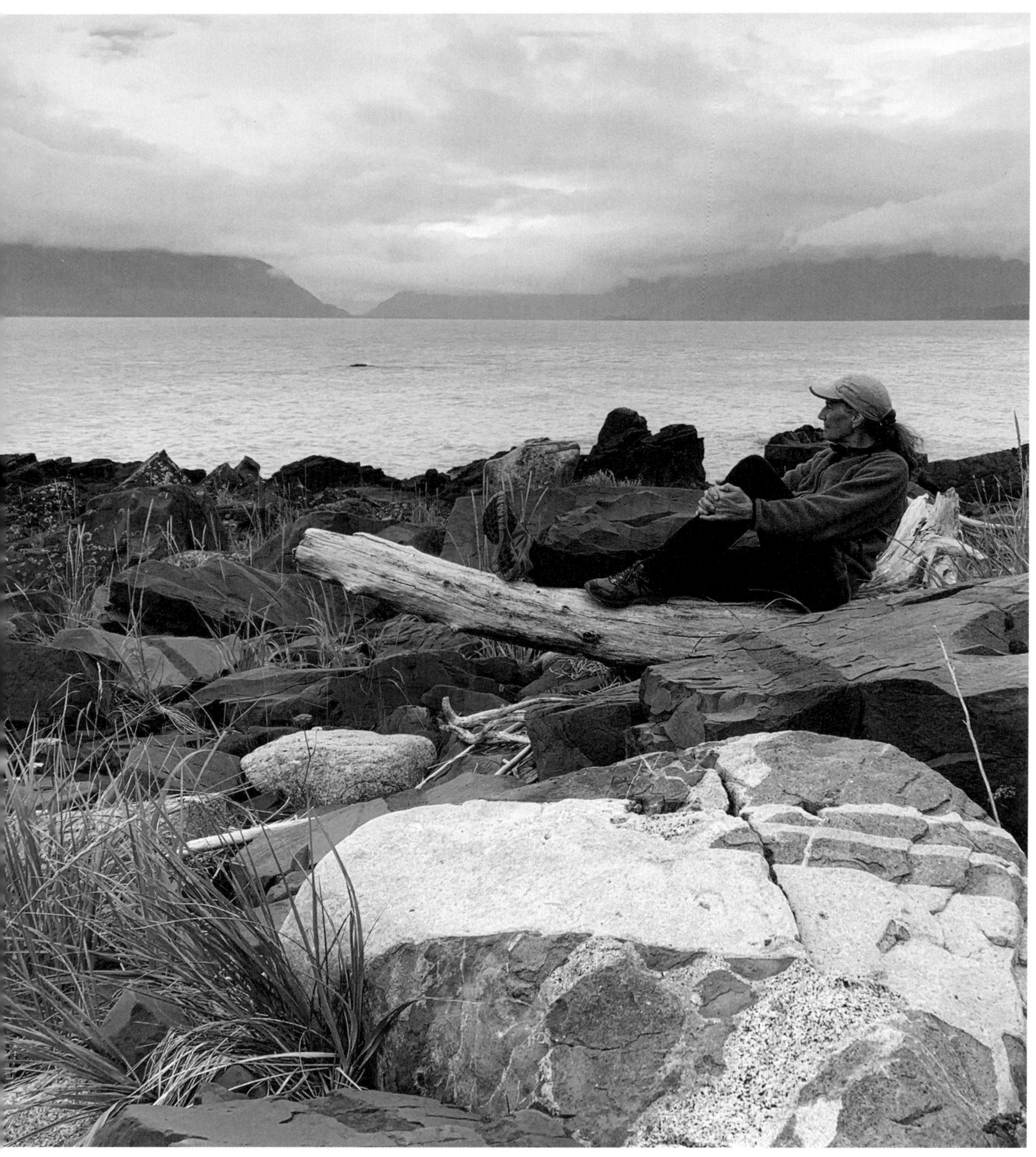

Joyce Majiski

Painter, Printmaker, and Sculptor

"I've always been inspired by people who live life the way they want to, deliberately following their dreams and passions and living unconventional lives."

What is your first memory of art?

I distinctly recall my very first painting, one made in kindergarten. We had to pick one primary and complementary colour and paint them side by side in thick poster paint. My mom still has my bright orange and blue painting tucked away in her cedar chest. In high school, I was one of two girls in class whose work was held up as an example to the others, something that was mortifying on a number of levels.

Prior to pursuing art full-time, you were a biologist and wilderness guide.

I have always been an artist, even while working as a biologist and running the guiding business with Jill Pangman of Sila Sojourns. In the winter of '86, I went to Mexico to study printmaking and paper making and built on that knowledge whenever I could in studios elsewhere.

In the 90s, as our guiding business ramped up, I took time in the winter to "play" mostly in California, Idaho and Utah, honing my whitewater kayaking and rock-climbing skills with friends. Between these bouts of being an adrenalin junkie, I sought out studios to create my artwork before returning to the Yukon for summers of guiding.

Around that time, I started a body of mixed media work that was to become my first big art installation. It took five years to create this work as it developed in different places/studios during a very challenging time of my life.

A series of inter-related events, including an overuse injury, death of my father, my relationship coming to an end and turning forty, caused me to question everything in my life. I'd watched my father pass away with regrets, and this made me question whether I was really doing what I wanted to in my life. The injury meant I couldn't guide in the way I had been anyway, so I decided to devote myself to being an artist full-time. I dipped my toe in and out of the guiding world for another year or two, but I think of my fortieth year as the year I walked into my new life.

The biggest challenge for me was the mental shift of not being out guiding all summer long, especially as I healed from this injury. It was my self-identity in question—if I wasn't a guide, then who was I? My circle of friends and acquaintances knew me as a biologist first and could easily see the transition to being a wilderness guide. But when I stopped doing that, it left me with a bit of an identity crisis.

Letting myself off the hook with explanations around this overuse injury and how I wasn't able to guide because of it was a personal challenge. There was definitely a period of adjustment for me.

That decade of my life was full of huge growth and change as I stepped more into my creative career. I had to trust that it would be ok and believe in myself. Being a full-time artist is risky business on a number of levels.

In the mid-90s, a series of interrelated events, including an overuse injury, the death of my father, my relationship coming to an end, and turning forty, caused me to question everything in my life. The injury meant I couldn't guide in the way I had been anyway, so I decided to devote myself to being an artist full time. I dipped my toe in and out of the guiding world for another year or two, but I think of my fortieth year as the year I walked into my new life.

My circle of friends and acquaintances knew me as a biologist first and could easily see the transition to being a wilderness guide, but when I stopped doing that, it left me with a bit of an identity crisis.

That decade of my life was full of huge growth and change as I stepped more into my creative career. I had to trust that it would be okay and believe in myself. Being a full-time artist is a risky business on a number of levels.

What made you decide to call the Yukon home?

As a single young woman, I could live in a small cabin in the woods hauling water and wood, and work in the wilderness. It was not unlike everyone else I knew who chose to live like that. As a cohort, the people my age worked hard all summer in the north, travelled in the winters, and returned to do it all again.

Being in the remote wilderness captured me from the start. The feeling of being out there in the quiet expanse, just living as another being on the land, gave me a sense of deep connection to the world around me and myself.

Being in the remote wilderness captured me from the start. The feeling of being out there in the quiet expanse, just living as another being on the land, gave me a sense of deep connection to the world around me and myself.

Who, what, and where inspires you?

I've always been inspired by people who live life the way they want to, deliberately following their dreams and passions and living unconventional lives. Whether scientists, artists, or explorers, I am especially inspired by women who, despite all odds, can live their passions.

Collaboration is a key component of your art and process.

I have a vivid recollection of the first time I invited someone to collaborate on a piece with me during an artist-in-residency. I laid down the ground washes on one side of our accordion book, and after it dried, I handed it to her to work on. As she added her first brush strokes, I remember my internal voice screaming, *Aaaahhh no, not that!* as I smiled on the outside. But once her first mark was down, I let it go, and we had a great time. We worked seamlessly to create a lovely mixed media two-sided accordion book. Letting go and trusting for the first time was a new experience and opened the door for more to happen.

Since 2010, I have been in a long-term weekly collaboration with Zea Morvitz, who lives in California. Each year, we set the parameters for our project; the format could be weekly postcards or pages for various bound volumes or long-form accordion fold books that develop over the year. For me, this collaboration with Zea is a grounding element, something I return to every Friday, even when I am not feeling a flow with anything else. Sometimes, the act of creating that week's work can kick-start me as well, so it is a valuable part of my practice.

"I am a keen observer and collector of objects and fascinated by the complex intricacy and interdependence of ecosystems and all living beings." How do you incorporate this into your art?

There is an intricate weaving of so many creatures and elements that creates this world as we see it and much that we do not see.

My house and studio are full of things that I have picked up on various travels, from fish skeletons and shells to stones and small artworks from other artists. I love colour and texture and integrate imagery and objects into books and boxes of collections that can be incorporated into installations.

A favourite piece that you've created?

A recent installation, "Song of the Whale," is currently the piece I feel proudest of. I knew this was a strong piece, but the reactions of people walking into the gallery for the first time still caught me by surprise.

My initial thoughts in creating this installation were to address issues around the abundant plastic pollution in oceans, our waste and consumption, and draw attention to how oceans connect to everything. As I recreated this young humpback whale, handling her bones, replicating each one carefully, and carving each bone by hand from ocean-salvaged Styrofoam, I learned her story and how she died, which touched me profoundly.

Why is art important?

Learning about human culture is almost exclusively done through the eyes of artists. Since the Homo species could hold a piece of charcoal, images depicting hunting scenes, lineage, mythology, stories, or whimsy have been captured by the creative ones in each culture. Through their eyes and dreams, we have learned the stories of people and how they lived throughout the ages. We glean stories from the shards of pottery found in middens, scraps of clothing, cave paintings, and glyphs carved into stones.

I aim for my work to be a platform for discussion and contemplation—a safe place to explore difficult issues.

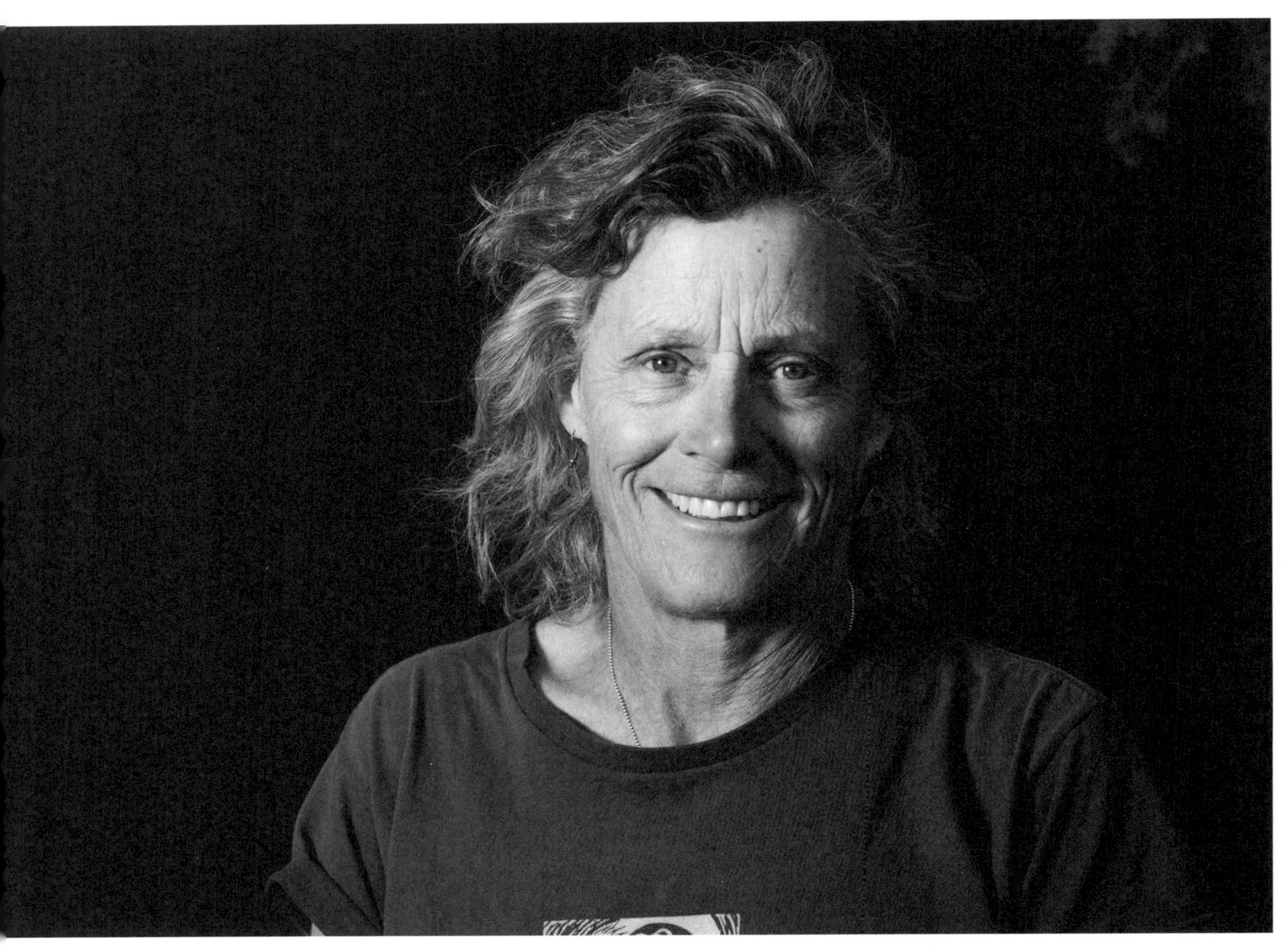

Jill Pangman

Co-founder, Conservationist, and Guide, Sila Sojourns

"The Yukon represented everything that I loved—wild country, untrammelled landscapes, natural beauty, amazing light, and a culturally vibrant and interesting community of people."

Your first memory of being in nature?

My life has always been about being in nature. My parents were outdoor enthusiasts, and the lasting memories I have of my childhood are of the hikes and skis we did as a family and my experiences in summer camps. I have very few memories of my early years that did not involve activities outdoors.

What brought you to the Yukon?

I was first introduced to the Yukon when I was barely twenty years old and working for the summer for Andy Russell, an Alberta-based nature photographer and writer. The focus of the summer was to get photos and material for his new book on the Rocky Mountains. However, we did one side trip, early in the season, to the Yukon at the invitation of the Kluane National Park and Reserve. We spent less than a week in the Yukon on that trip, but it left an impression. There I was on the edge of the world's largest non-polar icefield and the highest mountain range on the continent, photographing soaring towers of turquoise ice toppling into the frothing glacial silt-laden waters of the Alsek River.

When I spotted a job advertisement the next spring for a job in a remote camp along the Yukon/NWT border, I leaped at it.

The Yukon immediately came to mind. For me, it represented everything that I loved—wild country, untrammelled landscapes, natural beauty, amazing light, and a culturally vibrant and interesting community of people.

What fuels you as a wilderness guide, outdoor educator, biologist, naturalist, and conservationist?

I suppose *love* is what fuels me. My love of nature—all kinds of landscapes and environments, animals, and plant species. I care deeply about the future of wild spaces and wildlife habitat. As much as I love humanity and its potential, I am well aware of the damage we as a species have inflicted on the life-supporting ecosystems of this planet. I care enough to have chosen to devote countless hours to campaigns to protect wild country from the ravages of industrial development, to speak out on behalf of the needs of other species and our own, and to focus my life's work on trying to create educational and meaningful experiences in nature for the guests that come on my sojourns.

Sila Sojourns opened in 1992. What are the challenges and surprise benefits of starting a business?
The main challenge was juggling all the demands. Leading multi-day and-week journeys in the Yukon wilds is demanding enough on its own, and it was something that we were already familiar with, having been guiding for another company for several years prior, but to throw in having to simultaneously manage the business side of running trips added a whole other element. Along with needing to be skilled in whatever activity we were leading, we needed to be able to assess risk and manage it, perform wilderness first aid if required, manage difficult personalities, produce high-quality meals over open fires and camp stoves, and manage wildlife incidents, which meant being on call twenty-four hours a day for the duration of the journey. In addition to this, as a business owner, one needed to ensure that there were enough guests signed up on the trips to pay all the bills, which are significant with remote wilderness journeys.

As for benefits, the greatest one was being able to create the kinds of journeys we personally wanted to lead, and we felt our guests would benefit the most from. We could manage our own schedules since we were the ones setting the trip dates. And of course, the friendships developed over the years and the chance to spend meaningful time with people that one might never have met otherwise. It has been very rewarding work, witnessing how guests not only have an experience of being inspired by the beauty of the natural worl, but hopefully also see their own beauty reflected back to them.

Who, where, and what inspires you?
People who follow their passions, are enthusiastic about life, are generous and kind-hearted, are concerned about the future of this precious planet and all its life forms and do their best to be a positive force in the world.

There are so many places and types of environments that inspire me, and they are scattered across all the planet's continents—deserts, oceans, coral reefs, rain and temperate forests, rivers, wetlands, mountains, and glaciers. Human-made structures and spaces can inspire me, too, if they are constructed artfully and beautifully with elements of the earth and blend into the landscape.

You were President of CPAWS Yukon (the Yukon chapter of Canadian Parks and Wilderness Society) for ten years, are currently still a board member, and were on the board of the Wilderness Tourism Association of the Yukon (WTAY) for over twenty years.
My involvement in both organizations has allowed me to be a voice for the preservation of wilderness, wildlife habitat, and ecosystem health, as well as areas of high scenic and outdoor recreational value. Even though one is a conservation and the other an *industry* organization, they both promote the preservation of our natural wonders.

To be honest, I would not have stayed on the board of WTAY for nearly as long as I did if it were not for the fact it was also an avenue to speak up for conservation. As *industry professionals,* we could have the ear of government in a way that a conservation organization did not, especially during the years we had a very conservative government in power that promoted industry at the expense of the environment. WTAY represented an economic interest,

What I love about this northwest corner of the continent is the combination of light, vastness, wildness, rich wildlife, varied terrain, and a mix of mountains and tundra. To me, it brings together all the elements that I love the most about wilderness travel.

the industry of tourism, yet we were a consortium of wilderness tourism operators who relied on intact and expansive tracts of *wilderness* for our product.

You're also a parent.

I admit I had some trepidations going into motherhood, as I was very attached to my adventuring lifestyle and was unsure how a child would fit into that. However, when he was two and a half, I had a memorable moment of affirmation that my fears were unfounded. My husband and I, and a friend, were hiking up a mountain in the Rockies, Caelan strapped to my back. It was a glorious day, and I was in bliss being back on an alpine ridge in the Rocky Mountains, which I hadn't hiked in for some years. When we were almost at the peak, Caelan announced he wanted out of his carrier. He strode off on his short legs, clutching my outstretched hand, and as he peered over the edge at the all-encompassing view, his eyes grew really big. He took a big breath and excitedly exclaimed, "Oh, Mummy, it's SO beautiful!" It was then that I knew that this seed of mine had not fallen far from the tree, and that we were destined to have a lifetime of adventures together.

A place you want to explore.

I've been dreaming to have enough free time in the summer to do an extended wilderness sojourn of up to two months in length. This would be long enough to truly immerse in the rhythm of the journey and the place. For years I thought it may take the form of a canoe trip, across an expanse of sub-arctic and Arctic terrain, likely in the Northwest Territories or Nunavut. However, lately, I seem to be leaning more towards a combination of backpacking and river trips in the Brooks Range of northern Alaska's Arctic National Wildlife Refuge (ANWR). I have travelled extensively by raft and on foot in northern Yukon's Ivvavik National Park, just across the border from the refuge, many times over the last few decades, but have only once been into ANWR. It is vaster, more rugged, and has more access and egress options with at least one small tundra airstrip in most of the drainages. What I love about this northwest corner of the continent is the combination of light, vastness, wildness, rich wildlife, varied terrain, and a mix of mountains and tundra. To me, it brings together all the elements that I love the most about wilderness travel.

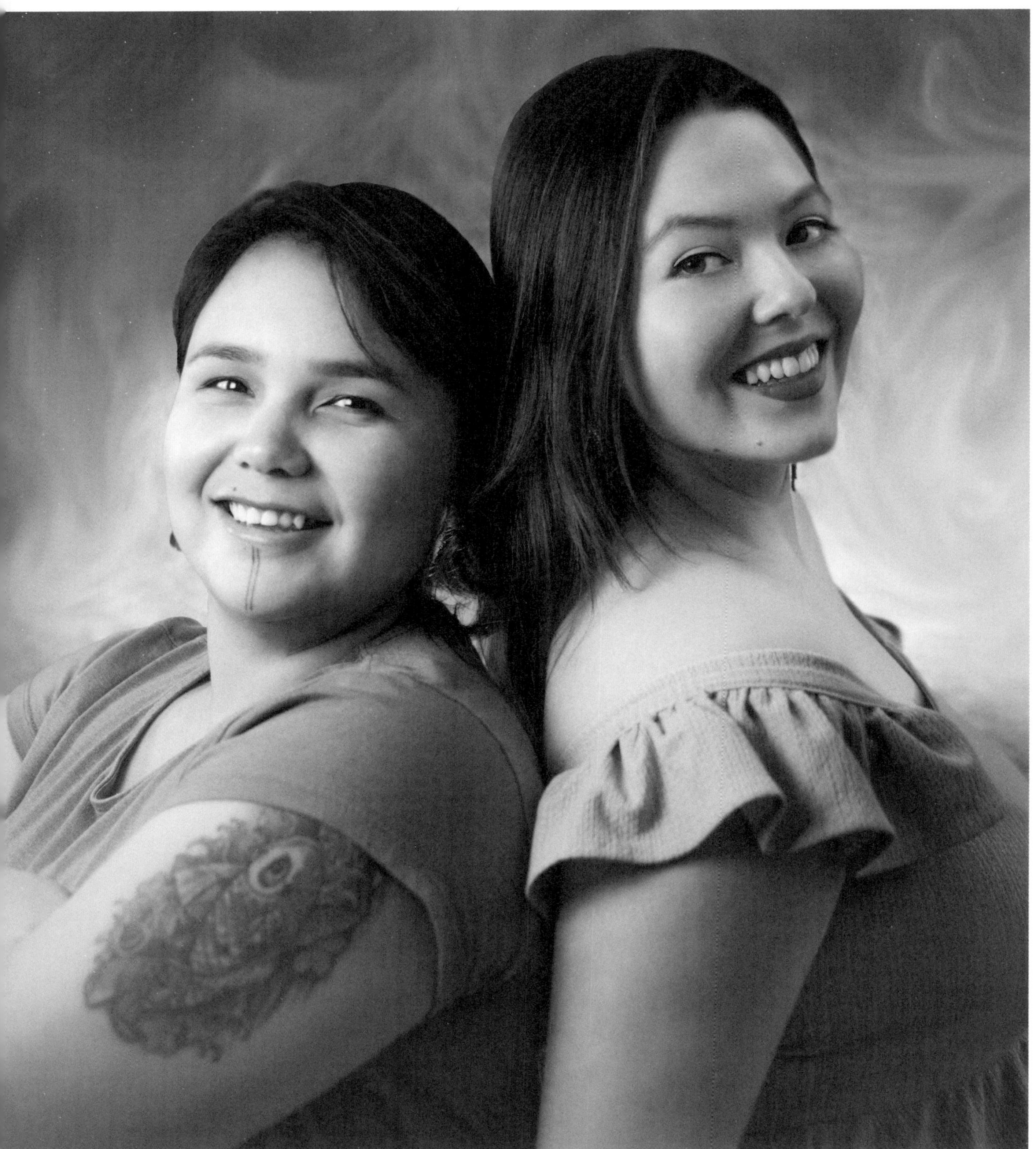

Sarah Elaine McLay & Shauna Seeteenak

CEO and Performance Coach, Hitmakerz; Hip-Hop Artist and Political Rapper

"I believe music is a powerful way to tell stories and connect with one another on a deeper level."

SARAH

"It's important that I be authentic as an artist, because I know that it will help people get through their struggles if they have someone to relate to."

SHAUNA

What is your first memory of music?

Sarah: My mom sang to me from the time I was a baby. She has the sweetest voice, and I remember her singing "Dream a Little Dream of Me" as a lullaby. It's one of my favourite songs, and I often sang it as an adult for auditions or performances.

Shauna: My first memory of music is listening to Salt-N-Pepa in bed. That's when I fell in love with hip-hop. I was maybe four years old; it was summer, and the sun was shining into my room. The music was playing on a cassette tape, and I fell asleep shortly afterwards. When I hear Salt-N-Pepa now, it reminds me of this time that inspired me to want to be a singer.

Sarah, you're a graduate of Toronto Metropolitan University (formerly Ryerson) with a BA in Creative Industries (Music Industry, Acting, and Dance Studies), and a minor in Music and Culture. How did this prepare you for your current role as a performance coach and CEO at Hitmakerz?

Sarah: What I took away from this experience is that learning is a lifelong journey that doesn't end when we leave school. My education taught me how to wear many different hats and be adaptable in various environments. I often use these skills in my career at Hitmakerz by helping facilitate communication between different perspectives in the industry and hearing the viewpoints of the artists, creatives, and businesspeople.

Shauna, you're originally from Baker Lake, Nunavut and are currently based in Iqaluit. How did the physical and cultural surroundings of Baker Lake shape and inspire you?

Shauna: There was not much to do in Baker Lake as a teenager other than going to a youth drop-in centre or playing sports. Music was both a form of expression and inspiration, but it also gave me something to do to pass the time during quiet and dark periods. I learned about struggles at a very young age. Addictions, poverty, high cost of living, poor housing situations. I feel like I need to touch upon these topics to not only help Inuit people move through these struggles, but also inspire others to believe that things do get better.

How soon after graduation did you begin working with Hitmakerz?

Sarah: I graduated from what felt like Zoom University in the midst of the pandemic. The whole experience was unique and truly reflected the zeitgeist of the bizarre time we were living in.

After graduation, I was teaching vocals and piano lessons at a couple of studios in the Greater Toronto Area. I started working at Hitmakerz in January 2021, initially as a part-time project manager during the day, while still instructing music in the evenings. I officially transitioned to working full-time as Hitmakerz' Chief Operating Officer that September.

Tell me more about what drew you to work with Hitmakerz and what makes it unique?

Sarah: Hitmakerz helps artists navigate the daunting process of getting their music out there in an often overwhelming system. Music is a huge part of culture and identity, and it has the potential to bring people together.

When I saw the opportunity to work in a space that matches my passions and prioritizes highlighting Indigenous voices, it was a dream. Hitmakerz helps create sustainable careers in the arts, and our roster has the opportunity to share their voices through music while also having a hand in the narrative of telling their story authentically by being involved in the branding, marketing, and release of their art.

Can you recall the first song that you wrote or perormed?

Shauna: The first song I wrote was called "Struggle." It's about how I felt I wasn't being heard and how it seemed like everything was going wrong for me. I was very young at the time, maybe fourteen. The first time I sang in front of an audience was in elementary school. A friend and I sang in front of the entire school, and I loved how it made me feel when everyone clapped.

> We operate with the idea that we are like a family and try to support each other accordingly. We try to foster creativity and push each other to do our best.

Is the process of expressing and sharing your experience through music therapeutic?

Shauna: It's definitely therapeutic. I was not taught ways of healthy expression growing up. It was hard to talk about my feelings with others. I took poetry in English in junior high, and I loved how I was able to express how I felt through words. I then heard Eminem's angry rap, and it caught my attention. He was able to express how he felt without taking negative action. That's what inspired me to write my own lyrics. It's like talking to a therapist.

Your songs address "the truths and challenges facing Inuit culture, including mental health, sobriety, breaking stereotypes, overcoming barriers, surviving the north, and trying to heal."

Shauna: It's important that I be authentic as an artist because I know that it will help people get through their struggles if they have someone to relate to. I also want people from around the world to know who we, Indigenous people, are, what we went through, and how resilient we are today.

How has your relationship evolved?

Sarah: Shauna's single marketing for "Better With You" was the first project I worked on when I started at the label. Over the last couple of years, we've gotten to know each other in studio settings, working on vocals together, being her manager, or just hanging out. The time we have spent online, in Ottawa, Iqaluit, and Toronto together has been wonderful. I feel lucky not only to have the opportunity to work with her, but also for the genuine friendship we have developed.

Shauna: I first met Sarah in 2021. I was pretty shy and closed off because that's just who I am as a person when I first meet someone. But I warmed up to Sarah after a few vocal lessons. We did quite a few lessons together, which helped me a lot. During this time together, I learned a lot about her and her about me. Sarah has always been open, patient, and flexible, which helped me trust her as a teacher, colleague, and friend.

Hitmakerz focuses on creating an encouraging, inclusive, and positive company culture.

Sarah: We operate with the idea that we are like a family and try to support each other accordingly. We try to foster creativity and push each other to do our best. I care about the people I work with. I want to see them succeed and achieve their dreams, so I do what I can to help those dreams become reality. Like a family, we are there for each other in good times and bad by motivating one another to continue working on our art when we feel uninspired and checking in on each other.

Shauna, congratulations on your debut album, *Therapy Sessions*, which was released in August 2021. How did it feel putting a record out into the world?

Shauna: Thank you. Releasing an album on major music streaming services made me nervous, but also excited to finally share my art with the world. *Therapy Sessions* has given me a lot of opportunities around Canada and positive feedback from fans, radio shows, blogs, and news stations. I really hope to soon get to a place where my music is being played across Canada.

What is it like being female in the music industry today?

Sarah: The biggest benefit is being able to network with other females in the music industry, represent female executives at record labels, and be inspired by the wonderful women around me. As a young female executive in a male-dominated industry, I often don't see myself reflected.

I often deal with a level of imposter syndrome as a young woman as I continue to gain experience and find my way, often learning as I go. It's important to develop a strong female support system to check in with.

The passion and heart with which you walk the journey is everything.

Acknowledgements

THIS BOOK would not exist without the incredible group of people featured on these pages. The passion and heart with which you walk the journey is everything. Thank you for sharing your stories and for being a pivotal part of the writing process, inspiring me, encouraging me, and being true to your path.

Thank you to the group of individuals who were part of the first *Bloom* book. The magic of that experience gave me the momentum to keep going, and to keep searching for and sharing the important work being done by so many wonderful people across Canada.

Lara Kordic, for her continued support and enthusiasm for this series and the stories within.

Monica Miller, for her commitment to making these books available to readers everywhere.

Setareh Ashrafologhalai, for being a designer extraordinaire who truly brought my vision onto the pages of both *Bloom* books.

Christine Jean-Baptiste, for her incredible edits and inspiring body of work. It was an honour to have you be a pivotal part of making this *Bloom* book.

To the entire team at Heritage House Publishing for bringing this second book to life.

The publicity team at Zg Stories for your support, enthusiasm and heartfelt efforts to share the stories in this book.

Lydia Okello, for penning the foreword to this book. Your story and the important work you do to shift conversations in the world of fashion inspire. Thank you for jumping on board again; it's an honour to have you share your words here.

Readers who supported the first book—to hear how the stories moved you reassured me that a second book was both necessary and would be well received.

To the independent bookstores and chain booksellers who carry the *Bloom* books on their shelves: thank you for bringing in books and authors, especially those of us just starting out.

Libraries, for making the *Bloom* books accessible to everyone.

Publications and platforms who have supported and shared about the *Bloom* books, thank you.

Friends and family near and far. Seeing photos of you with the book in your hands fills my heart. Your words of love and support are everything.

Aunt Janice—for your unconditional love and support.

Christian, Cali, and Elle. As we embark upon another adventure as a family, the following comes to mind. Although I've lived in a number of places, I've only ever really had one home. My home is my family. It's where the four of us are, together.

Ruth Michelle Shane—I miss you every day. Although you are no longer here in the physical world, your love and spirit have been with me throughout the process of putting this book together. I love you as big as the Universe. Always and forever.

Image Credits

PEACE AKINTADE Mason Neufeld

TARA AUDIBERT Self portrait

JOLENE BAILIE Kirsten Sawatzky

BRITT BERGMEISTER Bliss Braoudakis

CATHERINE BERNIER Gabriel Denis

JANE BROKENSHIRE Ryan L. Mackay

PRISCILLE BUKASA Sam Obadero, photographed at Arts Common *Now Listen* Cabaret

THANUSHI EAGALLE True Rosie Brix, Truzys Photos

BECKY FEASBY Nikki Collette Photography

CAROLYN GAVIN Virginia Macdonald

ANNA GILKERSON Zac Barkhouse

ANGELA GZOWSKI Self portrait

KAREN HOEKSTRA Karolina Turek

BREAGH ISABEL Mo Phùng

SARAH KEAVENY VOS Beth Johnston

LINDSAY KELLOWAY Megan Bodker Photography

JOËLLE (JOJO) LANDRY-BERGERON & MARIE-LAURENCE (MARLO) DESAULNIERS Joëlle Landry-Bergeron

SANDRA-LEE LAYDEN Victoria McEwan

LEAH LEGAULT Self portrait

KELLIE LODER Sandra-Lee Layden

OU MA Jasmine Macey

BRENLEY MACEACHERN & LISA MACISAAC Jen Squires

JOYCE MAJISKI Jennifer Massie

SARAH ELAINE MCLAY & SHAUNA SEETEENAK Myriam Sevigny, Mi Photography

MARA MENNICKEN Jurga Prakapaite

RACHEL MIELKE Jared Bautista

ANDRÉANNE MULAIRE DANDENEAU Danny Shumov

JAG NAGRA Agata Matyszczuk

TRUC NGUYEN Jenna Marie Wakani

AVIS O'BRIEN Nycky-Jay Vanjecek, Bluetree Photography

CHINENYE MARY OTAKPOR Ayobami Balogun

JILL PANGMAN Cathie Archbould

DAWN PEMBERTON Wendy D Photography

AMY ROBICHAUD Ida Magdalena Cummings

MARIKA SILA Rachel Barkman

LOURDES STILL Sierra Pries

MAYCIE-ANN ST-LOUIS Cameron Ugbodu

CARLA TAK Self portrait

KIM TAYLOR Sophie Vino

SYLVIA TENNANT Kristine Cofsky

KATRINA TOMPKINS Jane Brokenshire

SIGNY THORSTEINSON Carter Johann

MALLORY TOLCHER Angus Moylan, Frequency Photography

JANET TUENSCHEL Jen Short Photography

R.S. TWELLS Jazmin Hundal

OLIVIA VANDYKE Francis Eadie

LISA WALSH Paul Daly

TENE WARD Nath Martin

ANNA WILLIAMS Self portrait

JANICE WU Kaoverii Silva

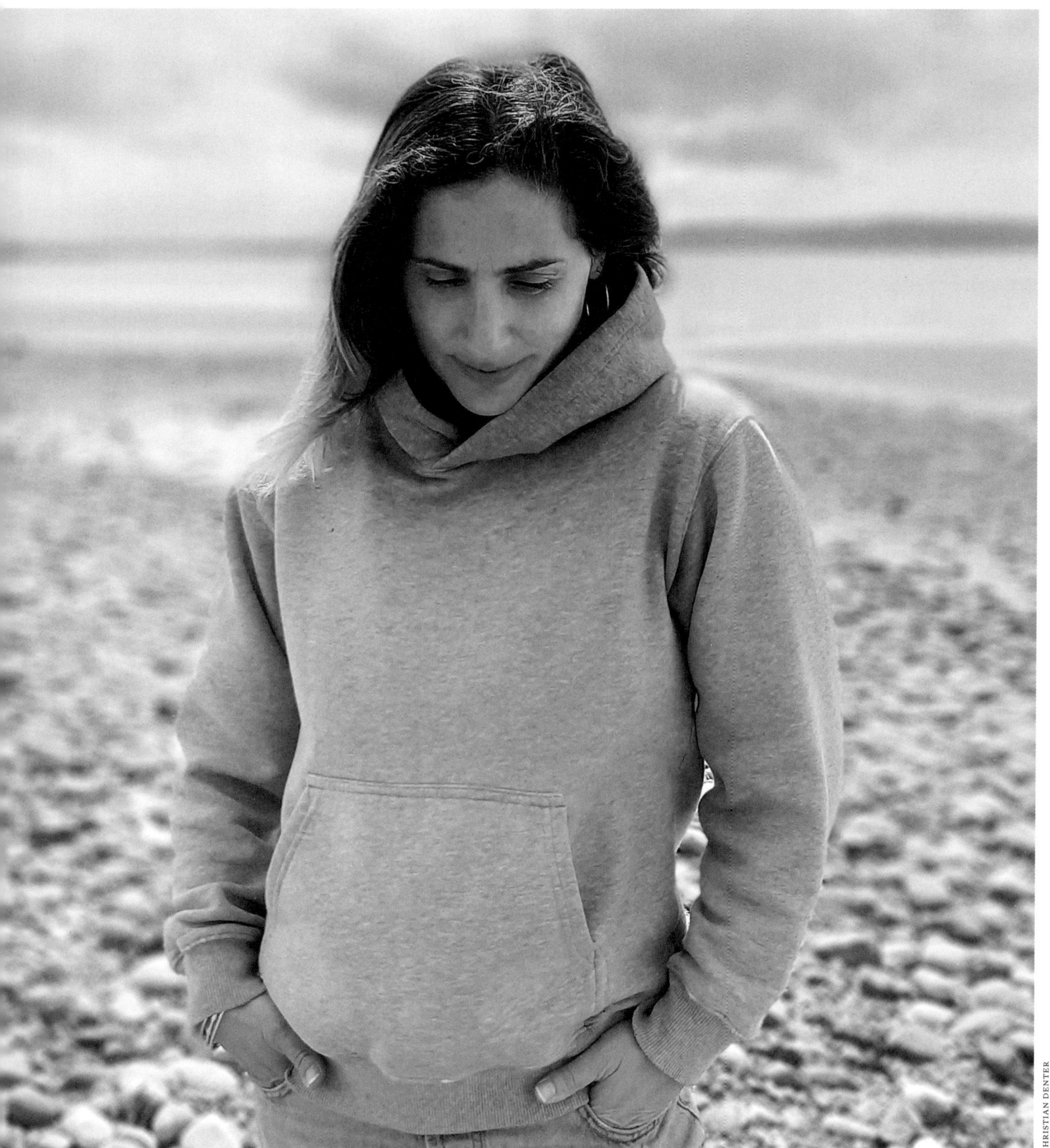
CHRISTIAN DENTER

About the Author

BEKA SHANE DENTER is a Canadian features and content writer currently based in Denmark, who has used her knowledge, passion, and nomadic lifestyle to fuel her writing career. Her work has appeared in *Scandinavia Standard*, *Elle Canada*, *Fashion*, NUVO, *Montecristo*, LUXE, *Ottawa Wedding*, BUST, *Today's Parent* and *The Inertia*. She holds a Bachelor of Arts in English, a Master's in Education, a certification in Web Writing and Social Media Communication from the University of Toronto, and a Graduate Certificate in Creative Writing from Humber College. This is the second book in the *Bloom* series.